SPIRITUAL
Mismatch

RESOURCES BY LEE STROBEL

SPIRITUAL
Mismatch

—

Hope for Christians Married to
Someone Who Doesn't Know God

LEE & LESLIE
STROBEL

Previously published as
Surviving a Spiritual Mismatch in Marriage

ZONDERVAN®

ZONDERVAN

Spiritual Mismatch
Copyright © 2002 by Lee Strobel

Previously published as *Surviving a Spiritual Mismatch in Marriage*

Requests for information should be addressed to:
Zondervan, *3900 Sparks Dr. SE, Grand Rapids, Michigan 49546*

ISBN 978-0-310-35035-4 (softcover)

ISBN 978-0-310-35040-8 (ebook)

Cover design: Curt Diepenhorst
Cover photos: Ursula Sander / Getty Images® / Shutterstock®
Interior design: Todd Sprague and Kait Lamphere

First printing January 2017 / Printed in the United States of America

Contents

For Linda Lenssen,

Leslie's spiritual mentor,
who influenced our whole family for Christ,
and to her husband, Jerry,
who preceded us Home.

I will give you a new heart
and put a new spirit in you;
I will remove from you your heart of stone
and give you a heart of flesh.

—Ezekiel 36:26

For Linda Lenssen,

Leslie's spiritual mentor,
who influenced our whole family for Christ,
and to her husband, Jerry,
who preceded us Home.

I will give you a new heart
and put a new spirit in you;
I will remove from you your heart of stone
and give you a heart of flesh.

—Ezekiel 36:26

How Leslie and I Wrote This Book

SEVERAL YEARS AGO LESLIE AND I PARTICIPATED IN A VALENTINE'S Day event in which we fielded questions from couples about marriage and the Christian life. Afterward, one young man came up, pointed to Leslie, and said to me, "Now we know who's got the brains in the family!"

He wasn't kidding! God has given Leslie a gift of wisdom. Her gentle spirit, sincere heart, and intensely practical biblical insights make her sought after by people who want counsel or guidance.

Since both of us have gone through an era of being spiritually mismatched, it made sense for us to write this book as a team so that we could draw upon our combined experiences and lessons. But when I brought up the idea for the book, Leslie protested: "I'm not a writer! Ever heard of stage fright? Well, I've got page fright!" As for me, writing is what I like best.

So we struck a deal: we would work together—mixing our ideas, insights, and advice—and I would actually write the bulk of the book. Besides, since much of the story is about what Leslie did during our time of mismatch, it's more comfortable for me to write about that than her.

So when you see parts written in the first person—with pronouns like "me" and "I"—that's me speaking. Leslie has added her perspective and input, and she has overcome her shyness long enough to write a chapter about her personal experiences during the time we were mismatched.

As they say on *Sesame Street*: "That's cooperation!"

—Lee Strobel

PART ONE

The Challenge of a
Mismatched Marriage

1 | Entering into the Mismatch

THE WEATHER WAS CRISP AND CLEAR ON THE DAY AFTER CHRISTmas 1966 when my friend Pete and I took the train from our suburban homes into downtown Chicago. We wandered around the Loop for a while, reveling in the bustle of the city, but then came time for me to bring him on a pilgrimage that I took as often as I could.

Fighting the wind, we trudged across the Michigan Avenue bridge and stopped in front of the Wrigley Building. There we stood, our hands shoved into our pockets for warmth, as we gazed across the street at the gothic majesty of Tribune Tower. I can't remember whether I muttered the word aloud or if it merely echoed in my mind: *"Someday."* Pete was quiet. High school freshmen are entitled to their dreams.

We lingered for a few minutes and watched as people flowed in and out of the newspaper office. Were they the reporters whose bylines I studied every morning? Or the editors who dispatched them around the world? Or the printers who manned the gargantuan presses? I let my imagination run wild—until Pete's patience wore thin.

We turned and walked up the Magnificent Mile, browsing through the overpriced and pretentious shops, until we decided to embark on the twenty-minute walk back to the train station. As we passed in front of the Civic Opera House, though, I heard a familiar voice beckon from the crowd.

"Hey, Lee, what're you doing here?" called Clay, another high school student who lived in my neighborhood.

I didn't answer right away. I was too captivated by the girl at his side, holding his hand and wearing his gold engraved ID bracelet. Her brown hair cascaded to her shoulders; her smile was at once coy and confident.

"Uh, well, um . . . just hanging around," I managed to say to Clay, though my eyes were riveted on his date.

By the time he introduced us to Leslie, I wasn't thinking much about Clay or Pete or the fact that my hands were getting numb from the cold and I was standing ankle-deep in soot-encrusted snow. I made sure, however, to pay close attention when Clay pronounced Leslie's name; I knew I'd need the proper spelling to look it up in the phone book.

After all, everything's fair in love and war.

FROM FAIRY TALE TO NIGHTMARE

As for Leslie, I found out later that she wasn't thinking about Clay as the two of them rode the train home that afternoon. When she arrived at her house in suburban Palatine, she strolled into the kitchen and found her mother, a Scottish war bride, busily preparing dinner.

"Mom," she announced, "today I met the boy I'm going to marry!"

The response wasn't what she expected. Her mother barely looked up from the pot she was stirring. In a voice mixed with condescension and skepticism, she replied dismissively: "That's nice, dear."

But there was no doubt in Leslie's mind. Nor in mine. When I called her the next night from a pay-phone outside a gas station near my house (with four brothers and sisters, that was the only way I could get some privacy), we talked as if we had known each other for years. People like to debate whether there's such a thing as love at first sight; for us, the issue had been settled once and for all.

Leslie and I dated almost continuously throughout high school, and when I went off to study journalism at the University of Missouri, she moved there so we could be close to each other. We got married when I was twenty and she was nineteen. After I graduated we moved to Chicago, where my lifelong dream of becoming a reporter at the *Chicago Tribune* was realized. Leslie, meanwhile, began her career at a savings and loan association across the street from my newspaper office.

We lived a fairy-tale life. We enjoyed the exhilaration and challenge of climbing the corporate ladder while residing in an exciting, upscale neighborhood. Leslie became pregnant with our first child, a girl we named Alison, and then later gave birth to a son, Kyle. Buoyed by our deep love for each other, our marriage was strong and secure—until someone came between us, threatening to shipwreck our relationship and land us in divorce court.

It wasn't an affair. It wasn't the resurfacing of an old flame. Instead, the someone who nearly capsized our marriage was none other than God himself. At least, that's who I blamed at the time. Ironically, it was faith in Jesus Christ—which most couples credit for contributing to the strength of their marriage—that very nearly destroyed our relationship and split us apart forever.

All because of a spiritual mismatch.

A MARRIAGE WITHOUT GOD

I can describe God's role in our courtship and early marriage in one sentence: *He just wasn't on our radar screen.* In other words, he was irrelevant.

Personally, I considered myself an atheist. I had rejected the idea of God after being taught in high school that Darwin's theory of evolution explained the origin and development of life. I figured Darwin had put God out of a job! Freed of accountability, I decided to live purely for myself and my own pursuit of pleasure. As for Christians, I tended to dismiss them as naive and uncritical thinkers who needed a crutch of an imaginary deity to get them through life.

Leslie, on the other hand, would probably have considered herself an agnostic. While I tended to react with antagonism toward people of faith, she was more in spiritual neutral. She had little church influence growing up, although she has fond childhood memories of her mother gently singing traditional hymns to her while she tucked her in at night. For Leslie, God was merely an abstract idea that she had never taken the time to explore.

Without God in my life, I lacked a moral compass. My character slowly became corroded by my success-at-any-cost mentality. My anger would flash because of my free-floating frustration at not being able to find the fulfillment I craved. My drinking binges got out of control a little too often, and I worked much too hard at my job, in effect making my career into my god.

Despite all of that, our marriage remained stable. Our love for each other smoothed over a lot of rough edges. When we were together, we were happy. That is, until everything exploded in the fall of 1979. That's when harmony dissolved into hostility. The reason: Leslie announced that after a long period of searching and seeking, she had decided to become a follower of Jesus Christ.

To me, that was the worst possible news! I was afraid she was going to turn into a sexually repressed prude who would forsake our upwardly mobile lifestyle in favor of spending all of her free time serving the poor at some skid-row soup kitchen.

"Look, if you need that kind of crutch," I said in a snide and patronizing tone, "—if you can't stand on your own two feet and face life without putting your faith in a make-believe god and a book of mythology and legend—then go ahead. But remember two things: don't give the church any of our money, because that's all they're really interested in, and don't try to get me to get out of bed to go anywhere on Sunday mornings. I'm too smart for that [bleep]!"

Nice guy, huh?

"THIS ISN'T WHAT I SIGNED UP FOR!"

That was the opening salvo in what turned out to be a turbulent, strife-filled, emotion-churning phase of our marriage. Our values began to clash, our attitudes started to conflict, and our priorities and desires were suddenly at odds. Arguments erupted, iciness replaced warmth, and more than once I let my frustration and anger spill over into an epithet-laced tirade of shouting and door slamming.

I can remember when everything culminated on one hot and humid day while I was mowing the lawn after another one of our quarrels. My blood was boiling.

"That's it," I muttered as I plowed through her flower bed in a childish display of passive/aggressive anger. "I don't need this anymore. This isn't what I signed up for! Maybe it's time to get out of this marriage altogether."

That was the low point. Our future hung by a thread. Maybe you can relate to that kind of emotional turmoil. Or perhaps you're frightened about your own marriage's future because your faith is driving a deeper and deeper wedge between you and your spouse. Through the years, Leslie and I have counseled many Christians who have tearfully told us how their union with a nonbeliever has increasingly brought them anguish, anger, and arguments.

Once Leslie and I got a phone call at 3:30 p.m. on Easter. Theresa was crying. "Holidays are always the worst," she said between sobs. "But today, he really went too far. He's been making fun of me, saying I'm weak, saying I believe ridiculous things, saying the church is just trying to get my money. I'm tired of defending myself. I don't know what to do anymore. Why won't he just let me believe what I want? Why does he have to ruin everything? It was bad enough having to go to Easter services by myself; why does he have to destroy the rest of my day too?"[1]

Theresa isn't alone. Rita's husband is a lawyer who is openly antagonistic toward anything Christian. Rita said, "He actually told our son that church is where bad people are, that people will try to make you think like them if you go to church, that little boys who go to church get molested, and if Mommy ever tries to take you to church again, you tell her you won't go."

Or consider Kathy. She said her anguish over her marital situation has only been amplified by her church and Christian friends who inadvertently make matters worse for her. "There's this underlying implication that if I would just be a better witness, if I'd just pray harder, if I'd just get him to come to Christmas services, if I'd give him the right book to read or tape to listen to, that somehow everything would work out," she said. "They don't come right out and say it, but I get the feeling that I'm the one at fault—and that hurts!"

Linda Davis, who lived for years in an unequally yoked marriage until her husband became a Christian, said the only lonelier plight for an unequally yoked person would be the death of her spouse. "I doubt, however, that even physical widowhood makes a woman feel as rejected and inadequate as does 'spiritual widowhood,'" she added. "The spiritual widow receives no flowers or sympathy cards. She simply grieves in silence for a union that never was."[2]

DON'T GIVE UP HOPE!

More than once while Leslie and I were spiritually mismatched, I predicted our marriage would end in divorce. Mentally, I had thrown in the towel. But through a variety of circumstances we were rescued from that fate.

Before it was too late, Leslie figured out how to live out her faith in a way that began to attract me rather than repel me. She learned how to grow and even flourish in her relationship with Christ despite discouragement from me. Although she would be the first to admit that she made mistakes from time to time, she was able to restore equilibrium to our relationship. Gently and lovingly, she started to point me toward Christ—and, ultimately, God used her to open my eyes to my need for a Savior.

Today we're celebrating twenty years as a Christian couple and thirty years of marriage. In an absolutely astounding display of God's grace, he not only forgave me for my immoral and atheistic past, but he gave me a ministry as a pastor and evangelist. Together, Leslie and I are experiencing a depth of intimacy, adventure, and fulfillment that we never could have imagined during those shallow years we spent without God.

Now, it's important to stress that—unfortunately—not every spiritual mismatch will end with both spouses joyfully serving Christ. The sobering truth is that some couples travel radically different spiritual paths for the rest of their lives. That's reality. No matter how much you want to, you cannot force your spouse to become a Christian.

Yet it's equally important to emphasize that if you find yourself in a spiritually mismatched marriage, there *is* hope. Don't despair! You can learn to thrive despite your differences. You can learn to encourage your spouse in his spiritual journey without inadvertently chasing him away. You can learn to earnestly seek the best for your partner without unfairly burdening yourself with undue responsibility for his salvation. In short, a spiritual mismatch does not have to be a death sentence for a marriage.

That may seem hard to believe if you're currently embroiled in conflict with your spouse over your differing views of God. But that's why Leslie and I are writing this book—to help you learn from what we did both right and wrong in this rocky period of our relationship. Believe me, we fumbled our way through, but we did walk away with some hard-earned lessons that we hope will both encourage you and give you concrete, practical, and biblical steps to take.

More importantly, you need to remind yourself on a regular basis that God has not forgotten you. He isn't gleefully punishing you because you're married to a nonbeliever. In fact, all of heaven is cheering you on as you seek to humbly and sincerely live out your faith in an often stressful and difficult environment. Your heavenly Father graciously wants to offer you courage in the face of strife, peace in the midst of turmoil, and optimism when everything seems shrouded in gloom.

With his help, you really *can* learn to survive a spiritual mismatch.

THE "WHY" BEHIND GOD'S COMMAND

If you've experienced the anguish of being a Christian wed to a nonbeliever, then you can readily understand why God has prohibited his followers from marrying outside the faith. He loves us so much that he wants to spare us from the emotional anguish, the clash of values, and the ongoing conflict that can result when one spouse is a Christian but the other isn't. His goal isn't to unnecessarily limit our choice of prospective mates but to lovingly shield us from the kind of difficulties that Leslie and I faced during the nearly two years we were spiritually mismatched.

"Do not be yoked together with unbelievers," Paul wrote in 2 Corinthians 6:14–16. "For what do righteousness and wickedness have in common? Or what fellowship can light have with darkness? What harmony is there between Christ and Belial? What does a believer have in common with an unbeliever? What agreement is there between the temple of God and idols? For we are the temple of the living God . . ."

Paul was not issuing a blanket prohibition against Christians having any association with nonbelievers. He was far too realistic to expect that.[3] In short, observed one scholar, Paul was saying: "Do not form any relationship, whether temporary or permanent, with unbelievers that would lead to a compromise of Christian standards or jeopardize consistency of Christian witness. And why such separation? Because the unbeliever does not share the Christian's standards, sympathies, or goals."[4]

Paul uses a Greek word that has two components: "other" and "yoked." This is a reference to the command in Deuteronomy 22:10 against harnessing two different kinds of animals together to plow a field or pull a load.

The reason for this prohibition is simple: the yoke was a rigid wood and metal device that was fitted around the necks of two animals. If the animals were of the same kind and similar strength, they would work harmoniously together, equally sharing the load. But if they were from different species, like an ox and a donkey, or if one was smaller or weaker than the other, their out-of-sync gait would cause the yoke to pinch and choke them, bringing severe pain.

So Paul was sternly warning Christians that pain would result if they allowed themselves to be harnessed to a nonbeliever in marriage. The natural consequence of being wed to someone outside the faith would be conflict over a myriad of issues, ranging from child-rearing to finances, and the possible choking of the Christian's faith.

The Old Testament tells us what happened when the wisest man who ever lived, Solomon, violated God's command against marrying outside his faith. "This act almost destroyed him," wrote Jo Berry, author of *Beloved Unbeliever*. "In his twilight years he was a broken man; depressed, despondent, and guilt-ridden, because he disobeyed God's law about intermarriage."[5]

Similarly, marriage to Jezebel quickly prompted the Jewish king Ahab to abandon his allegiance to the true God and to begin worshiping the false god Baal. With his faith in God drained away because of the corrupting influence of his nonbelieving wife, Ahab "did more to provoke the Lord, the God of Israel, to anger than did all the kings of Israel before him."[6]

The pattern is clear: we risk grave consequences if we don't heed God's loving commands for our life.

THE ROAD TO A MISMATCH

Even so, many Christians find themselves in an unequally yoked marriage—in many cases, a situation they had not intended at the outset. For instance, some couples started out as non-Christians, like Leslie and I did, and became spiritually mismated when one of them—usually the woman—became a follower of Jesus.

Others end up mismatched because the nonbeliever deceived the Christian during the dating process by pretending he was a follower of Christ. That may sound bizarre, but it happens more than you probably think. In fact, it was the topic of a memorable episode of *Seinfeld*.

It seems George Costanza was dating a woman who told him over dinner—unfortunately, after she had ordered an expensive lobster meal—that she was breaking up with him because she was a "Latvian Orthodox" and he wasn't.

"I've actually thought about converting," he said later to his friend Jerry.

"To Latvian Orthodox?" he asked, astonished.

George shrugged. "Who cares?"

George went to visit two elaborately dressed Latvian Orthodox priests who seemed perplexed by his desire to convert. "Is there one aspect of the faith that you find particularly attractive?" one of them asked.

"I think the hats," he said.

The other priest asked, "Are you familiar with our theology?"

George smiled and said modestly, "Well, perhaps not as much as you are. But I know the basic plot."

Obviously, George wasn't really a sincere seeker who wanted to find God. Instead, he went on to cheat on his "conversion exam" as part of a grand plot to fool his girlfriend into thinking he embraced the same faith.

The *Seinfeld* episode was comedy, but at its core was the recognition that some guys on the "dating hunt" will do whatever it takes—even to feign interest in spirituality—in order to fulfill their mission of winning over the woman of their dreams. That's what happened to a friend of ours named Sally.

"He talked a good game when we were going out together," she said. "He had been to church enough to use the right words and act the right way. He knew I wanted to marry a Christian and probably saw no harm in playing the part. But a few months into the marriage, he stopped going to church with me, and it became clear his heart had never really been changed by Christ. I was devastated—but it was too late."

When we pressed Sally for details, though, it became obvious that she had let her love for Mike obscure her discernment. She wanted to marry him so much that she had overlooked little signs along the way that should have warned her that he was not truly a born-again believer in Christ.

"In a way," she conceded, "I guess I let myself get fooled. I didn't ask the hard questions. I ignored the yellow flags, like the profanity he would use and the way he always relied on himself instead of God. And he hung around with friends who were definitely not Christians. I sort of let myself think everything would turn out fine in the end."

Other times, Christians are so new in their faith that they were simply unaware that God wants them marrying someone who's a Christian. Or perhaps they had never been taught what the Bible says about marriage.

Unfortunately, many liberal pastors don't adequately delve into the spiritual status of the people they're marrying—and if they no longer believe in the inspiration of Scripture, they themselves may not even agree with the biblical teaching against unequally yoked relationships.

Once the couple is married, however, and the Christian begins to grow in her faith, inevitably the tension starts to mount. In fact, the more she pursues God and takes her relationship with Christ seriously, the more likely that marital problems will erupt.

THE DANGER OF CONJUGAL EVANGELISM

Then there are some Christians who decide they know better than God. They're aware he doesn't want them to marry outside their faith, but they're convinced that their spouse will give his life to Christ very soon after the wedding vows are uttered. They mentally gloss over the conflict they're going to encounter over spiritual matters and underestimate how far their fiancé is from Christ. Christian journalist Terry Mattingly calls it "conjugal evangelism."

I'll never forget the time I spoke at a church about the dangers of unequally yoked marriages, describing all of the turbulence that Leslie and I experienced when we were spiritually mismatched. After my forty-five-minute talk, a young woman came up and said with complete sincerity, "I'm dating a man who is checking out Christianity, and I just know he's going to become a Christian before too long. So don't you think it would be all right for us to get married? Really, it's just a matter of time before he makes a commitment to Christ."

It was almost as if she had plugged her ears during my warnings! I wanted to shout: "Read my lips: 'Do not be yoked together with unbelievers!' For his sake, for your own sake, for your future children's sake—*heed God's Word!*"

In a newspaper column, Mattingly described an article written by a pastor. In it, the pastor imagines an inner voice—one of unvarnished honesty—that speaks to a minister as he gets ready to unite a Christian and a non-Christian in marriage. The voice in his head wishes it could speak this way to everyone who was present for the nuptials:

> Dear friends, we have gathered here today to witness a disaster in the making. Martha here has decided she wants to marry Chester. Martha—church-goer, hymn-singer, happy, raised right—is throwing it all away in order to marry Chet here, a smug, ungodly rascal . . . Why Chester and Martha want to lock themselves into marriage is beyond me . . . [But] I'll say some religious words over you as we all pretend that somehow God is blessing what He has forbidden. You will exchange rings and vows and saliva and leave here seeking the lowest common denominator in your values, your beliefs and your convictions . . . So let us pray, and pray, and pray.[7]

Frankly, Leslie and I can't understand how any self-respecting, God-honoring, Bible-believing pastor could preside over the wedding of an unequally yoked couple in direct defiance of biblical teaching. Yet sometimes ministers compromise because of church politics or they rationalize that perhaps conjugal evangelism actually will succeed in this case.

The problem is that just about everyone has heard at least one story of how conjugal evangelism *did* work in a particular instance. Unfortunately, that can give Christians false optimism as they weigh whether to trust God's teachings or their own wisdom.

But how can we expect God to bless a marriage that blatantly violates his own command? He can't protect us from the dire consequences of a mismatched marriage if we turn a deaf ear to his warnings. Says Job 4:8: "Those who sow trouble reap it."

Regardless of the road that led them there, unequally yoked spouses all find they have common challenges, problems, and concerns. Despite the difficulties, though, Paul cautioned against taking divorce as the easy way out. "If any brother has a wife who is not a believer and she is willing to live with him, he must not divorce her," Paul wrote. "And if a woman has a husband who is not a believer and he is willing to live with her, she must not divorce him."[8]

In other words: keep the marriage intact if possible—and seek God's help in coping with the mismatch.

WHAT'S THE MATTER WITH MEN?

You've probably noticed by this point that when we talk about mismatched couples, we usually refer to the woman as being the Christian. That's because this is the case in the vast majority of unequally yoked marriages. Perhaps that's understandable in light of statistics that show women tend to be more receptive to spiritual matters than men.

For instance, pollster George Barna has found that among Americans as a whole, men are less likely than women to read the Bible, attend church, contribute to a charity, agree the Bible to be true, believe in the resurrection of Jesus, or pray to God.

While three-quarters of American women say religion is "very important" in their life, only about half of men would agree. Half of females say their religious views have a great impact on their life, yet less than a third of males say the same thing. Four times more men than women identify themselves as atheists, and seventy percent of women claim to have made a personal commitment to Jesus, compared to sixty percent of men.[9]

We shouldn't be shocked by those findings in light of the way men are raised in our culture. The same factors that discourage men from forming close personal friendships with others are the very same reasons why many of them are reluctant to reach out for a personal relationship with God.

Among the factors that David W. Smith lists in his book *Men Without Friends* are the fact that as youngsters most males were encouraged to suppress their emotions, to be competitive, to keep their personal needs and longings deep inside, and to look up to role models who are independent and impersonal.[10] Sounds like a formula for a spiritually repressed person, doesn't it?

Contrast the independent, insulated, emotion-denying, self-reliant perspective of most men with the kind of attitudes necessary to follow Jesus: humility, a willingness to candidly admit failures and wrongdoing, a recognition of our need for a Savior, and absolute dependence on God.

One well-known sociologist has even raised the controversial possibility that hormones may be partly to blame for some males rejecting God. Rodney Stark of the University of Washington said elevated testosterone levels have been associated with men who are likely to engage in risky behavior.

"Being irreligious is risky," Stark told a convention of the Religion Research Association. He cited "Pascal's wager," an observation made by the seventeenth-century French scientist Blaise Pascal that a person has nothing to lose if he believes in God and it turns out in the end he was wrong, but he has everything to lose if he wagers that God doesn't exist and it turns out in the end that he really does.

Stark said that men, stimulated by their hormones to take risks, are more willing than women to take the ultimate gamble on the hereafter. He bolstered his theory by pointing out that in Judaism, where there's little emphasis on an afterlife, the number of religious men and women is about equal. The more a Christian denomination stresses heaven and hell, the greater the gap between the number of religious males and females, he said.[11]

Stark conceded that more research needs to be done in this area before firm conclusions can be drawn. And of course, a surplus of testosterone is ultimately no excuse for rejecting God. In the meantime, though, the reality is that most unequally yoked marriages involve irreligious men matched with religious women. As a general rule, however, the principles in this book apply regardless of the marriage makeup.

WHY DOES HE DO WHAT HE DOES?

Jan's husband was a skeptic. "Atheist, agnostic—I don't know exactly which he is. I just know he doesn't believe in God. And the more I grow in my new faith in Jesus, the more he digs in his heels," she said.

Her biggest problem, she added, was that she couldn't understand why he acts the way he does. "He isn't the most communicative guy in the world," she said with a smile. "You know—the strong, silent type. I just can't figure out what's going on in his head. What causes his outbursts? Why is he so sarcastic? Why does he seem interested when I talk about church, but gets really mad at other times?"

Ironically, your nonbelieving spouse is probably experiencing the same bubbling cauldron of emotions you are—for entirely different reasons. The more we can get in touch with why each partner feels the way he or she does, the more harmony we will experience and the more likely we can live out our faith in a way that will intrigue rather than repel our spouse.

So that's what we're going to talk about next. Leslie will tell her story, and then I'll tell mine—and we hope you'll walk away with some new insights to help smooth your spiritual mismatch.

But please let us encourage you one more time before we proceed. Never forget that God hasn't left your side! He knows your struggles, your frustrations, your fears, and your uncertainty—*and he cares*! He will help you if you let him.

If you knowingly entered into a spiritual mismatch, hoping in vain that conjugal evangelism would work, confess it to him and experience his forgiveness. If you've heaped condemnation on yourself because you've been blaming your spouse's spiritual disinterest on your failure as an evangelist, then forgive yourself. You're not responsible for his spiritual choices!

Together, we'll explore some ways you might calm the turbulent waters of your relationship and help you live out your faith in a way that honors God while being winsome to your mate. For now, though, we want to share some words of comfort and encouragement with you.

Undoubtedly, you're familiar with the Twenty-third Psalm, which begins, "The LORD is my shepherd . . ." In fact, you may be *too* accustomed to those words, having heard them to the point where they have lost some of their punch. So take some time to meditate on the way Leslie F. Brandt has put these ancient words of King David into modern language in his book *Psalms/Now*. Perhaps the fresh words of his paraphrase will open your mind and heart to experiencing this psalm in a powerful new way:

Spiritual Mismatch

The Lord is my constant companion.
There is no need that He cannot fulfill.
Whether His course for me points
to the mountaintops of glorious joy
or to the valleys of human suffering,
He is by my side.
He is ever present with me.
He is close beside me
when I tread the dark streets of danger,
and even when I flirt with death itself,
He will not leave me.
When the pain is severe,
He is near to comfort.
When the burden is heavy
He is there to lean upon.
When depression darkens my soul,
He touches me with eternal joy.
When I feel empty and alone,
He fills the aching vacuum with His power.
My security is in His promise
to be near me always
and in the knowledge
that He will never let me go.

From *Psalms/Now* by Leslie F. Brandt.
© 1973 Concordia Publishing House.
Used with permission.

2

In Leslie's Words: A Story of Loneliness, Fear, Perseverance, Faith

I REALIZED FROM THE OUTSET THAT SOMETHING WAS DIFFERENT about Linda Lenssen. Our new apartment was chaotic, filled with stacks of unopened moving boxes, when Linda knocked on the front door with a big plate of chocolate chip cookies in one hand and her three-month-old daughter in the other. She was pleasant and welcoming, and we hit it off right away. I was thrilled that her daughter was about the same age as Alison.

She called a few days later to invite me to her apartment for coffee. When we sat down at her kitchen table, I noticed a Bible and open workbook on the counter. That wasn't something I was used to seeing! During our conversation she mentioned she was involved with Christian Women's Club and some activities at her church, but she didn't seem pushy about it. Frankly, I had never heard anyone talk about those sorts of things. But because she was so friendly, I didn't feel threatened by it at all. It just seemed . . . different.

As Lee mentioned in the introduction, I had very little exposure to church as a child. I did take some confirmation classes at a Presbyterian church, but my only recollections are boys throwing spitballs, girls passing notes, and the frustrated pastor trying to get our attention. I don't remember hearing anything about what it means to be a Christian. Instead, it was mainly looking at maps of ancient locations and memorizing the names of people, places, and a list of things we should never do. None of us was the least bit interested.

Still, I found myself being interested when Linda would gently raise spiritual topics during our long talks over tea. I remember the time she asked about what kind of moral training we were going to provide for Alison. When I told her we really had no idea, she wasn't judgmental or condescending, although she did caution me that there are a lot of terrible things kids can get involved with and that it might be a good idea to look into some sort of spiritual education for her. That got me thinking about my own lack of spiritual knowledge.

About five months into our friendship, Linda invited me to go to church with her. I felt a little uncomfortable about this. It was obvious to me that God played a very important part in her life. It was equally clear that Linda was the nicest and most generous person I had ever met and that the way she parented was so much calmer and more serene than my own style. I felt like there was a lot I could learn from her. But I was skeptical about the idea of getting entangled with religion.

Even so, I eventually decided to say yes—if for no other reason than it seemed like she would keep inviting me until I gave in! She had included Lee in the invitation, but I knew that there was no way he would go with us, although he did agree to watch Alison while we went one Sunday morning.

I didn't realize when we drove off to a local movie theater, where a new but growing congregation called Willow Creek Community Church was meeting, that my life was about to radically change forever.

EXPERIENCING GOD

I remember thinking it odd that instead of taking me to her own church, Linda took me to a church she had read about in the newspaper. What I didn't know at the time was that this was a church designed to appeal to people like me, with little or no church background. And I loved it!

Instead of organ music and dusty old hymns with words I couldn't understand, this church featured vocalists who sang contemporary and upbeat songs that seemed to make spirituality accessible. They had a drama that was like a slice out of my own life, and they used the theater's big screen to show a multimedia presentation that touched my heart. The pastor looked like he was about my age, and he was dressed in a business suit instead of the robes I had seen in church as a child. Most important, though, was that he talked about God in language I could comprehend, describing the Bible's relevance to everyday life situations.

I remember coming home and enthusiastically saying to Lee, "You wouldn't believe it—this church was really exciting!" To him, "exciting church" was an oxymoron—words that people use together but actually conflict, like "jumbo shrimp" or "congressional ethics."

Lee simply wasn't interested in hearing about the church service. Nor was he interested in baby-sitting Alison another Sunday morning when he could be sleeping. But I wanted to go back. In the end, we struck a deal: I would take Alison with me to church so Lee could have a quiet house for sleeping late. He wasn't happy about it—I suspect he was concerned about what influence church might have on me—but he didn't put up a big fight over it.

This started a pattern: I would go to church, where I would learn something new about God each Sunday, and then Linda and I would talk about it over tea during the following week. I had a million questions, and fortunately Linda was very good at answering them. Through it all, our friendship grew deeper and deeper.

Then came the day in the autumn of 1979 when Linda once again explained God's plan of salvation to me. This time, I was ready! With all of my heart, I wanted to know Jesus personally, to be fully forgiven for my sins, and to be assured of spending eternity in heaven. That day I prayed to receive Jesus as my forgiver and leader.

Linda was ecstatic! She bought me *The Living Bible*, a paraphrase that helped me better understand what the text was saying. I was like a sponge—reading Scripture, asking questions, praying, learning, growing, exploring, stretching. It should have been the most exhilarating time of my life. Instead, it became the most difficult.

My decision to follow Jesus ushered in the most tumultuous era of my marriage to Lee. It was a time of harsh words, stony silence, open anger, and raw emotions. "Why are you wasting your time with that junk?" he would shout at me. "Why do you need that crutch in your life?"

The more I tried to explain that this wasn't a crutch—rather, it was a source of fulfillment, joy, and peace unlike anything I had ever experienced before—the more Lee would react in anger. Why was he being so cruel? Why was he so defensive? Why was it that when I would take one step toward him with the Bible, he would take two steps back?

With the benefit of hindsight, I will let him try to explain all of that in the next chapter! For now, though, let me describe our relationship from my point of view, emphasizing the kind of emotions that had me tied into knots for the nearly two years of our spiritual mismatch.

A FORMULA FOR FRUSTRATION

One of the most corrosive emotions that ate away at me during our spiritually mismatched era was a strong feeling of frustration. As my relationship with Jesus grew stronger and deeper, it became such an exciting and thrilling part of my life that I wanted to be able to share it with the man I loved the most. But he would always rebuff me, ridicule me, or ignore me when I tried to help him understand. It was the first time since we met when we were fourteen years old that there was something we couldn't experience together.

One incident crystallized my discouragement. At the time our finances were a mess. We were living a self-indulgent lifestyle and obviously not following biblical principles regarding spending, saving, and giving. If you have ever wrestled with money problems, then you know how deeply disheartening they can be.

Late one afternoon I went into our bedroom and reclined across the bed while I was reading the Bible that Linda had given me. I was hoping to find some specific wisdom about our finances that would ease the burden I was feeling. Instead, I kept coming upon verse after verse after verse that simply reaffirmed God's love for me. I began to understand in a fresh way how he wanted to ease my anxiety and infuse me with peace. Filled with gratitude and wonder and awe, I started to weep. I was just so relieved and happy to be reminded that there was a God who wanted to help me as a good father helps a treasured daughter.

At this extremely tender and vulnerable moment, I realized that it was time for Lee to come home from work. I glanced out the window and, sure enough, he was coming up the sidewalk. For a split second I wished Lee could understand the joyful and worshipful feelings that were churning inside of me and that he could share this moving experience I had just gone through. I wished he would embrace me and cry with me and revel with me in the love of God.

But I quickly put those thoughts aside. I knew the reality of the situation—if Lee saw my face damp with tears, he would sigh and throw down his briefcase and demand, *"Now* what?" I knew if he saw the Bible, he would probably use it as an excuse to pick a fight—"Why are you filling your mind with mythology and make-believe and wishful thinking?" I knew that if I were to bring up the subject of God, he would slam his fist on the table and say, "Look—I've had a long, hard day; don't make it worse by bringing up religion!"

So I did what I had to do—I quickly dried my tears, shoved the Bible under the bed, plastered on a smile, and emerged from the bedroom as if absolutely nothing had happened. I had just caught a wonderful glimpse of God's love and grace—so much that my heart was overflowing with worship—but I couldn't breathe a word about it to my own husband. That's a formula for frustration!

This happened to me over and over again as I continued to experience God on deeper and more profound levels. I would learn a new spiritual insight that was bursting with implications for our lives, but I couldn't share it with Lee. I would receive an answer to prayer that was so lavish and unexpected that I would want to explode with gratitude, yet I knew Lee would only scoff if I told him about it. I would feel a powerful desire to worship God, but I knew better than to mention anything about it to him. I would come across Christians who would make great friends for us, but I would hesitate to introduce them to Lee because their connection with church would only fuel his cynicism.

The only analogy that comes close to capturing the depth of my frustration was if I had visited a distant, beautiful, and romantic city, drinking in its wonderful sights and sounds, but Lee was neither interested in going with me nor hearing about it when I got back. As terrific as it would be to have explored that city for myself, an important part of marriage is being able to share those kinds of experiences with each other. Enjoying it alone would feel hollow. If you were to magnify that analogy a hundred times, you would begin to sense the frustration of being spiritually isolated in marriage.

WHEN VALUES COLLIDE

When Albert Einstein was celebrating his fiftieth wedding anniversary, he was asked the secret to longevity in marriage. "When we first got married, we made a pact," he said. "In our life together, it was decided I would make all of the big decisions and my wife would make all of the little decisions. For fifty years, we have held true to that agreement. I believe that is the reason for the success in our marriage. However, the strange thing is that in fifty years, there hasn't been one big decision!"[1]

Marriages work best when both partners see eye to eye on the decisions they face as a couple. For years that was true of Lee and me. We had the same values, the same outlook on life, the same attitudes, the same goals and desires. Decisions sort of made themselves; we rarely got embroiled in arguments or even extended discussions about which direction to go in life.

All of that stopped after I became a Christian. I was developing a Christian worldview—seeing everything through scriptural lenses—and Lee was still filtering everything through the lenses we had both formerly worn: the perspective of expediency, of selfish pleasure, and of blind ambition. Clashes were inevitable, and they came with increasing frequency and intensity.

Finances are a good example. In the past, we had never seen a dollar that we didn't want to spend. We lived far beyond our means and got mired in debt—but at least we both were in agreement on our lifestyle. Now as a Christian I wanted to apply the Bible's teachings about living within our means, saving a percentage of our income for future needs, and giving a portion of what God had provided us to support his work in the world.

In fact, I remember going to a church meeting about a fund drive to raise money so that Willow Creek Community Church could move out of the cramped movie theater and into its own building, where its various ministries would have elbow room to flourish. My heart was beating out of my chest! It was obvious to me that this expansion was so needed to reach the unchurched of our community—*including Lee!* I was really anxious to be part of this venture and contribute in some way to this fellowship that I had grown to love.

I went home, prayed, and waited for what I thought would be an appropriate time to bring this up to Lee. But when I did, he went ballistic! "Under no circumstances are we going to give *one cent* to that church!" he bellowed. "I've told you, that's all they want—your money! How can you be so blind? Don't you understand they're all con men who are playing you for a fool?"

The next morning Linda got an earful. "He's awful!" I whined. "Why is he so open-minded about so many things, but his mind snaps shut when it comes to church? It's like his attitude is, 'Don't confuse me with the facts!'"

I will tell you later in the book about the near-miraculous way God came through for me in the midst of this specific situation. In the meantime, though, I was realizing that finances were just one area where our values were at odds. As I peered down the road into the future of our marriage, I was disheartened to see it paved with arguments and conflict over one fundamental issue after another.

A MISGUIDED QUEST FOR MEANING

I knew that our values would soon clash over the way we would raise our children. I wanted Alison and Kyle to become authentic and enthusiastic followers of Jesus, exhibiting his morality and his attitudes of humility, servanthood, love, and self-sacrifice. Yet I knew Lee had a totally different goal. He would want to "toughen them up" so they would be more savvy, more cynical, and more ruthless than their peers.

In addition, our perspective on Lee's career began to differ. He was relentlessly devoted to success as a journalist, working extremely long hours under highly stressful circumstances to beat the competition at two other daily newspapers, four local TV news organizations, and two all-news radio stations. His life was like a whirlwind. He faced seven deadlines a day. Once he wrote nine articles in one day; another time he had three articles on the front page. He was focused like a laser beam on winning awards, promotions, and front-page bylines.

For years I had cheered him on, even though his obsession with the *Chicago Tribune* increasingly pulled him away from me and the children. But now, as my values were shifting, my perspective of what's really important in life started to change. Family mattered to me. Time together with Lee became more and more valuable to me. The money from his career couldn't compensate for the deterioration of his health that was inevitable under his unrealistic and ever-demanding schedule.

I began to recognize that Lee's never-ending pursuit of journalistic success was really a desperate, misguided, and unconscious quest to find meaning in life. In a way, he was striving for immortality by trying to make a splash in the world and leave behind a pile of newspaper clippings for historians to see that he really had made a difference with his life. He was trying to achieve security by making himself invaluable to the newspaper, knowing he was only as good as his last front-page exclusive.

As a Christian, I was able to see what he could not: that only knowing Jesus Christ and helping build his kingdom could ever satisfy Lee's desire for meaning. He would never really be fulfilled until he started living out God's plan for his life. He would never find security apart from Jesus. And he would always work feverishly in a frantic desire to achieve immortality through leaving a journalistic legacy until he received Christ's freely offered gift of eternal life in heaven.

In a similar way, Lee's drinking began to bother me. He was a "recreational drunk," someone who would periodically get plastered for the sheer fun of it. What I once saw as a harmless release of pent-up tension I now viewed as a twisted pursuit of the happiness he could never find until he personally encountered Jesus.

I could see these things but Lee couldn't. If I had tried to point them out, he would have exploded in anger. Increasingly, we were going through life reading different scripts. While I knew mine would ultimately have a happy ending, I was also convinced that his was destined to end in disaster.

Unless God intervened.

FEAR OVER THE FUTURE

These emotions—frustration over my spiritual isolation and discouragement over our differing values—were compounded by a recurring sense of fear. Some of it was anxiety over our marriage. Would Lee decide that divorce was the answer to our radically different lifestyles? Would he decide that I had changed too much from the person he once pledged to spend his life with? Even though divorce was never an option for me, I suspected there were times when he came close to calling a lawyer.

But my biggest fear concerned what I knew was going to happen someday after Lee's death. A holy God would look at him and say, *Lee, you rebuffed my offer of forgiveness and heaven for your entire life. You heard my message of mercy and hope, but you rejected it time after time. You made the choice to remain separate from me during your lifetime, and I let you have your way. Now I've sealed your decision. You can have your way throughout eternity by being separated from me and my people, forever.*

No human being on this side of death can imagine the abject horror of being separated from any influence of God for all of eternity. That's what hell is about. It's a place of utter hopelessness, despair, and torment where people will gnash their teeth in an eternity of regret. I tried to rationalize away hell by saying it's not as bad as fire-and-brimstone preachers make it out to be, but the clear teachings of the Bible paint it in terms too horrible to contemplate. I tried to soft-pedal the gospel by imagining that nice-but-ungodly people like Lee would somehow find their way to heaven, but again I knew I was playing games. Jesus himself taught otherwise.

I feared for Lee's soul! I loved him and didn't want to see him suffer and realize too late that he could have spent eternity in the blissful and perfect presence of God. I wanted the best for him, and that meant him having a redemptive relationship with Jesus Christ. It meant him knowing and experiencing God and unreservedly following him during his time in this world, and then enjoying heaven throughout the rest of time.

Sometimes my anguish over Lee's future was so intense that it would start to generate another corrosive emotion in me—guilt. I found this vague, free-floating sense of self-condemnation difficult to shake.

PLAGUED BY MISPLACED GUILT

The guilt didn't start right away. It developed after many months as I began to despair that Lee would never receive Christ. Slowly, I started to experience misplaced feelings of responsibility for Lee's spiritual condition.

If only I were a better Christian, I told myself, *then Lee would clearly see Christ in me and have no choice but to conclude that he's real. If I were only more loving, more sacrificing, more humble, more serving, then Lee would respond to the gospel. Maybe it's my lackluster Christian life that's hindering him from developing any interest in spiritual matters. If I would cooperate more with the Holy Spirit in his efforts to transform my character, then I would become a compelling witness. If I could just explain the gospel better or stop losing my patience with Lee, he'd certainly be a Christian by now.*

The problem, of course, is that I would never be a perfect Christian! My shortcomings were always glaring at me. And as long as Lee resisted the gospel, I could find reasons to blame myself for his response. Unfortunately, this feeling of self-reproach is common among unequally yoked women. In fact, during the years she was wed to a nonbeliever, author Linda Davis found that some well-meaning Christians actually reinforced the idea that she was somehow to blame for his rejection of God:

They said things like: "If you ladies with unsaved husbands would just be more sweet and loving, your husbands would get born-again in no time." (This direct quote came from a retreat leader whose husband had been a Christian since age six.) "As soon as the Lord finishes working on you, then he'll start working on your husband." (Can't he work on both of us at the same time?) "Just pray longer." (Fifteen years isn't long enough?) "You just need to love your husband to the Lord."[2]

You can imagine how those devastating comments would fuel feelings of inadequacy among unequally yoked people! They play on their worst insecurities. On top of that, they're just plain unscriptural!

It took my friend Linda to set me straight one day when I was feeling sorry for myself and moping around because of Lee's continued resistance to God. "Listen to me," she said sternly. "You're not responsible for Lee's decision to receive or reject Christ. There isn't one example in the Bible of anyone failing to come to Christ because his or her spouse wasn't a good enough Christian. If a wife had to be perfect to win her spouse to the Lord, no husband would ever receive Christ!"

In his grace God does not put the burden of heaven or hell on any marriage partner. It would be too much to bear if a wife knew that her husband's eternal destiny hinged solely on how well she lived out her faith in front of him or how compellingly she explained the gospel. I have seen wives who are paragons of Christian virtue and yet whose husbands are stone-cold toward God, and I have seen wives who could be poster children for Hypocrisy Anonymous whose husbands have become fully devoted to Christ.

In the end, the issue of salvation is strictly between your spouse and God. It's the Holy Spirit's role to convict him of sin (John 16:8–11); only the Father can draw someone to Christ (John 6:44). God won't strong-arm your partner into following him; instead, God will honor his spiritual choices. As for you, the Bible gives Christian wives and husbands this responsibility: *love your spouse.* Love him or her unconditionally. Love him or her regardless of whether he or she ever bends the knee to Christ. Be devoted, be prayerful, be encouraging—but don't try to be responsible! You're not. Your spouse is. *Period.*

If you have been plagued by pangs of guilt due to feeling responsible for your husband's ongoing disinterest in God or church, you need to release yourself from that sentence. Yes, live out your faith as authentically as you can. Yes, confess to God those personal failures and flaws that don't reflect well on Christ. Yes, apologize to your spouse when you haven't behaved in a Christlike way. Yes, cooperate with the Holy Spirit as he works his transformational power in your life.

But, no, *don't* assume responsibility for what you cannot control. Don't wallow in blame for what ultimately is someone else's decision. Don't weigh yourself down with a burden that God never intended you to carry.

YOU DID THE RIGHT THING!

There you have it: emotional isolation and loneliness. Frustration. Clashing values. Fear. Guilt. Then add anger over the way Lee would constantly demean my faith; resentment over the way some Christians treated me like a second-class citizen because of my unequally yoked status; and anxiety over the way Lee and I were inexorably growing apart as a couple. Mix that toxic concoction with the similarly disorienting emotions that Lee was experiencing at the same time (and which he will describe in the next chapter). Sounds pretty hopeless, doesn't it?

I don't want to leave that impression. Despite the tensions my conversion to Christ caused in our home, I never regretted making the decision to follow Jesus. And through everything, God answered my prayers in remarkable ways, flowed peace and contentment into my life when worry seemed ready to engulf me, and lived up to his promises to me over and over again. I don't think I could have ever gone through this alone—but, fortunately, I never had to. The Holy Spirit lived inside of me the whole time, closer than any mere friend could be. And God sent Linda into my life to be Jesus in flesh and blood to me.

If you have made the decision to become a Christian, you have done the right thing! Never second-guess that, regardless of whatever trials come your way. As Jesus said to his disciples: "These things I have spoken to you, so that in Me you may have *peace*. In the world, you have tribulation, but take courage; I have overcome the world."[3]

Peace and courage—aren't those the very things we need in the midst of a spiritual mismatch? Peace to deal with the now, the emotional vertigo that makes our heart sick at this very moment. And courage to deal with the future—whatever tomorrow and the next day and the next month and the next year and even the next decade might hold.

Isn't it just like our loving and gracious Savior to offer the exact help that is desperately needed by every person who is wrestling with being unequally yoked?

3

In Lee's Words: A Story of Anger, Resentment, Conviction, Renewal

IT WAS SUNDAY MORNING AND MY BRAIN WAS POUNDING. I PRIED open one eye wide enough to see raindrops running down the bedroom window. Thunder rumbled in the distance. *Ugh!* I put the pillow over my head and turned over. A drinking binge the night before had left my mouth as dry as cotton. I debated about whether to get up for some aspirin and water but decided I was too tired. It was better, I figured, to ride out the hangover in bed.

Then I heard the sound of a drawer closing. Someone was in the bathroom. A few moments later, Leslie crept into the bedroom to get her watch from the dresser. I peeked out at her and she realized I was awake.

"How do you feel?" she asked.

I groaned. "Not good," I managed to grunt. "What're you doing?"

"Getting ready for church." There was a pause, and then she asked in a very pleasant voice, "Do you want to come with me?"

I wanted to growl, *Do I look like I want to go to church? I feel like an elephant is dancing on my head, it's pouring rain outside, I'm exhausted and irritable, and I don't even believe in God! Just take a wild guess about whether I want to go with you!*

But do you know what I said instead? "Yeah, okay," I snapped. "I'll go."

I threw off the covers and stormed into the bathroom to shave and take a quick shower. Then I stomped around the house, slammed some

42

doors, refused Leslie's offer of breakfast, and got dressed. Leslie knew better than to try to engage me in conversation when I was in an ornery mood like that. Basically, she tried to stay out of my way.

"Where the [blank] is the umbrella?" I shouted as I ransacked the closet. When I couldn't find it, I said, "Well, we're just going to have to make a run for it."

I had left the car on the driveway overnight. We ran to it as fast as we could, but we still got drenched. That only made me angrier! Muttering under my breath, I drove down the highway so fast and recklessly that when we hit puddles the car would start to hydroplane. That would elicit more swearing from me.

Before long, Leslie started to cry. At first she fought the tears, but soon they were flowing down her cheeks. "Look, I'm not twisting your arm!" she said. "If you don't want to go to church, don't. Just let me go in peace!"

Now I felt bad. Why had I agreed to go with her in the first place? Why hadn't I stayed in bed and let her attend church by herself? Why was I seething with so much rage and resentment that I was emotionally abusing the very woman I loved the most?

If you had asked me back then what emotions were prompting my behavior that morning, I wouldn't have had a clue. Like most men, I wasn't in touch with that side of my life. All I knew was that the recent changes in my newly converted wife, though positive for her, were feeding the worst side of me. My world was unraveling and I couldn't figure out how to put it back together again!

Do you recognize any of these symptoms in your spouse? The chances are you're perplexed by why he acts and reacts the way he does. And most likely, he himself doesn't even understand the emotional cauldron that is bubbling inside of him. That's a dangerous combination! Without discerning the reasons behind his behavior, it's going to be extremely difficult for you to restore calm to a contentious relationship and to prevent your spiritual mismatch from degenerating.

But now I have the advantage of many years of hindsight and analysis. Looking back, especially now through spiritual lenses, I can better diagnose what was driving me in those days—and maybe talking about it will help you gain a few insights that will avoid future turbulence in your own mismatched marriage.

THE "REVERSE HALO EFFECT"

Now I understand what got me out of bed that Sunday morning and set the stage for such an obnoxious display of anger. Frankly, I didn't want to get out of bed, but I felt I *had* to—because, in my eyes, I was losing my wife!

I felt like she was being lured away from me into a new sphere of relationships where I didn't fit in. The issue in the back of my mind wasn't whether she was just going to attend church for an hour on that particular Sunday; from my perspective, this represented one more step away from me and toward a whole different world where I felt excluded.

So I made the decision to go with her that morning because I wanted to hang onto her—and my anger flashed because I would rather have stayed in bed, because I was feeling sorry for myself, and because I felt helpless in winning her back from these insidious church folks.

What's more, I felt like I was losing respect from Leslie, and that made me feel hurt. All of a sudden, after years of being each other's biggest admirers, she was being attracted toward a whole new bunch of people. The kind of individuals she was starting to look up to and emulate were Christians who had authentic, vibrant, and growing relationships with Jesus. So where did that leave a non-Christian like me? Although she never had a bad word to say about me, I felt that in her eyes I was being diminished.

In a way, I was suffering from what psychologists call the "reverse halo effect." The "halo effect" is when a person demonstrates competency in one area of life and people assume—often with no real basis—that he or she is equally accomplished in other areas. For instance, people might give extra weight to the political opinions of an actor just because he has achieved status in the movies, even though reciting lines in a film doesn't necessarily qualify a person to offer weighty insights on an election.

On the other hand, the "reverse halo effect" is when people learn about a shortcoming in an individual and assume—again, perhaps with no real basis—that the person is similarly flawed or inept in other areas of life. An example would be people drawing the conclusion that an attorney who has marital problems would therefore also lack competence in his law practice.[1]

How did this apply to me? Deep down inside, I felt that because I now had a significant shortcoming in the eyes of my wife—that is, I wasn't a follower of Jesus like other people she admired—that this would lessen her opinion of me in all other areas of our life. Suddenly, my judgment would be suspect, my decisions would be questioned, my opinions would automatically be considered flawed, and she would respect me less.

In short, I felt that since the qualities Leslie now found more and more appealing—such as faithfulness to Christ, a Bible-centered morality, and spiritual maturity—were beyond me as a nonbeliever, then I was doomed to lose her love and watch helplessly as she slipped further and further away from me.

SEEING JESUS AS A RIVAL

To put it bluntly, I was jealous of Jesus! I felt like Leslie was cheating on me by having a relationship with the Son of God. That may sound strange, but those were the emotions coursing through me. Jesus was attracting my wife with all kinds of exotic gifts—including all the promises of Scripture—and I didn't have any way of fighting back.

For the first time in our marriage, her emotional needs were increasingly being met by someone other than me—specifically, through her relationship with Christ. That meant I wasn't as needed as I used to be—and marriage counselors will tell you that most husbands have a strong desire to be needed. I felt victimized because I believed that Leslie had unilaterally broken our marriage agreement by seeking comfort, solace, and encouragement from someone apart from me.

Since then I have found that this feeling is common among nonbelievers whose wives become Christians. Media mogul Ted Turner, founder of CNN, said it was a "shock" when his wife, Jane Fonda, announced to him that she had become a Christian. Said one report: "Turner's daughter Laura doesn't think religion per se was the real basis of their disagreement. She says, 'It was another male'—Jesus. 'It took time away from him.'"[2] Their marriage didn't survive.

Another husband, who did later become a follower of Christ, captured the emotions of many husbands this way:

> When a man's wife becomes a Christian, it's a whole different kind of threat. Suddenly she has a love relationship with someone he can't even see. He can't understand anything she tries to tell him about this new God she has come to know. All he knows is that she's in love with somebody else, and he is jealous. Instead of remaining the first priority in her life as when they first got married, he has suddenly been demoted to number two after God . . . It would be easier for him to understand if she had run off with another man; but she's in love with someone he can't even compete with. He feels helpless.[3]

My jealousy also extended to her new church friends. Why was it that so many of the church leaders were men? What were their real motives? I was suspicious about their intentions. I figured they must not be very fond of me, since I was an atheist, and in my mind this automatically put us in an adversarial posture. They were pulling Leslie away from me, and I had to find a way to do something about it.

In reality, none of Leslie's new Christian acquaintances or anyone in the church had ever done anything that could possibly be construed as inappropriate. Yet in my mind, I saw them as rivals for my wife's attention. They shared many things with Leslie that I didn't. They talked about spiritual experiences and biblical teachings that I knew nothing about. They had an entire language—with terms like "spiritual gifts," "quiet times," and a whole raft of theological and biblical terms—that I didn't speak. They all admired evangelical Christian leaders who I had never heard of. That made me the odd man out.

Now, I admit I have a lot of flaws, but jealousy wasn't generally one of them. People would not have labeled me "controlling" in my marriage. Even so, you can see how my mind was distorting what was really going on. The more I felt excluded from her newfound world of Christianity, the more my imagination would conjure up reasons for being jealous and wanting to rein in Leslie before she got away from me.

Now, consider this: what if your partner already has a tendency toward being overly possessive? What if he's naturally the suspicious type? In that case, you can see how easily these circumstances could quickly heat him from a simmering jealousy into a full boil of resentment.

WHEN VALUES COLLIDE

In addition to these feelings of hurt and jealousy, I also experienced a great degree of frustration over our increasingly different values. One of the reasons we had enjoyed a stable marriage was that we shared a common viewpoint about basic matters of life, such as how to spend our money and our free time. But Leslie's commitment to Christ began to change her opinions about a wide range of issues. Her faith was not just a small compartment of her life; it influenced the way she saw everything.

For example, we used to be pretty loose with our finances, feeling free to indulge ourselves whenever we felt we deserved it and dipping into debt quite significantly. Not content to merely live within our means, we tended to be wasteful and extravagant.

But now Leslie didn't think debt was such a good idea. Having been taught what the Bible has to say about handling finances, she wanted to pay off our heavily laden credit cards and adopt a more responsible lifestyle. That rankled me, because her newfound financial conservatism had implications for what I did and didn't purchase.

To make matters worse, she actually wanted to give some of our money to the church. That infuriated me! As a journalist, I had seen plenty of naive people fleeced by con men. I figured that the church was really after our cash but that Leslie was too blinded by her faith to recognize it.

I envisioned pastors living lavish lifestyles at the expense of hardworking folks who entrusted them with their money because they assumed it was going to help the less fortunate.

Leslie felt so strongly about giving to the church that she actually got a part-time job with the idea that she would contribute some of her income to the ministry. I agreed to this at the outset—but when it came time for her to fork over a portion of her paycheck, I balked. To me, this would be like pouring it down the drain.

"Come on, Leslie, you can't give that much money to the church!" I implored her. "Think of all the fun we could have with it. You're robbing us and giving money to a place that probably has more than it needs."

We later reached an accommodation, as we'll describe in a coming chapter. But this was indicative of the way our values were changing.

On Sundays, I preferred to sleep late, linger over the newspaper, go out to a nice restaurant for brunch, and doze in front of the television during the football or basketball game. Now Leslie's desire to go to church threw a monkey wrench into everything. While I told her I didn't care if she went alone, often I felt an internal pressure to accompany her—again, because I felt that otherwise I was losing her. That further fueled my indignation.

Our attitudes toward entertainment also began to conflict. In the past, we had attended some on-the-edge movies, splashed with profanity, violence, and worse, but now Leslie shied away from them. Instead, she suggested we should see more uplifting and positive films, which certainly didn't interest me.

My own behavior, which never seemed to bother Leslie in the past, now made me feel guilty because I sensed she no longer endorsed some of the things I did. For instance, my language was often filthy and raw. After all, that's the way reporters talk in the newsroom. While Leslie didn't scold me when I let loose with a string of profanities, I could see her wince ever so slightly. Using God's name in vain seemed to especially upset her. She no longer found my off-color jokes to be funny. To avoid offending her, I began to censor myself, but that only made me more resentful.

And if she disapproved of my language, I knew she was opposed to my drinking. My attitude toward liquor was that mere social drinking made no sense. Why sip alcohol when I could guzzle it? Why get tipsy when I could get blitzed? My goal was to get drunk so that my inhibitions would slip away and I could laugh and have fun with abandon. I wasn't an alcoholic, because I wasn't dependent on liquor, but I did use it liberally to lubricate my lifestyle.

Leslie, on the other hand, was never much of a drinker. And now I sensed she didn't like my occasional binges. I wasn't even sure anymore whether I should order wine at a meal. I felt like I had to walk on eggshells with her. She never demanded that I stop drinking, but I knew her well enough to read her body language—and the message was clear enough!

I began to resent her because, as I told myself in a fit of self-pity, I was the one who was always feeling subtly pressured to compromise and give up things. Of course, I conveniently overlooked the many times when she quietly let me have my way rather than further inflame the situation. I was mostly concerned about me—and I wasn't happy!

FEARS OVER THE FUTURE

Then there was fear. I began to be afraid for our future together if Leslie continued to take her faith more and more seriously. The more she changed, the further we were in danger of drifting apart, and that concerned me greatly.

Also, I worried about whether she would embarrass me in front of my friends by shaming them for their language or attitudes. Would she even pressure me to dump some of my long-standing buddies because she now considered them to be a corrupting influence?

Once, when I sensed she no longer liked me to hang out with a particularly hard-drinking, foulmouthed pal, I said in a huff, "Why don't you just give me a list of people I can and can't hang out with?"

Ironically, she hadn't actually said a word to me about my friends. But since I knew she was embracing Christian values, I began to assume she didn't want me associating with certain people whose attitudes represented the opposite. So I was getting upset with Leslie due to what I figured she was thinking. Leslie couldn't win! If she confronted me about my friends, I'd get angry, but if she didn't say anything, I'd *still* get mad!

In addition, I was disturbed that she may begin to disclose private details about our personal life in her prayer groups. I didn't know what happened in those secret get-togethers, but I feared the worst. I didn't want strangers knowing what went on in the privacy of our marriage or hearing about the unguarded words that spewed from my mouth during one of my angry tirades behind closed doors. I had a public image to protect!

I was afraid Leslie might say to her prayer partners, "Please pray for Lee. He's spiritually lost, he has closed his eyes to the truth, he arrogantly refuses to admit he's a sinner, and behind the phony façade of his success he's insecure, immature, immoral, stressed out, and bitter. And you know how much I love him!"

There was no evidence she had been doing that. But when you find yourself circulating in different arenas and among different people than your spouse, you only have your suppositions and suspicions to go by. And I tended to imagine the worst.

WHAT ABOUT THE KIDS?

I was especially troubled about what was going to happen with our children. I could see endless arguments down the road about how to raise them. Practical issues abounded. Should I take the kids to R-rated movies when they're in junior high school? Should I let them have access to contraceptives when they're teenagers? Should I teach them how evolution puts God out of a job? Where would we go to get parenting advice: Dr. Spock or Dr. Dobson?

And if Alison and Kyle became Christians, how would they regard me? I didn't want my own kids seeing me reading the newspaper instead of going to church on Sunday morning and whispering behind my back, "Poor Daddy! He's just a lost pagan headed for hell! I feel so sorry for him!"

I didn't want my children to pity me! A father wants to be admired by his children and to be their primary male role model. I didn't want them to think I was a miserable wretch or hell-bound reprobate. I didn't want them judging me for my drinking, my language, and my friends. I didn't want them seeing their youth pastor as their role model instead of me. I didn't want to become their pet evangelism project. I feared I would lose their respect and thus lose credibility with them.

I remember one Sunday when we picked up little Alison from her Sunday school class after church. "What did they teach you today?" I asked.

"That God loves me," she replied. "He loves all of us—you and Mommy too."

Leslie thought that was wonderful; I was more critical. I was troubled that these Christians were force-feeding their theology to my child before she was old enough to think critically about what they were saying.

They were imparting principles and ideas that were diametrically opposed to my own atheistic position. What right did they have to program my child to parrot back mythology as being truth? Their goal was to turn my child into a Christian, when to me this only meant creating a big gulf between us. At the same time, I knew that if I were to try to correct what she was being taught at church, this might confuse Alison even more, making her feel like she was in the middle of a tug-of-war between her parents.

I treasured my children. I wanted the best for them. To me, that meant "toughening them up," making them self-reliant, skeptical, and independent, and preparing them to compete in a nasty and unforgiving world.

The farthest thing from my mind was what they really needed the most: a loving, personal relationship with their Creator, who would give them an unshakable self-esteem, strength, and courage for the difficulties of life, a moral compass to guide them, and a rock-solid confidence in their eternity.

THE "BAIT AND SWITCH"

Lurking in the back of my mind was the fear that Leslie had gotten involved in some sort of cult that was going to try to control every aspect of her parenting, her lifestyle, and her relationships. And what about her personality? With her values and character changing so significantly, I was concerned that the Leslie I once knew was going to gradually morph into a Leslie who I wouldn't love as much.

In a sense, I felt like a victim of "bait and switch." This is a form of consumer deception in which a store advertises a product in an especially attractive way, but once the customer enters the premises the salesperson tries to discourage him from buying that product and instead tries to switch him to a more expensive—and more profitable—item.

That's how I felt about Leslie becoming a Christian. I had married one Leslie—the fun-loving, risk-taking, try-anything-once Leslie—and now she was being transformed into something else. Yes, I would admit there were aspects of her new persona that I liked, but I still felt cheated. I wanted the old Leslie back!

Faced with circumstances like these, some non-Christian husbands actually go through a kind of "bereavement." This is when they mourn the loss of the partner they once had such a close—and unshared—relationship with. Depression and disorientation can result.

"People go through the bereavement process at any time in life when they experience severe loss," said British pastor Michael Fanstone, who has counseled many mismatched couples. "A non-Christian husband may go through similar anguish if he feels that his spouse is no longer 'his.'"

Fanstone added:

> She has found a person called Jesus with whom she claims to have a love relationship. To the partner left on the sidelines, this can be devastating news. He perceives that their marriage has been attacked by an outside agency claiming his wife's heart. He senses the loss of the earlier relationship with his spouse very deeply, even though the

two of them still share the same home and bed. He feels that the exclusive, mutual love they had earlier is no longer there.[4]

THE MAN IN THE MIRROR

All these emotions—hurt, jealousy, frustration, fear—contributed to an underlying anger that seethed just below the surface. Sometimes I would erupt with shouting and even physical displays of fury. For example, one day I got so enraged that I kicked a hole in our living room wall. Leslie stood there speechless; Alison started to cry. I immediately felt like a jerk.

If you had asked me what had triggered that childish outburst, I couldn't have told you at the time. But today, with the benefit of hindsight, I can now identify one important contributor to my anger that I never would have understood back then. And it might explain some of the unexpected outbursts from your partner that have left you perplexed.

The insight is this: *the more Leslie opened her life to Christ and pursued a God-honoring way of life, the more her behavior had the effect of unmasking the ugliness, selfishness, and immorality of my own lifestyle.*

In other words, the more she sought after purity, integrity, honesty, and forgiveness, the more readily apparent it became to me that my own life and relationships were corroded with cynicism, bitterness, superficiality, and self-centeredness.

Leslie didn't have to confront me, lecture me, or criticize me. In fact, she studiously avoided doing that. But merely living out her Christian life in my presence was like holding up a mirror to me. I was suddenly faced with seeing the blatant contrast between my cynicism and her sincerity, my self-promotion and her God-devotion, my inner ugliness and her inner beauty, my anxiety and her peace, my greed and her generosity, my Lee-driven immorality and her God-centered morality.

For the first time, I was seeing myself as I really was—*and I didn't like the picture!* I wanted to cling to the illusion that I was a wonderful guy who was doing great. But Leslie's authentic Christian lifestyle exposed the real me by comparison. I was being convicted of sin, and it made me angry because I didn't want to face it.

On the negative side, this tended to create an unfocused kind of antagonism, outrage, and resentment inside of me. I couldn't put my finger on why I was so upset—I just was.

On the positive side, though, God was using this experience to help me recognize the depth of my depravity. In light of Leslie's godly lifestyle, it was increasingly difficult for me to maintain my positive self-image as an independent-thinking, successful, basically good person. In other words, I was beginning to make spiritual progress by recognizing my sinfulness—and that's an essential step toward God.

I hope that will be an encouragement to you if you're seeing some of the same reactions in your own spouse. Yes, your partner's anger can be frightening, his silent treatment can be disconcerting, his sulking can be childish, his resentments can be unfair. But maybe . . . just *maybe* . . . they might actually represent a sign that God is starting to deal with him about his sin.

Remember: just as God hasn't forgotten you in the midst of the turbulence of your mismatched marriage, he also hasn't forgotten your spouse. "The Lord is not slow in keeping his promise, as some understand slowness," said Peter. "He is patient with you, not wanting anyone to perish, but everyone to come to repentance."[5]

INSIDE YOUR PARTNER'S MIND

Not long ago, our unequally yoked friend Betty was having lunch with Leslie and me in a suburban Chicago café. "I just don't understand why Ed reacts the way he does," she told us in obvious frustration. "I'm not trying to shove Christianity down his throat. So why is he getting so angry? Why is he so suspicious about what I'm doing? Can't we just agree to disagree about God without him getting riled all the time?"

I spent the next several minutes explaining how and why I had reacted the way I did when Leslie became a Christian. As I talked, her eyes got wider and wider.

At the end, she said, "Ohhh, *now* I get it! To me, the changes God was doing in my heart were all positive. I never considered the possibility that they would be negative from Ed's perspective. This really helps!"

Similarly, I hope that delving inside the mind of one former skeptic has been helpful to you too as you ponder how to survive your mismatch. Of course, every individual reacts differently to changes in marriage, and so you will have to decide how much of my own experience is applicable to your situation.

In any event, insights about the nonbeliever's motivations are just one ingredient in living harmoniously. There are a lot of other lessons we learned through trial and error that kept our marriage from flying apart. As we continue, we'll talk about some concrete suggestions for making the most of your spiritual mismatch.

PART TWO

Making the Most of Your Mismatched Marriage

4

The Players: God, Your Spouse, and a Mentor

LESLIE IS AN OPTIMIST BY NATURE. SHE ALWAYS EXPECTS THE best to eventually happen. Her attitude is that if people have good intentions and a common goal, everything will work out in the end. But several months into our spiritually mismatched era, when there was still no prospect that my attitude toward God was ever going to change, Leslie was suddenly slapped with a cold realization: *her husband might never come to Christ.*

At first this thought plunged her into despair. This would mean that those toxic emotions that were churning inside of her—the fear, loneliness, frustration, guilt, anger, resentment, and anxiety—could persist unabated into the future. It would mean that my free-floating anger, sarcasm, and hostility might continue to generate tension in our marriage as long as we were together. She was nearly overcome with hopelessness.

She refused to give up, however. Her desperation was soon followed by a fresh resolve: she *must* make the most of our unequally yoked relationship! With God's help, she became ever more determined to make our marriage as fulfilling, as joyful, as intimate, and as satisfying as it could be. She pledged that she would not just *survive* our spiritually mismatched marriage but she would actually *thrive* in the midst of it. She vowed to create a positive and nurturing environment for our children and to raise them with Christian values and beliefs as far as she was able.

In effect, Leslie drew a line in the sand and said, "I'm in this for the long haul. From here on out, I'm not going to focus so much on our mismatch as I am on our potential to grow together into the future as a couple. As far as I can, with the power of the Holy Spirit, I'm going to *make this marriage work.*" She began clinging tenaciously to Philippians 4:13: "I have the strength to face all conditions by the power that Christ gives me."[1]

That was a defining moment for her and for us. Her decision not to go get mired in angst, anguish, and anger, but instead to move ahead in an affirmative quest for a richer and deeper marriage started to change her attitudes at the deepest level. In fact, the entire environment of our marriage began to change. Many of the tensions that had arisen because of her initial overanxiousness to convert me now began to slowly subside.

Christians who are unequally yoked often arrive at this kind of turning point in their relationship. "I came to the realization that if I continued to define our marriage in terms of our conflict over God, we were going to get stuck there and stop growing," said one Southern California friend whose spiritual mismatch has now stretched for nineteen years. "If I was going to wait until my husband became a Christian to be happy, I was giving him far too much control over my life. I needed to build on our common ground, to accentuate the areas where we were compatible, and to find ways to be happy and fulfilled in spite of our mismatch."

Nancy Kennedy, who has written about her unequally yoked marriage for Christian magazines and books, said she used to wonder why God didn't do something about her unbelieving spouse. Then came her turning point when she realized he is doing something: "He custom-designed this situation expressly for me and my husband: that he might be glorified and I might be made more like him."

This relieved a lot of her anxieties and helped her decide to make the most of their marriage while she is waiting for the day when her husband might come to Christ. "Since [God] is in control, I don't have to fret and worry," she said. "I can relax and enjoy my husband just as he is. So I've resolved that if it takes another forty years [for him to receive Christ], I want them to be good years. Years of laughter and joy. I owe that to my husband, and I think it's what God wants as well."[2]

But how can Christians cultivate that kind of upbeat and intimate atmosphere in their marriage if their spouse remains on a different spiritual wavelength? "I think I learned more from my mistakes than I did from anything else," Leslie said. "A lot of what I did was trial and error, taking two steps in a positive direction and then taking one step—or three steps—backwards. I wish I knew then what I know now!"

While there's no step-by-step, one-size-fits-all formula that will instantly revolutionize your relationship, Leslie found twelve helpful insights that contributed immeasurably to the longevity of our marriage. We'll be dealing with most of them in the next two chapters. Right now we want to concentrate on the top three, because they deal with a trio of relationships that are absolutely essential if you're going to thrive in your mismatched situation.

These key relationships are, first, with God; second, with your spouse; and third, with a spiritual mentor who can take you by the hand and guide you through the minefield of your spiritual mismatch. So here are the principles that rescued our marriage.

1. INSTEAD OF FIXATING ON YOUR STRUGGLES, FOCUS ON YOUR SAVIOR

When you're being pulled simultaneously in two directions—toward God by the Holy Spirit and away from him by your spouse—it's critically important to remember where your priorities should lie. The very first of the Ten Commandments tells us to put God before anything and anyone.[3] The first part of the Great Commandment given by Jesus tells us to "love the Lord your God with all your heart and with all your soul and with all your mind and with all your strength."[4] As Eugene Peterson renders 2 Corinthians 5:14 in *The Message*: "[Christ's] love has the first and last word in everything we do."

It's all too easy to turn our primary attention away from God and to stay riveted instead on the plight of our mismatched marriage. But that keeps us bogged down in our troubles rather than lifting our eyes toward our Solution. There are at least seven reasons why we must continue to keep God first in our lives:

We Keep God First Because He Deserves Our Primary Allegiance

God is our Creator who made us in his image, our Sustainer who keeps us alive, our Redeemer whose Son died for our sins, and our Father who adopted us as his children. "For great is the Lord and most worthy of praise," said the psalmist. "He is to be feared above all gods. For all the gods of the nations are idols, but the Lord made the heavens."[5] First and foremost, we put God above all else because that's the place of honor that he so obviously warrants by virtue of who he is and what he has done. And the Bible makes this promise to those who draw close to God: "Come near to God and he will come near to you."[6]

We Keep God First Because This Perspective Recalibrates Our Life

"The remarkable thing about fearing God," said Oswald Chambers, "is that when you fear God, you fear nothing else, whereas if you do not fear God, you fear everything else." In other words, when you give God the reverence, honor, and awe that he deserves as your First Love, then all of a sudden you realize that nobody—and no circumstances—can ultimately harm you. "The Lord is my light and my salvation—whom shall I fear?" asked King David.[7] You're reminded God is in control and that your eternity is secure. Fears over marital turmoil begin to fade.

On the other hand, if you allow God to slip from preeminence in your life, you will find yourself afraid of every uncertain circumstance. Everything beyond your control will generate anxiety and fret within you. "When I set God at the center of my life, I realize vast freedoms and surprising spontaneities," said Peterson. "When I center life in my own will, my freedom diminishes markedly. I live constricted and anxious."[8] As our friend Phil Callaway wrote,

Faith chases away fear
Fear imprisons. Faith frees.
Fear troubles. Faith triumphs.
Fear cowers. Faith empowers.
Fear disheartens. Faith encourages.
Fear darkens. Faith brightens.
Fear cripples. Faith heals.
Fear puts hopelessness at the center of life.
Faith puts fear at the feet of God.[9]

We Keep God First Because He Will Meet Needs That Our Spouse Never Could

Marriage counselor Gary Smalley said that many people enter into marriage or even friendships with the misconception that other individuals will be able to meet all of their needs. "We rely on one person or a group of folks to meet our needs for love, purpose, excitement, fulfillment, and ego gratification," he said. "And you know what happens? They eventually let us down because they are human."[10]

It's fundamentally unfair to expect our marriage partner to fulfill needs that only God is truly capable of meeting. If he or she could do that, we would no longer have any use for God! By focusing on God as the One who will fulfill our deepest longings and give our life purpose and meaning, we release our spouse from unrealistic expectations that can only lead to disappointment.

We Keep God First Because He Empowers Us to Love Our Spouse When He's Not Very Lovable

First Corinthians 13 contains that classic description of love: "Love is patient, love is kind. It does not envy, it does not boast, it is not proud. It is not rude, it is not self-seeking, it is not easily angered, it keeps no record of wrongs. Love does not delight in evil but rejoices with the truth.

It always protects, always trusts, always hopes, always perseveres. Love never fails."[11] Great sentiments—but try carrying them out on your own!

There were many times when my outbursts, antagonism, and smug arrogance made it difficult for Leslie to love me. Fortunately, God enabled her to persevere. Galatians 5:22 says that if we stay closely connected with God, the Holy Spirit will actually increase our capacity to love others. Mother Teresa used the analogy of electricity: "The wire is you and me; the current is God," she said. "We have the power to let the current pass through us, use us, and produce the light of the world—Jesus."

We Keep God First Because He Can Create Something Good from the Pain of Our Mismatch

"And we know that in all things God works for the good of those who love him, who have been called according to his purpose," says Romans 8:28. God doesn't promise to intervene and instantly "fix" your mismatch, but he does promise to use your circumstances—painful though they may be—to accomplish something good in your life or character.

James put it this way: "Consider it pure joy, my brothers, whenever you face trials of many kinds, because you know that the testing of your faith develops perseverance. Perseverance must finish its work so that you may be mature and complete, not lacking anything."[12] If we abide in Christ, he can use our experiences as an unequally yoked Christian to develop and mold our character in ways that never would have been possible without the struggles and difficulties we have faced.

We Keep God First Because He Will Be Our Spouse When Our Earthly Spouse Is Distant

At those times when the conflict from your mismatch makes you feel like a spiritual widow—isolated, lonely, and separated from your spouse by his icy attitude—God is there to comfort, encourage, and reassure you. "For your Maker is your husband—the LORD Almighty is his name— the Holy One of Israel is your Redeemer; he is called the God of all the earth," said the prophet Isaiah.[13] Promises God: "Though the mountains be shaken and the hills be removed, yet my unfailing love for you will not be shaken nor my covenant of peace be removed."[14] He reaffirms in Hebrews 13:5: "Never will I leave you; never will I forsake you."

Finally, We Keep God First Because He Loves Our Partner Even More Than We Do

When the first-century religious elite groused that Jesus had been welcoming sinners into his presence, he did something unprecedented. To adamantly drive home his response, Jesus decided to tell three rapid-fire stories—the only time in the Bible where he barraged his critics with a trio of parables to make sure they could not miss the lessons he wanted to teach them.

Jesus described a distraught shepherd venturing off into the bramble and bush in search of one errant sheep; a widow frantically sweeping her hovel in search of one missing coin; and a desperate father searching the horizon daily for the return of his prodigal son.[15]

My mentor, Bill Hybels, points out that these stories have three common threads: (1) something of great value was missing; (2) that which was missing was important enough to warrant an all-out search; and (3) retrievals result in rejoicing. Jesus' unmistakable message to those hard-hearted religious leaders was that spiritually lost people matter greatly to him, that they're worth both his efforts and ours to bring them to faith, and that the salvation of one individual warrants a huge party.[16]

Those are lessons unequally yoked Christians must learn and relearn time after time at the feet of Jesus. Despite their often-distasteful lifestyle, their foul language, their drinking, and their indifference toward God, spiritually lost people are of incalculable value to Jesus. Second Peter 3:9 says God "is not wanting anyone to perish, but everyone to come to repentance."

When you stay closely related to God, he will continually soften your heart toward your unbelieving spouse so that you don't become like those first-century religious snobs, whose judgmental attitudes made Jesus recoil, and you don't fall into an "us versus them" mindset that subtly puts your partner into the role of "the enemy" rather than being the object of God's affection.

These are just a few of the many reasons why we should continue to place God in the supreme position in our lives. As Luke 12:31 reminds us, "[God] will give you all you need from day to day if you make the Kingdom of God your primary concern."[17] Everything hinges on that word "if." When we make God and his ways our supreme focus, it's like pointing the compass of our life toward True North—everything else sort of falls into place.

That leads to an obvious question, however: *How can we ensure that God will occupy the premier position in our heart?* That can be a problem in the sometimes-harsh environment of an unequally yoked relationship.

Under the Radar Screen

Some of the best ways to cultivate an ongoing intimate relationship with God—talking to him through prayer, studying about him through the Bible, and learning about him at church and through fellowship with other Christians—are the very activities that spouses frequently discourage in a spiritually mismatched marriage. When Leslie would pray in my presence, I complained that she was putting on a pious show. When I would see her reading the Bible, I would want to argue over the reliability of Scripture. When she wanted to go to church or hang out with her Christian friends, I would complain that she wasn't spending enough time with me.

"I learned very quickly that if I wanted to pursue various spiritual disciplines to keep close to God," Leslie said, "I had to do them under Lee's radar screen."

For example, Leslie would get up early in the morning, while I was still asleep, to pray and study the Bible at the kitchen table. This became a special time for Leslie to commune alone with God and to orient her day around him. So for the nearly two years of our mismatched era, the first thing I would see in the morning as I turned from the hallway into the kitchen was Leslie quietly closing her Bible and getting up to greet me with a warm smile and hug. Without speaking a word, she was communicating: *I've just had my spiritual nourishment for the morning; now, let's not let the subject of God come between us today.*

Leslie also arranged to meet with her prayer group at times when I was either at the office, away on a trip, or involved in some other activity. There were many opportunities for spiritual growth—special retreats, classes at church, group Bible studies—that she didn't feel she could participate in without worsening the friction in our marriage. That's why it was so important for Leslie to have a very active mentoring relationship with her friend Linda.

We'll talk about the need for a spiritual mentor in the next section, but in the meantime we just want to stress that Leslie's growth as a Christian in those early years was largely the result of Linda doing Bible studies with her, answering her questions, praying with her, and providing godly guidance. In short, Linda helped Leslie stay close to God by fulfilling the functions that church would normally fill in a Christian's life.

Let me stress that Leslie never tried to hide from me that she loved Jesus and wanted to grow in her relationship with him. She wasn't living a life of duplicity—pretending to be one thing when she was with me, then revealing her true self in those hidden moments with God. I was quite aware of her devotion to Christ and the fact that she was praying, studying the Bible, and that these times were becoming more important to her.

However, Leslie was being sensitive to me and our marriage by pursuing her spiritual growth out of my presence whenever possible. It was merely a practical concession to my sinful hostility toward God. And you might need to take similar steps to insulate yourself from your spouse's criticism or hostility. Think through the various ways you could cultivate your relationship with Christ in a way that falls under the radar screen of your spouse.

All of this was helpful in Leslie's ongoing spiritual development. Staying intimately connected with God enabled her to take this next step in keeping her relational priorities straight.

2. MAKE YOUR SPOUSE THE NUMBER ONE HUMAN BEING IN YOUR LIFE

As I described in the previous chapter, I was afraid that I was losing my wife to a rival male—Jesus—and this generated feelings of anxiety and insecurity in me. I was relieved to find, however, that Leslie's devotion to Christ actually reinforced her love for me and made her want to strengthen our bonds. Instead of increasingly ignoring me in favor of Christ, church, and her Christian friends, Leslie actually redoubled her efforts to be an attentive, caring, and thoughtful spouse.

Over time, I developed the unmistakable feeling that I was still the Number One person in her life—just as she was in mine. She lived out an attitude of gentle servanthood that put my needs ahead of her own. This is contrary to everything in our culture that tells us to selfishly put ourselves first—but that's what marriage is about. And it's what Christianity is about—following the Savior who "did not come to be served, but to serve."[18] Leslie's constant efforts to reassure me of her love and devotion were vital in calming the turbulence of our relationship.

The apostle Peter said one of the keys to living in an unequally yoked marriage is that the Christian should exhibit "respectful, pure behavior" in dealing with her spouse.[19] Respect is a crucial ingredient in marriage, especially to husbands. It tells your spouse that you appreciate him, that you value him as a person, that you regard his opinions as being important, that you have faith in him, that you admire him, that you're thankful for who he is and what he does, and that you hold him in the highest esteem.

If you lose respect for your husband, you may very well end up losing your husband, because he will sense your disappointment in him. Your low opinion of him will inevitably leak out in disparaging comments and wound him deeply. He will withdraw emotionally and maybe even physically.

In her book *When a Believer Marries a Nonbeliever*, Bebe Nicholson (whose skeptic-turned-Christian husband, ironically, is also named Lee) makes this observation:

Respecting the other person, refusing to attack the other's most vulnerable area, and viewing the other person with kindness and love, even in the heat of battle, are crucial if we are to avoid a downward spiral of negativity. We must learn to see our partner in a positive light, even when the fires of disagreement are raging. We must stick with the issue being discussed instead of attacking the other personally. We need to refrain from arguing in front of others or discussing our spouse in a negative light with other people. We need to let positive thoughts replace negative ones.[20]

So what does Peter mean when he emphasizes that Christian spouses must exhibit "pure" behavior? Some experts have translated this word as "chaste."[21] As one scholar pointed out, however, this concept "is not to be limited to sexual chastity; it denotes that purity in character and conduct that should characterize all of the Christian life."[22]

Though I disagreed with Leslie's religious beliefs, I couldn't deny that the purity and authenticity of her faith were winsome and attractive. It's hard not to respect people whose beliefs match their behavior and whose character is consistent with their creed. In a wishy-washy world, where the national motto might as well be "What's in it for me?" and where expediency usually wins out over ethics, people like Leslie—whose behavior was marked by a humble fidelity to Christ and his teachings—often win the admiration of nonbelievers.

The beauty of a spouse winning her partner to Christ through her "respectful, pure behavior" was illustrated many centuries ago by Monica, the mother of Augustine, the great Christian philosopher. Augustine watched the process happen, later writing to God that his mother unselfishly served her spouse "and did all she could to win him to you, speaking of you . . . by her deportment [that is, by her behavior], through which you made her beautiful and reverently lovable to her husband . . . Finally, when her husband was coming to the very end of his earthly life, she won him to you."[23]

How did Leslie live out this "respectful, pure behavior"?

Leslie Actively Searched for Ways to Serve Me

Billy Graham once said that the greatest enemy of marriage is self-ishness. Both partners in a relationship are supposed to be servants of each other, mutually meeting each other's needs and seeking out ways to please one another. As my mother told me on the eve of my wedding: "Marriage isn't a fifty-fifty proposition; it takes one hundred percent from both parties." Each partner must give to the other, serve the other, and love the other with his or her total capacity.

One Christian author suggested that we ask ourselves when we awake each morning: "How can I make my partner happy today?" As the Christian does this, "very often, the partner begins to sit up, to take notice, to ask significant questions about God and his way of doing things."[24]

And that's what happened in our relationship. When Leslie did little things to serve me—like made my favorite dinner, bought me a book she knew I would enjoy, or surprised me at the office and took me to lunch—it communicated volumes about what she thought of me. And inevitably the more Leslie would find new ways to serve me, the more motivated I became to find ways to serve her!

One key: Leslie made sure she was serving me in the way I wanted to be served rather than the way she might have wanted to serve me. "Study his response to what you do," suggested writer Carole Mayhall. "For instance, he may prefer your canceling a social engagement when he's 'peopled out' to having *I Love You* spelled out in M&M's on his pillow."[25]

Leslie Didn't Just Hear Me When We Talked, But She Listened to Me

There's a big difference! "*Hearing* is basically to gain content or information for your own purposes," said marriage expert H. Norman Wright. "*Listening* is caring for and being empathetic toward the person who is talking. Hearing means that you are concerned about what is going on inside *you* during the conversation. Listening means you are trying to understand the feelings of *the other person* and are listening for his sake."[26]

When Leslie and I would have a conversation, I had the distinct impression she was riveted to that moment. I didn't feel like I had to fight for her attention, and that told me she respected me. Says James 1:19: "Everyone should be quick to listen, slow to speak."

Leslie Allowed Me to Feel Needed

Although I never could have articulated it at the time, one of my fears was that I would become unnecessary or superfluous to Leslie. As her husband, I had a strong desire to protect her, provide for her, and care for her. But if she was going to look more and more toward God to meet those needs, was I going to be less and less valuable to her?

In their book *Caught in the Middle*, authors Beverly Bush Smith and Patricia DeVorss deal with this subtle but significant issue: "The Lord promises to be the supplier of all our needs . . . and we no longer are so dependent on other people. The independence feels good, but our husbands were attracted to us in part because they wanted to take care of us. It is important that we continue to give our husbands the gift of needing their protection and care."[27]

They go on to suggest some of the very things that Leslie naturally did in our relationship: "Appreciate your husband's efforts at earning a living . . . Be grateful for all that he provides instead of dwelling on what you don't have . . . Don't turn him down when he offers to carry in the groceries. Of course, you could do it, but enjoy his effort to care for you . . . And when he is wary about your driving at night or traveling alone far from home, don't resent his concern. He is simply fulfilling God's call to be your protector."[28]

Leslie Honored Our Relationship by Building on Our Common Ground

Yes, there was a schism between us due to our differing religious beliefs. But that didn't mean we had to stop relating in other areas. Leslie and I got married because we enjoyed each other's company and shared a lot of mutual interests. Leslie made a special effort to identify those activities and make sure we continued to pursue them together.

For instance, we enjoyed traveling together and exploring new restaurants and sights, so at Leslie's urging we took an extended vacation to a picturesque resort area in Wisconsin. We left behind our disagreements over God and spent that time connecting through long walks in the woods, deep conversations over dinner, and evening bicycle rides down country lanes.

"Chains do not hold a marriage together," said Simone Signoret. "It is threads, hundreds of tiny threads which sew people together through the years."[29] Leslie made sure that our spiritual mismatch didn't cause our overall relationship to unravel. She identified the strands that knit our lives together and did what she could to make sure they remained strong.

Leslie Refrained from Comparing Me with Christian Husbands

All of us muse from time to time about what it would be like to be married to someone else. But Leslie made it a point not to compare me with Christian husbands or so much as hint that I didn't measure up to their level of spirituality or kindness. "Such comparisons are dangerous because they dishonor our spouse (we're really saying we'd prefer to be married to someone else) and allow us to avoid responsibility for our own actions," said writer Elizabeth Cody Newenhuyse. "Instead of resolving the discontent we may be experiencing in marriage, we take refuge in saying, 'If only we could be like the Smiths.' Naturally, we can't be, so we're absolved of our obligation to change."

Her advice: compare marriages, not mates. "If I brood because I wish my husband could be more like our friend Greg, who always takes his wife out, I'm edging toward dishonoring my spouse," she said. "But if I casually say, 'Don't the Johnsons seem to have fun together? They went to that dinner theater—maybe we should go,' I'm making a positive, nonthreatening suggestion."[30]

The same is true in unequally yoked relationships. Rather than Leslie comparing me unfavorably with our neighbor Bill because he provides strong spiritual leadership in his home, it would be better for her to say, "Bill and Janet are taking their kids to a program at church to give them strong moral values. Maybe we should consider something like that for Alison and Kyle to reinforce their good behavior." Again, that's a positive, nonthreatening suggestion that keeps my ego intact.

Leslie Loved Me as Her Partner, Not as Her Project

It was important that I never sensed Leslie's love was conditional or that it was being motivated by her evangelistic zeal. I was her husband, not her "conversion project," and I needed to know that she still respected me as her spouse even though we didn't see eye to eye on religion. Looking back, I know that there were many times when I aggravated or frustrated her. Even so, she never once made me feel like she would love me more, value me more, or appreciate me more if I were a Christian instead of a skeptic.

By following these six principles during our mismatch, Leslie was tugging on the tiny threads that sewed our lives together, pulling them tighter and tighter. At the time, I wasn't aware how much her relationship with Christ empowered and equipped her to continually reach out to me in love. All I knew was that whenever I feared that the centrifugal force of our spiritual mismatch was going to cause our marriage to fly apart, Leslie moved closer to me, reassured me, and served me—all of which made me want to draw closer to her too.

But there was yet another relationship that was critically important in this process—even though at the time I was mostly oblivious to it.

3. HARNESS THE SUPPORT OF A SPIRITUAL MENTOR TO GUIDE, SUPPORT, AND ENCOURAGE YOU

Have you ever been at a summer camp where they gave you narrow strips of leather or plastic to braid together into a bracelet? If you use two strands, the result is rather flimsy. But *three* strands—well, that makes all the difference in the world! The Bible recognizes this principle in Ecclesiastes 4:9–12:

Two are better than one, because they have a good return for their work: If one falls down, his friend can help him up. But pity the man who falls and has no one to help him up! Also, if two lie down together, they will keep warm. But how can one keep warm alone? Though one may be overpowered, two can defend themselves. A cord of three strands is not quickly broken.

The truth is that you need a close friend to help you cope with the emotional trauma of living in a spiritually mismatched marriage. But these two relational strands will never really be strong until both of you fully weave the third strand—God—into your lives. Then you can have a supernaturally powerful connection. God can work through this friend to accomplish his will in your life and to speak the truth to you in love.[31]

This is the role Linda played with Leslie. As God knit together their hearts with his, he created strong three-way bonds that were able to fend off the stresses of an unequally yoked marriage. If you were going to advertise for someone to fill this role, you might write something like this:

Wanted: Spiritually mature Christian. Must be wise, discerning, kindhearted, and savvy. Needed for prayer, encouragement, and guidance. Must have waterproof shoulders to cry on, durable knees for long periods of prayer, and strong backbone to stand up to a friend when necessary. Sense of humor essential. Must be available 24/7. No compensation, but plenty of rewards.

That is a good description of Linda. Although she had never personally experienced a spiritual mismatch, her God-given empathy gave her the capacity to understand and appreciate Leslie's situation. Fundamentally, she fulfilled three roles in Leslie's life.

She Was a Patient and Careful Teacher

As we mentioned earlier, Leslie desperately needed Linda to help her grow in her understanding of God and the Christian life. Linda accomplished this by going through introductory Bible studies with Leslie, discussing Christian books that they were reading at the same time, and answering Leslie's many questions about the faith. Since she lived in the same condominium building, it was easy for the two of them to get together on a moment's notice when I would go out for a while.

"In a way, Linda was my pastor, my Sunday school teacher, my mentor, and my coach all rolled into one," Leslie said. "Fortunately, God gave her the right gifts, personality, and temperament to do all of that well. This wasn't something she did begrudgingly; she really loved getting together and helping me grow."

She Was an Authentic and Sincere Role Model

Leslie and I had never been friends with a committed Christian couple before, and so for a long time we subtly scrutinized the marriage of Linda and Jerry even before Leslie became a Christian.

We wanted to see whether we could detect a holier-than-thou attitude toward those who didn't subscribe to their theology. We wanted to see how they would handle conflict in their marriage. We wanted to see whether they would put on a Christian smiley face and pretend they never got angry, worried, or frustrated. We wanted to see whether they would be truth tellers and whether they would ask for forgiveness when they made a mistake. We wanted to see whether they would hold a grudge if we did something to hurt them. We wanted to see if they were honest about the little things in life. We wanted to hear the comments they would make about people who weren't around.

We watched for a long period of time, and guess what we found? We discovered they weren't perfect. But then again, they never claimed to be.

Primarily, what we saw was a gentle spirit of acceptance toward us, a lot more humility than pride, a willingness to admit when they were wrong, an anxiousness to reconcile when there was a conflict, a readiness to acknowledge the rough edges of their character and a sincere effort to smooth them out, a refusal to playact by pretending that the Christian life is always happy, and an admission that they struggled with their faith from time to time. But most of all, undergirding everything, we saw an honest desire to become a little more like Jesus, bit by bit, as time went by. In short, they were *real*.

Their sincere and wholehearted faith embodied the kind of salt and light that Jesus told his followers to be for the world.[32] He wanted them to be like salt by living a life that causes others to thirst for God, that spices up the world, and that retards the moral decay of society. And he wanted them to be like light that illuminates his truth for people, that shines his compassion into dark places of hopelessness and despair, and that draws people toward Jesus—because he, ultimately, is the light of life.

God used Linda and Jerry's genuine Christian lifestyle, with its salty and gently illuminating qualities, to help draw Leslie to faith in Christ. He used their marriage to illustrate for Leslie, day in and day out, what it means to have a relationship anchored firmly to Jesus Christ. As Leslie quietly observed them interact in an ongoing way, they gave her a living picture of what a New Testament relationship could be like. And though Leslie was closer to them than I was, I also was tugged toward Christ by the winsome and attractive way in which they related to each other as a couple.

She Was a Kind and Committed Companion

"There were so many times when I was so mad at you that I could have screamed," Leslie said to me as we were talking about this chapter. "Actually, sometimes I *did* scream—but fortunately not at you. That only would have made things worse! Instead, I'd go over to Linda's place and she'd let me vent and cry and dump my emotions on her. She was never too busy for me to drop by. She didn't care if the sink was full of dirty dishes or if she was still in her pajamas—she always made me feel welcomed. I honestly don't know what I would have done without her!"

But while she allowed Leslie to express her raw, unvarnished emotions, Linda was careful not to cultivate an environment where the situation became Leslie, Linda, and God *versus* Lee. It would have been easy to always side with Leslie in the disagreements she was having with me and to begin to see me as the enemy. Linda made it a point to stress my positive virtues and to help Leslie understand that all of our marital woes were not solely tied to the fact that I wasn't a Christian.

"Linda never let me get bogged down in feeling sorry for myself," Leslie said. "She would listen, she would empathize, she would console, but she would always get to the point where she would dry my tears and help me get back on my feet. She would stress the positive and give me specific ideas for how I could get our marriage back on track. She didn't allow me to get stuck; she was always pointing me forward and toward God."

She Was a Firm But Loving Counselor

Linda resisted the temptation to always tell Leslie what she wanted to hear. Rather, she consistently offered Bible-centered advice even though at times it meant saying things that were difficult for Leslie to accept.

For example, once I had asked Leslie not to go to church on a certain weekend because I wanted us to do something else. Leslie got angry and went to Linda to express her frustration. "I told Linda that I didn't care what you said or did; I was going to go to church regardless of how you felt, and you could just deal with it," Leslie recalled.

It would have been easy for Linda to have jumped to her defense and declared, "You're right! You go to church whenever you feel like it, and Lee can just learn to live with it."

Rather, Linda was sensitive to the damage this would cause in our fragile relationship. So she said to Leslie: "God doesn't want you to go to church out of an attitude of getting even with Lee. I think God would rather you stay at home and show Lee he's important to you and that you want to honor him, even though you disagree with him."

How did Leslie react to Linda's suggestion? "I was totally annoyed," she recalled. "It felt good to be mad at you—you deserved it! I really wanted to get even with you. But as I thought and prayed about it, I realized that Linda was right. I decided to compromise—and the result was that we became less polarized than we would have been if I had stubbornly insisted on getting my way."

Linda's firm but loving counsel ended up saving us from a lot of heartache—and it played an important role in an amazing incident that reminded Leslie that God had not forgotten her.

A Minor Miracle

The incident involved Leslie wanting to give money to the church's building project. As Leslie mentioned in an earlier chapter, I blew up at this idea and insisted that none of our money go to the church. Well, now we want to tell you the rest of the story.

The next week, Leslie saw an ad in the newspaper for people who wanted to do work on the telephone from their home. This was a great solution, she thought: she would get her own job so she could contribute her own money to the church. How could I object to that? After all, none of my money would go to these "charlatans."

Well, I *did* object. When Leslie told me she was going to earn her own money, I said, "That's great, but we can use that cash for vacations or savings or a new car! Don't give it to the church! That's just pouring it down the drain!"

The next day Leslie went to Linda. "I just know God gave me this job so I could give to the church's building drive," she said. "I'm going to have to figure out a way to hide some of the money and somehow sneak it to the church."

Again, Linda's counsel wasn't what Leslie wanted to hear. "Leslie, God doesn't need your money," she said. "God wants you to keep your marriage together and to honor your husband."

"You can't be serious!" she replied in frustration. "I specifically got this job so I could contribute. The deadline for the building fund is only a few weeks away, and I'll be heartbroken if I can't participate. Does God want *that*?"

Linda clung to her wise advice. "If God wants you to contribute," she said, "he'll find a way of allowing you to do it without you lying to Lee or sneaking around behind his back. Being deceptive isn't the way to build trust in your marriage."

Both Linda and Leslie then decided on a positive course of action: they committed to praying in earnest that God would change my attitude.

The tension was thick between Leslie and me for the several days after our argument over her job. But behind the scenes, God was at work tenderizing my heart, softening my attitude, and reminding me of how much I loved Leslie. One evening she was in the kitchen when I walked in and sat down at the table.

"Look, I've been thinking about how you want to give this money to the building fund," I said. "I don't understand why you want to do it, but you're right—you're the one who earned the money. We would never have had the money in the first place if you hadn't gotten the job to give to the church. So I guess it's okay with me if you make the contribution."

Leslie was thrilled. "Thanks!" she said, giving me a big hug. "I know you don't understand why, but this is very important to me."

I shook my head. "No, I don't understand," I said. "But I love you and if this is what you want, then it's fine with me."

Leslie went ahead and wrote the check to the church. Linda had been right: she felt much better than she would have had she sneaked around my back. But her putting the check into the offering plate wasn't the end of the episode. God had not only been busy in my heart, he also wanted to teach us both a lesson about his faithfulness—and his sense of humor.

The next day the telephone rang. It was Leslie's supervisor. He explained that they had just realized she had been filling out her time sheets incorrectly.

With trepidation, Leslie asked, "Does that mean you overpaid me and I owe you money?"

"Oh, no," he exclaimed. "Actually, we owe you money."

"How much?"

He proceeded to tell her—*and it was exactly the same amount that Leslie had donated to the building fund at the church!*

What an amazing God! He used this minor miracle to reaffirm his goodness and love to Leslie. Thanks to Linda's advice, she had done the right thing by refusing to be deceptive, and God had rewarded her for it.

As for me—I was flabbergasted! It was one of those amazing "coincidences" that kept me awake at night, wondering whether there really is a God who cares and provides for his children.

Finding a Linda for You

If you're spiritually mismatched, then we don't have to sell you very hard on your need to have someone like Linda in your life. As God "knit" together the souls of David and Jonathan, you need him to create a supernatural connection between you, another person, and God.[33] As one plaque defined friendship: "A friend is one who knows you as you are, understands where you've been, accepts who you've become, and still gently invites you to grow."[34] Here are some ideas for how you can find someone who might be a friend like that to you:

- Ask God to bring someone like Linda into your life. Specifically pray that he would provide you with an encourager, mentor, and friend who can help deepen your faith and carry you through difficult times.
- Ask the women's ministry leader at your church (or men's ministry director if you're a guy) if he or she knows someone who would enjoy having a mentoring relationship with you. Look for an individual who has some of these spiritual gifts: encouragement, shepherding, discernment, wisdom, or teaching. It's a plus if the person had once been spiritually mismatched. Obviously, this would give him or her a special understanding of your situation.
- If you can't find a suitable mentor at your church, you might try joining a small group that your church may offer. A small group composed of people the same gender as you, meeting at a time that would not be disruptive to your marriage, can be a lifeline to someone in a spiritual mismatch. You might find a whole bunch of Lindas—or perhaps you might become especially close to one member of the group who can informally mentor you.

A few churches actually offer small groups specifically for those who are unequally yoked.

- Some parachurch organizations also can be helpful. For example, after we moved away from Illinois, Leslie got involved with Stonecroft Ministries, which sponsors Christian Women's Clubs around the country, and she connected very deeply with a woman named Anita Gamble, who picked up in Leslie's life where Linda left off.[35] Another option is the Christian Business Men's Committee (CBMC), whose local chapters provide mentoring as part of the organization's Operation Timothy.[36]

It's important that you enter into this kind of relationship with the expectation that this will be a two-way street. Don't expect that you will only be on the receiving end of the friendship. When we enter into a relationship anticipating that we are the only ones who will benefit, we end up disappointed. Instead, God will use you to sharpen, encourage, and support the other person if you're both open to that possibility.

"You are allowed to keep only that which you consciously give away," said Ted Engstrom. "Give away your friendship, and you will receive friendship in return. Give away your self, and your 'better' self will return to you many times over."[37]

A Firm Foundation

Okay, you're cultivating a close, authentic, and dependent relationship with God. You're intent on keeping your spouse the Number One individual in your life. And you're bonding with a friend like Linda, who will help encourage and equip you to survive—and, yes, even thrive—in your unequally yoked situation. These are the crucially important first three steps in making the most of your mismatched marriage. These relationships will form a firm foundation for everything else that you do.

But this isn't all that you can do. When you turn the page, Leslie and I will continue to set forth nine more steps you can take in making the love of your life last a lifetime.

5 | Giving Your Spouse What God Gave You

ON THE TELEVISION SHOW *ROSEANNE*, A NEIGHBOR STROLLED over with a newspaper in hand. "Hey, Roseanne, what do you think of this headline?" she asked. "Utah housewife stabs husband thirty-seven times."

Without missing a beat, Roseanne replied: "I admire her restraint."[1]

She was just kidding! It's true, however, that the friction of marriage can sometimes spark animosity and even flashes of anger. And that's all the more true of spiritually mismatched relationships, where frustration and misunderstandings often run deep. Roseanne's quip aside, we are thankful to God that physical violence is rare. Yet sometimes the wounds from subtle psychological warfare and years of emotional abuse can almost be as painful.

The reality is that you're reading this book because you're in the midst of an unequally yoked relationship. And you're faced with a choice. You can passively allow yourself to be swept along by the turbulent currents of conflict and discord, or you can take steps to affirmatively seize the situation and make the most of your mismatched marriage.

Leslie and I want to help you choose that positive option, beginning first with the steps outlined in the previous chapter: making sure God reigns supreme in your life; making sure your spouse ranks top among people in your life; and making sure you have a spiritual mentor to help you cope with your life. With that groundwork in place, let's look at several other steps that you can take to thrive in the midst of your mismatch.

4. AS FAR AS YOU ARE ABLE, MAKE YOUR RELATIONSHIP A "CHRISTIAN" MARRIAGE BY LIVING OUT GODLY PRINCIPLES IN YOUR LIFE

You can't control your spouse's spiritual outlook; if you could, he or she would already be a Christian! But you have quite a bit of control over how *you* live. And it's possible to unilaterally live out your faith and influence your marriage and children with Christian values, even without the participation of your partner. Jo Berry, in her book *Beloved Unbeliever*, makes this important observation:

> Rather than wishing things were different, all of us have to admit that, for the most part, our marriages only will be as good or as bad as we make them. And any unequally yoked wife can have a "Christian" marriage, to the extent that she is willing to implement God's standards into her performance and the relationship itself.[2]

That's a liberating thought! The Christian principles, values, and morality that you decide to put into your marriage are going to change the entire flavor of your relationship. "Marriage, at the start, is an empty box," said relationship expert J. Allan Petersen. "You must put something in before you take anything out."[3] And if you put in biblical behavior and Christ-honoring choices, it's naturally going to change what you—and the rest of your family—get out of the marriage. Christian counselor Larry Crabb put it this way:

> Perhaps your spouse will not join you on the path to oneness. But you can maintain your commitment—first to obey God and then to minister to your spouse through each opportunity that arises. The result will *possibly* be a better marriage (and in many cases *probably*). The result will *surely* be a new level of spiritual maturity and fellowship with Christ for you.[4]

Of course, the degree to which you can implement biblical standards in your home is going to be affected by whether your partner is merely indifferent toward Christianity, in which case you will probably have a lot of leeway, or whether your spouse is hostile toward spiritual matters, in which case you probably won't be able to go as far.

"My husband really doesn't care very much about whether I go to church, whether I raise our kids as Christians, or whether I live out my faith in the marriage," said one woman who has been unequally yoked for twelve years. "He doesn't object to Christian values; he just has no personal interest in God. So I've had a lot of flexibility in creating a Christian atmosphere in our home."

Gary Oliver, who directs the Center for Marriage and Family Studies at John Brown University, told *Christianity Today* that the initial impact of a spouse's conversion to Christianity is "disequilibrium," in which unbelieving partners experience uncertainty and ask: "Will they be a Bible-banger? Will I be condemned? Will they be going to Bible studies all of the time? Will they still want to have fun? Will they not want to have sex anymore?"

He quickly added, though, that the long-term effect of the conversion on the marriage is often generally positive. Why? Because the Christian has "signed on" to a biblical perspective on relationships. "This almost always leads to increased . . . commitment to making marriage work," he said, adding that there is also a "significant impact of the support of Christian friends, the indwelling power of the Holy Spirit, and the encouragement of God's promises."[5]

So you don't have to wait until your spouse is a Christian to have a "Christian" marriage. You can have one, at least to some degree, right away. You can decide on your own to live out your faith as best you can—by being a truth teller, a servant, a forgiver, a worshiper, and a person of humility, integrity, compassion, kindness, and self-control. The extent to which your relationship can be "Christian" is the extent to which you commit yourself to following Jesus and letting his influence permeate your entire life.

5. INSTEAD OF PURSUING HAPPINESS, ALLOW YOURSELF TO RELAX IN GOD'S JOY

Living in a spiritual mismatch can put the Christian under a cloud of gloom. Unfortunately, this can start a downward spiral of negativity. For your own sake—and the sake of your spouse—it's important for you to break that cycle. This cannot be done, however, by merely trying to pursue happiness as an antidote; instead, you must learn to rest comfortably in God's joy. After all, there's a big difference between *happiness*, which is dependent on what's happening in your world, and *joy*, which depends on Jesus' presence in your life.

Too often we allow the circumstances of our life, and especially the up-and-down nature of a mismatched marriage, to dictate how cheerful we are. If your spouse is being tolerant of your spiritual growth and is even beginning to openly investigate Christianity himself, you may feel wonderful. When he picks fights over your belief in the Bible, digs in his heels when you ask him to go to church, or blows a gasket when you are at a Bible study instead of going to a ball game with him, then you plunge into depression. Because of changing external circumstances, your emotions are like a yo-yo: happy one minute, glum the next.

According to the Bible, though, true joy is a by-product of knowing the Savior, of experiencing him daily, of being confident in his provision for you, of being assured of eternal life. Galatians 5:22 mentions joy as the second quality that the Holy Spirit will manifest over time in the lives of Christians. The apostle Paul, who underwent terrible deprivation and suffering, wrote a letter to the Philippians while imprisoned under Roman guard—and yet its repeated theme is joy. As evangelist Billy Sunday observed, "If you have no joy, there's a leak in your Christianity somewhere."

In writing nearly a dozen books on the Bible, J. Stephen Lang has been struck by how often joy is mentioned, even in the midst of persecution and pain. "The person who knows where he or she stands with God can feel joy in any situation, for it is not dependent on externals," he said. "Joy, in the Bible's view, is not the same as pleasure or amusement. It is more enduring, for it is based not on the pleasant sensations of the moment but on the long view of things, enjoying the presence of God here and now but also looking forward to eternity."[6]

Don't assume you're going to have to wait until your partner becomes a Christian to experience joy. Your life can be buoyed right now by a positive outlook. Learn to laugh again! It may be easier than you think. Canadian humorist Phil Callaway says lightheartedness can be rekindled through a number of little things. He recommends we make friends with optimistic people, thank God for someone else's good fortune, praise others, listen to music with our eyes closed, sing loudly in the car, get help for chores we dislike, plant something each spring, rest on Sunday, learn a clean joke, talk to our neighbors, buy a flower and smell it before giving it away, thank God for the sunset, get enough sleep, and try something new.[7]

Or, we might add, enjoy a funny Christian book, like Callaway's *Who Put the Skunk in the Trunk* or *Humor for a Woman's Heart*, written by a variety of authors. Or read Chuck Swindoll's excellent biblical exploration of Christian joy, *Laugh Again*.[8] In fact, there's a whole bunch of Christian humor books to lighten your spirits. Honest, we didn't make up these titles: *Dated Jekyll, Married Hyde* by Laura Jensen Walker; *Days of Our Wives: A Semi-Helpful Guide to Marital Bliss* by Dave Meurer; *Help! I'm Laughing and I Can't Get Up* by Liz Curtis Higgs; *It's Always Darkest Before the Fun Comes Up* by Chonda Pierce; *She Who Laughs Lasts* by Ann Spangler; *Sometimes I Wake Up Grumpy . . . And Sometimes I Let Him Sleep* by Karen Scalf Linamen; and our personal favorite title: *The Lord Is My Shepherd—And I'm About to Be Sheared* by G. Ron Darbee.

Think of the positive impact that a pleasant and joyful disposition will have on your unbelieving spouse. A life that's upbeat and winsome is much more attractive than one that's gray and somber. And we all know that humor is one of the best lubricants in overcoming the inevitable friction in marriage. "The shortest distance between two people is a laugh," quipped Victor Borge. Humor releases tension, draws people together, and helps create a forgiving and loving atmosphere. Leslie and I couldn't begin to count the number of times that a well-timed quip managed to short-circuit the downward spiral of one of our arguments.

Experiencing joy begins with a decision. Paul said we should personally resolve to "rejoice in the Lord always."[9] Swindoll puts it this way:

> *Joy* is a choice. It is a matter of attitude that stems from one's confidence in God—that He is at work, that He is in full control, that He is in the midst of whatever has happened, is happening, and will happen. Either we fix our minds on that and determine to laugh again, or we wail and whine our way through life, complaining that we never got a fair shake. We are the ones who consciously determine which way we shall go.[10]

So make that conscious determination! *Decide on joy.* Cast your ballot for laughter. Choose cheerfulness. Rejoice always. Force a smile until it feels natural. Crack a joke. Resolve to see the bright side. That's not denial; that's acknowledging your difficulties and yet choosing to see the bigger picture. "Joy does not overlook our circumstances," one friend told us. "It overrides them."[11]

We like Callaway's perspective: "No matter what goes right, no matter what goes wrong, God is in control," he said. "And one day—maybe not tomorrow, or even next week—I'll see things His way. So I might as well just throw back my head and laugh."[12]

6. INSTEAD OF GIVING YOUR SPOUSE WHAT HE DESERVES, GIVE HIM WHAT GOD GAVE YOU

Leslie had enough. I had belittled her beliefs once too often. Inside, she was seething. Everything within her was itching to retaliate, to fight sarcasm with sarcasm, to give me a dose of my own medicine. After all, she had grown up in Chicago, where the city's unofficial motto is, "Don't get mad, get even!" She relished the thought of fighting fire with fire and putting me in my place. What could be more emotionally satisfying than verbally cutting me down to size?

But she resisted that impulse. With great difficulty—and through radical reliance on God—she was able to restrain herself. She knew that retaliation would only fuel a downward spiral in our relationship. Besides, it wasn't what Jesus would do. As A. M. Hunter said, "To return evil for good is the devil's way; to return good for good is man's; to return good for evil is God's."

One of the main reasons our marriage stayed intact during these tumultuous times was that Leslie courageously fought the temptation to sink to my level and to give me the tongue-lashing that I admittedly deserved. While she did stand up for herself, she managed to do it without dumping gasoline on an already explosive situation.

Unquestionably, this was difficult to do. What was Leslie's secret? She reminded herself on a regular basis that God hadn't given her what *she* deserved. "[The Lord] has not dealt with us according to our sins, nor rewarded us according to our iniquities," says Psalm 103:10.[13] If God were to pay us back for the way we have treated him, we'd all face instant annihilation. Instead, he offers grace to anyone who will humbly receive it. "But God showed his great love for us by sending Christ to die for us while we were still sinners," says Romans 5:8.[14]

Then Jesus tells all of his followers that they too must be gracious toward others—even those who mistreat them. He even went so far as to say in the Sermon on the Mount: "For if you forgive men when they sin against you, your heavenly Father will also forgive you. But if you do not forgive men their sins, your Father will not forgive your sins."[15]

When a man and woman say their marriage vows, essentially they are promising that they will forgive each other day in and day out. "A good marriage," said Billy Graham's wife, Ruth, "is the union of two forgivers."[16] That's all the more important in a spiritual mismatch, where tempers are often on the edge, where emotions are frequently at the boiling point, and where feelings are all too often bruised.

I picture forgiveness like a game of tug-of-war. When conflict arises because of the mismatch, it's like a knot developing in the rope that represents your relationship. If both spouses continue to pull hard on their end of the rope, the still-loose knot begins to get tighter and tighter and tighter. At some point, there's the danger that nobody can ever untie it.

But forgiveness means one spouse merely drops his or her end of the rope. This loosens the tension and preserves the possibility that the knot might be untangled by the two of you. The other person can continue tugging, but it doesn't do any good any more. As an ancient African proverb observes, "Whoever forgives ends the quarrel."

The apostle Paul put it this way: "If it is possible, as far as it depends on you, live at peace with everyone."[17] Sounds sensible, doesn't it? The real question is *how* to live at peace with someone who seems intent on making war. The answer lies in what I call the "PEACE process," a plan whose five steps each begin with a letter from that word. When you're feeling the urge to punish your partner rather than pardon him, take this course of action.

- **The *P* in PEACE stands for *Pray*.** Honestly express your emotions to God and ask for his help. If you don't feel like forgiving your spouse, candidly tell that to God. Sometimes Leslie would say: "I feel like wringing Lee's neck right now, but I know you want me to forgive him instead. Please, God, give me the power and grace to do that, because I'm simply not capable of doing it on my own." Then pray for your spouse—that God would bless him, encourage him, and draw him toward himself. You'll quickly find it's very difficult to remain angry too long toward a person for whom you're sincerely praying.
- **The *E* in PEACE reminds us to *Empathize* with our spouse.** Look at the situation from his perspective. Try to diagnose what might be motivating his behavior. Reread the chapter that describes my emotional response to Leslie's conversion and see if it might provide some insights into why your husband is acting the way he is. Remember that it's unfair to ask someone who isn't

a Christian to act like a Christian. I'm not saying you need to condone how he's behaving but merely try to understand what's driving him. Focus on loving the sinner without endorsing his sin. As Ralf Luther said, you don't have to love the mire in which the pearl lies, but you should love the pearl that lies in the mire.

- **The *A* in PEACE stands for *Act*.** Even when we don't feel like being forgiving, we should take concrete action toward forgiving our spouse simply because God tells us we should. Call a cease-fire in the war of words. "Bless those who curse you," Jesus said.[18] This means deciding that when your partner shoots bitter words your way, you'll make the conscious decision to respond with kind and considerate language. When you step out in faith by following God's ways even when it's difficult, you can trust that he will give you strength as strength is needed.

- **The *C* in PEACE reminds us to *Confess*.** More often than not, we share a bit of the blame for pushing our spouse into the role of being our adversary. Sometimes it's our own stubbornness, our own pride, or our own attitudes that contributed—at least in part—to the rift between you. The Bible says there's a direct connection between confession and healing.[19] When we assess the situation and honestly admit to ourselves—and then to God and finally to our spouse—that we share some of the blame, that can be a big step toward healing. I found that when Leslie sincerely apologized for playing even a minor role in our conflict, this would usually deflate my anger and make me more willing to confess that I was much more to blame.

- **The final *E* in PEACE represents the word *Emulate*.** Whenever we're not sure how to love our spouse when he's acting unlovable, whenever we hesitate to forgive because we're perplexed over how to proceed, whenever we wonder if we are going far enough to reconcile, we can look at the example of Jesus and model ourselves after him. After all, Jesus set a very high standard for forgiveness. He actually prayed that the Father would forgive the very soldiers who were torturing him to death! In light of God's undeserved forgiveness of our infinitely serious sins, how can we dare withhold forgiveness of our spouse's misbehavior? "Bear with each other and forgive whatever grievances you may have against one another," says Colossians 3:13. "Forgive as the Lord forgave you."

If you don't seek God's help in adopting a forgiving spirit, your mismatched marriage can become an ever-growing trash heap of hurts, wounds, anger, resentment, petty grievances, dashed dreams, and festering grudges. Yes, it's difficult to forgive—and even harder to resist the temptation to resurrect your spouse's mistakes from the past and throw them in his face during a weak moment in a future argument. As actress Marlene Dietrich quipped, "Once a woman has forgiven her man, she must not reheat his sins for breakfast."

But what we find when we offer our partner grace instead of grief is that we grow closer to God, our character becomes more developed, our need to get even dissipates, tension in the relationship is lessened, and we become unshackled from the bitterness that would otherwise weigh us down.

The Bible says that as a person thinks within himself, "so he is."[20] People who chronically think resentful and revengeful thoughts toward their spouse often become resentful and revenge-seeking people who end up subtly pushing others away from themselves. They don't hold a grudge as much as the grudge holds them in its claws. As an old adage says, "To forgive is to set a prisoner free—and discover the prisoner was you."

7. BEWARE OF FALLING VICTIM TO UNREALISTIC EXPECTATIONS

When I was still a hard-core spiritual skeptic, Leslie had a vision of what I would look like if I would only become a Christian. She imagined I would become transformed into the perfect husband. I would diaper the kids, mow the lawn, wash the dishes, clean the bathrooms, and take out the garbage without complaint. I would pamper her with romantic dinners. My angry outbursts would disappear. I would become patient, compassionate, and wise beyond my years.

Well, I *did* become a Christian and . . . let's just say I have never quite lived up to Leslie's rosy expectations! Fortunately, God has changed my values, priorities, and worldview over the years, for which we're both grateful. But I'm still me. God may have rounded off many of my sharp edges, but I am far from being the perfect mate.

"I'd caution any Christian in a mismatched marriage to be realistic about her spouse," Leslie said. "Not every annoying thing he does is a direct result of him not being a Christian. If you think he's going to be immediately perfected when he becomes a believer, you're putting an undue burden on him and you're setting yourself up for disappointment. Besides, if you blame his lack of spiritual interest for all of his shortcomings, you're giving him a convenient excuse for not continuing to grow as a husband and father."

One source of these unrealistic expectations is when unequally yoked Christians visit a church function and see how Christian couples relate to one another. In public, Christian couples are usually on their best behavior. Husbands are kind, caring, and solicitous toward their wives. When mismatched Christians see this kind of public conduct, they assume—incorrectly—that these husbands always act the same way at home.

The best thing to do, Leslie recommends, is to get beneath the surface-level niceties and find out what Christian marriages are really like. One way to do this is to be part of a small group where Christians are more willing to disclose the realities of their relationships. Or it may help to have an occasional lunch with a spouse from a Christian marriage and talk in confidential terms about the dynamics of her partnership.

"You'll see real quickly that their marriages aren't ideal, either," Leslie said. "They still argue, they still have disagreements, they still act childish from time to time—and they probably still squabble over who's going to take out the garbage. That's just life—and recognizing that really helped me become more realistic."

As a result, Leslie stopped banking on my conversion to turn me into the ideal mate at some undefined future time. Instead, she became more actively involved in gently encouraging me to continue growing as a husband. She had honest talks with me about how we could each better contribute to a more harmonious relationship. This also had the benefit of taking the spotlight off of our mismatched situation so that it didn't become the unrelenting focus of our lives.

8. KEEP FOCUSED ON WHAT YOU LOVE BEST ABOUT YOUR SPOUSE

There's a natural tendency in a mismatched marriage to become obsessed about the one big shortcoming in your partner—that he or she is not a Christian. The more this becomes your focus, the more he or she begins to feel like a disappointment to you. And those kind of attitudes are quickly picked up by the non-Christian spouse. For a while in our marriage, for example, I couldn't shake a vague and disquieting sense that I was letting down Leslie, that I was falling short of who she wanted me to be, and that I was in some sense a failure as a husband. That was very depressing to me.

Fortunately, Leslie began to realize that she was subconsciously sending negative messages to me. When she tried to "fix" me by stressing my shortcomings, she found that this actually reinforced the very behavior she didn't like. She came to the conclusion that it would be much healthier for our marriage if she would emphasize all of the things she loved about me. She quickly found that the more she accentuated my positive attributes, the more motivated I was to live up to her praises. "I learned the hard way that people tend to become what others praise in them," Leslie said.

There were several practical steps she took to accomplish this. First, she resisted labeling me. Yes, I was an atheist, but she refused to let that term define me. Instead, she tried to see me as God saw me: as a treasured part of his creation, a human being whose soul was etched with the likeness of God, a wayward son whom he longed to connect with. Unfortunately, labels can reinforce negative behaviors. Think of how many children are branded with a less-than-flattering label and who end up shipwrecking their lives in a subconscious attempt to fulfill that picture of themselves.

Second, Leslie tried to verbalize her appreciation for me as much as possible. She would do this through a few words of congratulations after I had done something right, through impromptu notes she would leave in my briefcase for me to find later, or by letting me overhear how she would praise me when talking to her friends. Leslie tried to maintain at least a ten-to-one ratio between uplifting, encouraging, and cheerleading words and words that were more critical. Of course, there are times when she needed to address my faults, but by then she had such a deep reservoir of goodwill built up and I was so secure in her love for me that I was better able to hear critical words without the defensiveness I used to have.

We have carried on this practice now that both of us are Christians. We go out of our way to praise the best qualities in each other, we let each other know that we accept each other unconditionally, we consistently reinforce our love for each other, and we try to paint a vision of what God can do with each other if we stay true to him. To give you an example, a few years ago when David Letterman's "Top Ten" lists were the rage, I wrote a note to Leslie on beautiful paper. It's not the most poetic thing that has ever been written; in fact, I never intended for others to read it. But these are the words I like Leslie to hear from me:

TEN OF THE MANY THINGS I LOVE ABOUT LESLIE

10. She's the most beautiful person I've ever known.
9. Sometimes she's just plain silly—and she lets me be silly, too.
8. She's the world's greatest mother.
7. She is full of love, joy, peace, patience, kindness, goodness, faithfulness, gentleness, and self-control. Hey, *she's a walking Bible verse!*
6. She's my biggest cheerleader!
5. She likes to hold hands and go for walks.

4. She cares deeply about her friends and lets them know it.

3. She loves to go on quiet rides together and either talk about everything or talk about nothing.

2. She thoroughly enjoys the adventure of our life together.

1. She introduced me to her best friend—Jesus.

Let me ask you this: *what do you want your spouse to become?* Paint a word picture for him or her! Write your own "Top Ten" list of the qualities you admire most in your partner and see if this doesn't become a subtle blueprint for how he or she continues to behave in the future. "Do not let any unwholesome talk come out of your mouths," said Paul in Ephesians 4:29, "but only what is helpful for building others up according to their needs, that it may benefit those who listen."

Remember that there were valid reasons why you married the person you did. Remind yourself of those when your spiritual mismatch seems to be sapping the life from your relationship. You have a lot in common—you like to stroll through the woods, or see the latest movies, or try out exotic restaurants, or play tennis together. Build on those similar interests and watch how they can keep your connection tight even when your differences over spiritual issues threaten to split you apart.

9. LEARN TO DISAGREE WITHOUT BEING DISAGREEABLE

Conflict is inevitable in any marriage, but especially in those where the spouses are at odds over a topic as potentially volatile as spirituality. But conflict can have its benefits. "The process of growing into an intimate relationship involves conflict," said marriage expert Gary Oliver. "Since many of us avoid conflict like the plague, we don't grow, we don't change, we don't get close, and we don't experience intimacy. We stay stuck in the rut of mediocrity."[21]

The Bible says in Proverbs 27:17: "As iron sharpens iron, so one man sharpens another." Have you ever seen steel being used to sharpen steel?

There's noise, friction, heat, and sparks. So this biblical imagery is suggesting that working through conflict will sharpen us as people and as couples.

Our spiritual mismatch certainly provided us with plenty of conflict to work with. Because Leslie handled it positively and prayerfully, our relationship didn't experience a meltdown, but instead God used it to deepen our understanding and appreciation of each other. What did Leslie do right? Here are a few specifics.

Leslie Learned When to Stand Firm and When to Compromise

This saved our marriage from degenerating into a battlefield where every little victory came at the expense of a hard-won fight. "If I had made a big deal out of every little problem that came up because of our mismatch—*whew!* We would have been fighting all the time," Leslie said.

For example, one Sunday the church was starting a new series on marriage at its weekend services. At this point, I was beginning to become more open to trying out church, and Leslie thought it would be ideal for both of us to hear a biblical perspective on what a marriage relationship should look like. When she asked me early in the week if I would be willing to go with her, I said, "Yeah, sure . . . maybe." The problem was that she saw this as more of a commitment than I intended it to be. By the time Friday rolled around, I was suggesting that we take a weekend jaunt to Wisconsin so I could chill out after an especially stressful week.

Leslie could have drawn a line and said, "You led me to believe you'd go to church this weekend! This is an important series! We're *not* going to Wisconsin; we need to work on our marriage instead." But as we began discussing the matter, she realized I could make a good case that in my own mind I never made a firm commitment to attend church that weekend. Besides, even if she did twist my arm and get me to change my mind, I certainly wouldn't have been in any mood to hear what the pastor was saying anyway.

So Leslie said, "I was hoping to hear the start of this new series on marriage, but I know you're exhausted and could use a few days in the woods. Actually, that does sound like fun—we could take some long walks together and relax. I've got a tape of an earlier message on marriage. Would it be okay with you if we listened to it on the drive to Wisconsin?"

That was fine with me. I just wanted to get away and clear my head for a few days. We did listen to that tape on the road, and do you know what? It was really helpful. Besides, it provided fodder for some conversations while we were taking those long walks in the woods. Thanks to Leslie's discernment, we avoided what could have been a divisive argument and instead reached a compromise that both fulfilled my desires while basically achieving Leslie's original goal.

Some issues just aren't worth fighting over. Even if you win the battle, you may very well have lost the war, because you will have alienated your spouse. "Don't major on the minors," Leslie advises.

Other matters, though, are more serious and may require you to draw a line and firmly say no. If your partner wants you to participate in something unethical or illegal, or wants you to do something that violates your conscience or Christian commitment, then it's appropriate to explain why you can't participate. When this happens, don't use an accusatory tone that demeans your spouse. Instead, talk about your own feelings and why participation would make you feel uncomfortable, scared, or violated. Personally, I found myself admiring Leslie when she stood up for what she believed. It showed me that her faith wasn't wishy-washy, but was truly the guiding force in her life.

Leslie Learned the "Stop-Look-Listen" Approach to Conflict

Whenever disagreements would arise in our relationship, especially concerning spiritual matters, Leslie would take three steps.

First, she would **STOP** being defensive and honestly consider whether there was a seed of truth to what I was saying. In the example I mentioned above, Leslie paused long enough to realize that in my mind I hadn't really made a firm commitment to attend the weekend services. While she thought I had, there was enough ambiguity that she figured she should give me the benefit of the doubt.

Then she would **LOOK** for mutually acceptable solutions that will not only resolve the immediate issue, but which might deal with this entire category of conflict. In this example, her goal was to expose me to biblical teaching about marriage; my goal was to escape to Wisconsin for the weekend. She looked for a solution that would meet both needs. Not only did this resolve the matter at hand, but it also created a paradigm for future disagreements in this same vein. If I were willing to listen to tapes as we went on drives together, then this opened up a lot of future opportunities to get spiritual input into my life even if I wasn't willing yet to attend church on a consistent basis.

Finally, she would **LISTEN** to what I was saying. "Everyone should be quick to listen, slow to speak and slow to become angry," says James 1:19. As we discussed whether I had made a commitment to go to church that weekend, Leslie didn't automatically assume that I was merely trying to weasel out of a promise in order to avoid hearing a sermon on marriage. Rather, she listened to what I said and how I said it, reaching the conclusion that I really was exhausted from work and needed a few days out in the woods to decompress.

Over time, Leslie became adept at what Theodore Reik calls listening with the "third ear." That means listening for the underlying emotions beneath the words that are said. For instance, sometimes we would be arguing over an inconsequential matter, but Leslie would say, "I hear a lot of hurt in your voice. I can tell you are upset over more than this little issue. What has really wounded you?" That opens the door to a whole deeper level of communication. Instead of just skating on the surface of our conflict, we can dig down to the roots of our discontent and talk about the subterranean emotions that might be secretly fueling our behavior.

Leslie Learned to Fight Fair

Disagreements due to spiritual mismatches are inescapable. They might center on parenting issues: Dad thinks it's okay to let his son view adult-oriented material on the Internet, while Mom knows that's inappropriate. They might revolve around moral issues: Mom wants to fudge on the income taxes, but Dad wants to be scrupulously honest. They might focus on practical issues: Mom wants to go on a women's retreat, but Dad isn't interested in watching the kids for the weekend. They might involve intellectual issues: Dad thinks there are good reasons for believing the Bible is historically reliable, while Mom isn't interested in hearing them.

Often, the question of whether these disagreements will escalate into an all-out battle, with wounded casualties on both sides, is determined by the manner in which the Christian handles the conflict.

Leslie's credo was found in Psalm 4:4: "In your anger, do not sin." In other words, it was okay for her to feel the anger that she often experienced when we would lock horns, but she tried to avoid attitudes and actions that would be harmful or counter-productive.

For example, she sought to honor me as her husband and thus refrain from biting, sarcastic comments that were meant to hurt me rather than illuminate the issue at hand. She tried not to muddy the waters by bringing up side issues or dredging up my misdeeds from the past. She was careful to accurately recite the facts of the situation and was quick to retract unfair remarks that slipped from her lips in the heat of discussion. She didn't throw common courtesy and politeness out the window just because we were arguing. She used humor, where possible, to defuse tension. She stayed with the discussion until we either reached a solution or mutually agreed to talk about it at another time.

Without even realizing it, she was living out the kind of advice offered by marital counselor Gary Smalley in his bestseller *Making Love Last Forever*, where he lists his "fighting rules" for couples. They include these suggestions, among many others:

- Maintain as much tender physical contact as possible. Hold hands.
- Don't use "hysterical" statements or exaggerations. ("This will never work out." "You're just like your father.")
- Resolve your conflicts with win-win solutions; both parties agree with the solution or outcome of the argument. Work on resolution only after both understand feelings and needs.[22]

I don't want to give you the impression that Leslie never let her emotions get the best of her. As committed as she was to fighting fair, there were times when both of us went for the jugular rather than responsibly searching for common ground and when we subjected each other to several icy days of silence instead of engaging with the issues. But her overall orientation was to work through our conflict in a God-honoring way, with an understanding spirit, a forgiving nature, and a humble disposition. And in doing so, she taught me something about Jesus.

Yet what happens when conflict leads to alienation? What steps should the Christian take when she senses that discord over spiritual issues is pushing her partner away? We've had to deal with that situation too, and we learned some lessons that we will be discussing in the next chapter as we complete the twelve ways to make the most of your mismatched marriage.

6

The Chill, the Children, and the Most Challenging Question

C.C. AND HER HUSBAND WERE DRIFTING APART IN MANY WAYS. Before they got married, he assured her that he believed in God, and yet now he was reluctant to go to church with her. On Sunday after Sunday, C.C. sat alone in the pew. They became immersed in their respective careers. "Too many missed communications, chilly silences, and unkind words led us further apart," she said. "We even stopped making love."[1]

It's ironic that the idea of God, who invented marriage in the first place and who deeply loves both spouses in every relationship, can actually become a wedge between couples in unequally yoked situations. Usually, religion is not the only source of discord in these marriages, but it can become the flash point for anger and arguments. Even when the Christian spouse is committed to working through conflict in a God-honoring way, emotions and hurt feelings can cause even the best of intentions to go awry. The result: an icy distance develops between the husband and wife.

We have already looked at nine ways to make the most of your spiritually mismatched marriage, and there are three other hard-learned lessons we want to share in this chapter. Let's begin by delving into what to do when you begin to feel an ominous chill in the air of your relationship. Often it takes quick action to avert your marriage from heading into the deep freeze.

10. WHEN YOU SENSE YOUR SPOUSE IS PULLING AWAY, GENTLY TAKE THE INITIATIVE TO RECONNECT

My gut-level response to conflict—especially over spiritual matters—was first to erupt in fiery anger and then to cool down, withdraw, and freeze out Leslie. That's a common response among men who are unskilled in relational dynamics. The silent treatment was my immature way of trying to punish Leslie while at the same time avoiding the issue at hand. Sometimes I would go several days without speaking to her.

Had Leslie responded the same way—by pouting, digging in her heels, and turning a cold shoulder toward me—this easily could have led to a marriage-threatening rupture in our relationship. But Leslie saved our relationship by lovingly and gently reaching out to reconnect with me when she sensed I was beginning to pull away from her. She did this before the coolness in our relationship had a chance to harden into solid ice. This wasn't a desperate attempt to control me. It wasn't a frantic effort to cling to me. Rather, it was a sincere expression of grace—and it kept our marriage from icing over.

She often did this by little acts that I barely noticed at the time but which quietly began to thaw our relationship. For instance, she would make sure she would go to bed at the same time I did. That sounds simple, doesn't it? But think about it: when one partner stays up late watching television and comes to bed only to find his spouse fast asleep, this accentuates the gulf between them. Going to bed at the same time creates a subtle connection, almost as if you were saying to your partner, "We may have our differences, but we're still in this together!" Besides, some spontaneous cuddling is almost unavoidable!

Also, Leslie would make sure we would sit down at the table and eat dinner together whenever possible. This provided a timeout in our hectic lives and established an environment where conversation could more easily flow. In addition, Leslie would suggest that we participate in activities that we enjoyed jointly. She might clip out a restaurant review from the newspaper and casually show it to me as she floated the idea of going out to eat, or she might point to a newspaper ad for a new movie featuring our favorite actors and propose that we catch the late show. Even if I wasn't willing to go along with her suggestion, she nevertheless was sending a subtle message to me: *Let's not let a silly grudge stand between us.*

Sometimes Leslie would tell me a joke to break the ice, or make my favorite meal for dinner, or put a note on my shaving mirror with the word "Truce???" written on it. But more important, Leslie would make sure that she maintained physical contact with me. She would come up behind me while I was eating breakfast and give me a quick hug around the neck. She would casually put a hand on my shoulder while we paused for a moment to talk in the hallway. She would give me a good-night kiss. She would take my hand and hold it while we were waiting in line at the grocery store.

There is something quietly reassuring and reaffirming about a simple touch. It represents tenderness, warmth, and forgiveness. "To touch is to communicate our acceptance of the other even as he or she speaks harshly, accuses falsely, behaves unkindly, or acts inconsiderately," said Bobbie and Myron Yagel, who have taught marriage seminars for more than twenty years. "One of the best ways for spouses to preclude angry eruptions in marriage is for one of us to touch the other the moment we sense trouble brewing. This way, we interrupt the separation before it occurs. It's almost impossible to hate someone whose hand you hold."[2]

But our physical contact didn't stop there. Even as we were starting to grow apart—in fact, especially *because* we were drifting apart—Leslie didn't hesitate to initiative lovemaking. This was extremely important in knitting our lives back together when our marriage was beginning to unravel.

Making Love, Not War

Like a lot of non-Christian men, I was under the impression that Christian women had an uptight, puritanical aversion to sex and were ashamed of their bodies. One of my biggest fears when Leslie became a Christian was that she would turn into a sexually repressed prude who would see sex as a necessary evil at best and at worst an abhorrent activity to be scrupulously avoided. My nightmare was that she was going to put up an "Off Limits!" sign on her side of our bed.

This stereotype runs so deep that researchers at the University of Chicago reacted with dismay when their in-depth study of sexual practices among Americans disclosed that the most consistently satisfied women are conservative Protestants. By a significant margin, these religious women ranked highest among those who always had orgasms during intercourse. They were followed by mainline Protestants and Catholics. It was women with no religious affiliation who finished last.[3]

"[This] may seem surprising," the scientists wrote, "because conservative religious women are so often portrayed as sexually repressed. Perhaps conservative Protestant women firmly believe in the holiness of marriage and of sexuality as an expression of their love for their husbands . . . Despite the popular image of straitlaced conservative Protestants, there is at least circumstantial evidence that the image may be a myth . . ."[4]

This stereotype of sexual frigidity is not rooted in the Bible. God intended sex to be a beautiful part of the bonding process between spouses. He designed it not just for procreation but for pleasure as well. The Bible says that sexual intercourse allows a husband and wife to experience a unique oneness.[5] When our sexuality is expressed in the context of the loving, secure, trust-filled, long-lasting, and safe environment of marriage, it's a mysterious method of mathematics in which one plus one equals one.

God's design is for husbands and wives to enjoy a vital, regular, and mutually satisfying physical relationship. Scripture tells husbands and wives that their bodies belong not just to themselves but to their spouses as well. Then the Bible adds, "Do not deprive each other except by mutual consent and for a time, so that you may devote yourselves to prayer."[6] Any nonharmful sexual activity that's mutually agreeable is permissible in the marriage bed.[7]

"Good sex begins in the Bible," said my friend Robert Moeller in a book he wrote for couples. "Rather than saying, 'Shame on you for having sexual desires,' our Lord says, 'Quench that sexual thirst by turning to your spouse. That person is my gift to you as a continual source of gratification and refreshment.'"[8] Christian author Mike Mason put it this way in his lyrical book *The Mystery of Marriage*:

Is there any other activity at all in which an adult man and woman may engage together (apart from worship) that is actually more childlike, more clean and pure, more natural and wholesome and unequivocally right than is the act of making love? For if worship is the deepest available form of communion with God (and especially that particular act of worship known as Communion), then surely sex is the deepest communion that is possible between human beings.[9]

There are three important reasons why it was vitally important for Leslie to reach out to me physically when we seemed to be drifting apart due to our spiritual mismatch:

- First, I had been hesitant to initiate lovemaking because I was uncertain how Leslie's conversion may have changed her attitude toward sex. I feared rejection, but instead Leslie took action and chased away those fears.
- Second, by signaling that she wanted our love life to continue unabated despite our spiritual mismatch, Leslie removed one of my big objections to her decision to become a Christian. Once I realized that this important dimension of our relationship wasn't going to change, some of my negative attitudes toward Christianity dissipated.
- Third, I harbored a secret fear that in Leslie's eyes I was no longer good enough for her because I wasn't a Christian. When disagreements over religion would push us apart, I quietly wondered whether Leslie would really want to reconcile with me or whether she would rather find someone else who shared her faith. Spontaneously suggesting lovemaking was a powerful way for her to reinforce that she still loved me despite our spiritual differences. She was making it clear that she was going to do whatever she could to prevent our mismatch from creating physical or emotional distance between us.

When the Christian spouse goes on the offensive to reconnect with her partner through kind words, small gestures, and physical affection, this is merely a fulfillment of God's directions to be forgiving, grace-filled, honoring, and respectful toward her spouse. In an equally yoked marriage, where each partner is indwelled by the Holy Spirit, both spouses should move toward reconciliation, but in a mismatched marriage the burden generally falls on the believer.

It's often an awkward step to take, however. To give an example of how to take this kind of action, let's finish the story of C.C., who we introduced at the outset of this chapter. She had been married to David for thirty years, and their different beliefs about God were just one of the reasons why they ended up living separate lives under the same roof. She became desperate to reconnect with the man she loved, and so she went to the best possible source for advice.

The Big Thaw

Looking for answers, C.C. turned to Scripture. First Peter 3:1–2 leapt off the page: "Your godly lives will speak to them better than any words. They will be won over by watching your pure, godly behavior." She understood what that meant, but she was at a loss concerning what to do. "How am I supposed to win David over by my behavior when my anger is so close to the surface?" she asked. After anguishing for a while, she prayed a simple prayer: "Change me, Lord—I'll do whatever you ask."

She tried little gestures to warm up their icy relationship. For instance, she celebrated her husband's half-birthday with half a cake. She even took time to express appreciation to him for going to work each day. "But touching—making that final sensory connection—scared me," she said. This is what happened next:

> It had been two years since we'd made love. Seven times in a row I'd initiated lovemaking, only to be rejected. Now, in the midst of my fear, I felt the Lord's gentle leading: *Start at the beginning.* So I touched David's arm when we talked or placed my hand on his back.

After several days of "thawing," I made my move. "David, I need a hug." Our first attempt was stiff, almost awkward. But each day I asked for and received these revitalizing moments of warmth. Then one day, I turned around to find David's waiting arms poised for a hug.

One ordinary Saturday, David grabbed my hand and looked at me with tender, pleading eyes. As we embraced, forgiveness melted our hearts. Apprehensions, awkwardness, and old hurts vanished. The timing, the place, the circumstance—all had been orchestrated by God. We came together as naturally and comfortably as when we were first married, and completed the final step in our journey back to each other.[10]

Who knows where C.C.'s marriage would have ended up if she hadn't been mature, godly, and courageous enough to make the first move toward reconciliation? Her approach—seeking wisdom from Scripture; praying to God for help; starting with a simple step of action; and gently persisting over a period of time despite initial rejection—is a model for all of us. And in the end, after years of living in a mismatched relationship, David finally said yes to Christ.

So when a bitter wind is blowing through your marriage and threatening to ice over your hearts, take immediate steps to warm up your relationship. Reach out in grace and love to your spouse. Not only will this bridge the gap between you, but it also will be a subtle illustration to him of how his heavenly Father has taken the initiative through Jesus Christ to reach out to him in the hopes of reconnecting for eternity.

11. RAISE YOUR CHILDREN WITH CHRISTIAN VALUES, BUT BE CAREFUL NOT TO TURN THEM AGAINST YOUR SPOUSE

Children are often buffeted by the turbulence of a mismatched marriage. They love both of their parents, yet even at a young age they have an uncanny ability to sense when there's tension in the house. Since children crave stability, they feel anxiety when they perceive that their parents are at odds. They really begin to get confused when their Christian mom and skeptical dad start to send them mixed messages.

Mom tells them how important it is for them to come to church, yet they wonder why Dad is lounging in his favorite reclining chair and watching the football game instead of going along with them. Mom tells them not to use foul language, but then they hear Dad utter those same words when he hits his thumb with the hammer or when his favorite baseball team loses. They see their mom reading the Bible, but Dad always seems to prefer the business section. Mom advises them to rely on God, while Dad cautions them not to trust anyone but themselves.

As they get older, Mom stresses why they should stay away from R-rated movies, and yet Dad caves in and takes them when they complain that all of their friends have seen the film. Mom counsels that premarital sex is wrong, while Dad's attitude seems to be, "All kids fool around. What's important is that if you decide to engage in sex, you do it safely." These conflicting signals—and a flurry of others—bring confusion, uncertainty, and apprehension into their lives.

Before Leslie and I were Christians, our naive plan was to raise our kids to be intelligent enough to draw their own conclusions about which path to take in life. The problem, of course, is that when you create a spiritual vacuum in your home, the false gods of the world will rush in to fill it.

Materialism lures them with the idea that their possessions determine their worth as a person. Hedonism insists that personal pleasure is paramount, despite how others might get hurt. Secular humanism seeks to divorce them from any transcendent moral order and mires them in situational ethics. New Age thinking tries to convince them they are each gods who can find fulfillment by looking within themselves. Ambition tells them to watch out for Number One and not to care about anyone else. And a cacophony of gurus offer conflicting spiritual guidance, insisting that it doesn't really matter which path you follow because they all end up in the same place anyway.

Then our Christian neighbor, Linda, pointed out to Leslie the folly of thinking we can let our children decide their morality on their own. After all, we live in an increasingly confusing world, where lines between right and wrong are blurred, ethics are fluid, virtue is passé, and nothing seems certain except uncertainty. Launching children into that kind of hostile environment without a solid moral upbringing would be parental malpractice!

After Leslie became a Christian, she became convicted by Bible passages like Proverbs 22:6: "Train a child in the way he should go, and when he is old he will not turn from it." She realized she needed to inculcate God's values, God's morality, and God's truth into Alison and Kyle, whether I was an active participant in that process or not. Here are some lessons she learned along the way.

Non-Christians May Be Open to Christian Education for Their Children If the Emphasis Is on Developing Moral Values

When Leslie approached me about the idea of having Alison and Kyle attend the church's children's program, she stressed that this was a way for them to develop strong moral values. That sounded all right to me. I wanted my kids to be tough and self-reliant, but I also wanted them to learn such values as honesty, respect, personal responsibility, courage, and gratitude. When she told me, "Those are straight out of the Bible," then I replied that it was fine with me if she brought the kids to church.

From a purely pragmatic viewpoint, Leslie was going to go to church anyway. If she left the kids at home, I would have to get up and take care of them. If she brought them with her, I could sleep off my hangover in peace. Besides, if I wanted my kids to make up their own minds about what to believe, they needed to be exposed to all possibilities, and so it didn't bother me that they would hear what Christians believe.

Non-Christians frequently acquiesce to their children going to Sunday school. One study showed that forty-eight percent of unchurched parents have their children enrolled for religious instruction.[11] "I'll tell you why I like having my kids in Sunday school," one agnostic father told me.

"When I was a kid, we got a certain amount of moral training in the public schools, but I'm not sure I can count on that these days. I want to teach my kids right from wrong, and if the church can help, then I'm all for it."

That's the same reason some non-Christian parents send their children to private Christian schools. They're seeking not only a moral dimension to their child's instruction, but they also want a higher quality of education than might be available from their local public schools. Our daughter, Alison, teaches at a Christian school whose reputation for educational excellence is so strong that people from a variety of faith backgrounds send their children there.

Not all non-Christian parents agree, however. For some of them—especially those in Generation X—"religious tolerance" is a foundational concept. To them, this doesn't merely mean respecting people from all religious faiths; rather, it means having the attitude that all religious beliefs are equally valid. Consequently, they may shy away from allowing their children to attend Sunday school if they think they will be taught that there's only one way to God.

If this becomes an impediment, sometimes it's a good idea to challenge your spouse to personally check out the curriculum that's being used in the children's ministry. Most of the time, he will find that he agrees with the lessons being taught, since in the younger grades they tend to revolve around God's love for the child, building a strong self-esteem, and learning about basic values through Bible stories. If he is still adamant that his kids not attend a Christian program, then this next point becomes even more important.

All Christian Parents Should Home School Their Children

I'm sure that statement raised your eyebrows! But hear us out: we're *not* saying all Christian parents should withdraw their children from public schools. While that's the right course of action for some, it isn't for many. For example, Leslie and I sent our kids to public schools. What we *are* saying is that all Christian parents should intentionally and strategically take advantage of day-to-day opportunities in the home to build biblical values into their children. In that sense, all Christians should be teaching their children at home. That's what Deuteronomy 6:4–9 tells us:

> Hear, O Israel: The Lord our God, the Lord is one. Love the Lord your God with all your heart and with all your soul and with all your strength. These commandments that I give you today are to be upon your hearts. Impress them on your children. Talk about them when you sit at home and when you walk along the road, when you lie down and when you get up. Tie them as symbols on your hands and bind them on your foreheads. Write them on the doorframes of your houses and on your gates.

In other words, as opportunities arise during the time you're with your children at home, teach them about God. Put Bible verses on the walls of their bedrooms. Weave scriptural values through as much of your interaction with them as possible. Look for life-lessons that can be drawn from everyday experiences. For instance, if the neighborhood children are ostracizing a kid who is different from them, this is a good chance to talk about how Jesus teaches us to be loving toward all people. Other real-life lessons about honesty, gossiping, bravery, and gratitude abound if we are just alert for them.

Another way to inculcate biblical teaching is to expose children to age-appropriate Christian resources. For instance, all children watch videos. Why not show them high-quality, Bible-based videos that educate them about God and how he wants them to live? The wildly popular Veggie Tales videotapes feature colorful cartoons of Bob the Tomato and Larry the Cucumber as they illustrate such biblical values as obedience, courage, thankfulness, and positive self-esteem. These upbeat and clever stories are actually promoted as being, "Sunday morning values, Saturday morning fun."

Most parents read to their children before they go to sleep. Why not choose Bible stories written for children? Christian bookstores are packed with top-notch books that you can read to your kids or that they can read themselves. For instance, Glen Keane, a directing animator for Walt Disney Pictures, has authored a series of books that creatively teach biblical values through the adventures of a raccoon named Adam. I actually got tears in my eyes when I read his book *Adam Raccoon at Forever Falls*! This poignant tale of how a lion named King Aren sacrifices himself to save his friend Adam from a dangerous waterfall is a powerful parable for the story of salvation. It's so well done that I once read it during a sermon I did for adults!

Other books are available for older youth. Both of my books, *The Case for Christ* and *The Case for Faith*, which describe the evidence that convinced an atheist like me that Christianity is true, have been published in Student Editions that are designed to be especially relevant and understandable for teenagers. Ravi Zacharias's excellent book *Jesus Among Other Gods*, which defends the absolute truth of the Christian message, also has been rewritten and repackaged in a special edition for students.

These kinds of resources can either supplement your children's Sunday school teaching or they can substitute for a children's ministry if your spouse refuses to let them attend one. In either case, unequally yoked parents need to constantly be on the lookout for spiritual input that they can provide for their children to compensate for the lack of religious instruction by the other partner.

Let Your Children Know That All Questions Are Permissible and That All Feelings Are Legitimate

British pastor Michael Fanstone stresses this point in his book *Unbelieving Husbands and the Wives Who Love Them*. "Nothing works better with children who have an endless supply of important questions than a steady stream of straight answers," he said. "The value of open and honest discussion is that misconceptions and unnecessary fears can be laid to rest quickly. What children sometimes imagine is often very much more sinister than the reality."[12]

Leslie remembers the time when Alison, who was four years old, picked up on some vibes that we were having strife over spiritual matters. When Alison was alone with her, she asked with concern: "Are you mad at Daddy?"

Leslie was glad that Alison felt secure enough to broach that subject rather than internalize her concerns and live with a festering anxiety that maybe her mom and dad were going to split up. I thought Leslie handled this exchange really well.

"I was able to tell her that Mom and Dad love each other very much and that sometimes we have different opinions about some matters, but that's okay," Leslie said. "I reminded her that she and her friend Sara sometimes had differences of opinion, but she was still her best friend. I also reiterated that both Mom and Dad love her and Kyle very much and always will. That seemed to satisfy her. I think she just wanted some reassurance."

Because the tension in a spiritually mismatched home can trigger emotions of fear, apprehension, and uncertainty in children, it's vital that they feel free to express their emotions to their parents. Let them know that whatever feelings they are having are valid and can be openly discussed. For instance, when they say they are afraid, don't correct them or tell them they are being silly. This sends the wrong message that their emotions are incorrect, when actually feelings are neither right nor wrong. Instead, validate their feelings and then lovingly address the underlying factors that are generating that response in them.

"I made bedtime a special opportunity for the children to say whatever was on their heart," Leslie said. "Whenever they would ask a question or express a feeling or concern, I would always thank them. That way, the lines of communication seemed to remain open—and they could drift off to sleep without being burdened."

Remember That You're a Walking Advertisement for Jesus

An old adage says, "Values aren't taught as much as they're caught." In a spiritually mismatched marriage, all eyes are on you to see how a Christian behaves. You're going to be the most influential Christian to your children. Your life will be the most irrefutable evidence to them that following Jesus is the very best way to go through life.

Leslie could teach the children as many Bible stories as she wanted about honesty, but what really impacted them was when they returned from the grocery store one day and Leslie realized the cashier had accidentally given her too much change. She promptly bundled up the kids and returned to the store to set matters straight.

Leslie could talk endlessly about the importance of prayer, and yet nothing would imprint that message on their hearts as much as walking into the kitchen early in the morning and seeing their mother at the kitchen table as she was quietly lifting up her family to God.

Your children don't expect you to be perfect. Just authentic. When we do fall short, our modeling of confession and repentance is very powerful for children to witness. One of my most poignant child-rearing memories was after I became a Christian and realized that my workaholism had caused me to slight my kids. I got down on my knees to be eye-level with Alison and Kyle, put my arms around them, and tearfully apologized. Then I vowed to be a better father, and we sealed the moment by praying together for God's help in that regard.

It's difficult for a non-Christian spouse to object to you modeling a Christian lifestyle for your children. After all, you are just being faithful to who you are. You are not trying to indoctrinate them or force them into becoming Christians. Instead, you are providing a daily example of what the Christian life looks like. Ultimately, they are going to have to decide whether they will follow Jesus. In the meantime, what could be wrong with sharing this most important part of your life with them?

Avoid Turning Your Kids against Your Spouse

Children pick up on logic faster than we sometimes think. If you are modeling a Christian life for your children, taking advantage of opportunities to inculcate biblical values into them, and exposing them to religious training, you are sending the message that it is wonderful to know Jesus personally. And if Daddy doesn't pray, go to church, or have his own relationship with God, then the logical conclusion is that there must be something not-so-wonderful about him.

It is critically important that Christian spouses avoid undermining the authority of the nonbelieving parent or showing anything less than respect and honor for him. Leslie always scrupulously avoided criticizing me in the children's presence. She didn't want the children thinking she thought less of me or looked down on me because I wasn't a follower of Jesus.

"When Alison would ask why Daddy didn't go to church with us, I told her it was because he and I had different opinions about God," Leslie said. "I told her everyone, including her, had to come to their own conclusions about Jesus, and that I loved Daddy and respected his opinion. Now, she was young at the time, so she didn't ask a lot of sophisticated follow-up questions! But it seemed very important to her that I continually reaffirmed my love for her and for her dad."

When Leslie and the kids walked out the door to go to church, she didn't give them the impression that I was a bad person for staying at home. She would give me a kiss and cheerfully say to them, "Say 'good-bye' to Daddy! We'll see him in a little while."

Matters get stickier as children get older. One mother of three told us that her husband got a raise at work shortly after she and the children began praying for the family's financial situation. "What an answer to prayer!" she spontaneously exclaimed when he brought home the news. The children clapped.

"There's another term for this," said the skeptical husband.

She asked, "What's that?"

"A coincidence!"

Another woman described how her son was learning about Darwinism in high school. She started poking holes in the evolutionary theory by recounting some scientific data that she had read in Christian books. Her husband, though, angrily cut the conversation short, accusing her of "indoctrinating the boy with religious propaganda" and saying she would hurt his grade in the class if she kept "confusing him" about the issue.

These situations require tact. One solution is to have a private conversation with your spouse where you ask him to be as respectful toward your beliefs as you are trying to be toward his. Tell him you need to be as authentic about who you are as he is about himself. Seek a compromise where both of you agree never to disrespect each other in front of the children. It's hard to argue with the viewpoint that if children are going to make up their own minds about important issues such as faith, then it's a good thing for them to hear different perspectives on the issue—including the Christian position.

That sounds logical, doesn't it? Unfortunately, when the volatile issue of faith is involved, sometimes logic goes out the window. There are non-Christian spouses whose hostility toward Christianity is so extreme that they don't want their children to have any Christian influence. In those rare cases, the Christian partner must rely on prayer for her children and implement these ideas only as far as she can without causing ongoing arguments in the home.

12. REGULARLY ASK YOURSELF THE MOST CONVICTING QUESTION OF ALL

We have covered a lot of topics as we have discussed how to make the most of your spiritually mismatched marriage. We have delved into parenting, reconciliation, conflict resolution, encouragement, expectations, forgiveness, attitudes, finding a mentor, and the importance of keeping God first and your partner second in your life. If we had to sum it all up into one point, however, it would be to ask yourself the "most convicting question of all." What question is that?

When I get a new calendar at the start of every year, the first thing I do is page through it and find the first day of each and every month. Then I take out a pen and write down the question I want to make sure I deeply ponder at least once every thirty days: *"How would I like to be married to me?"*

Wow, what a sobering question! Twelve times a year, it forces me into a painful period of self-examination. If I were married to me, what changes would I want in my behavior? What rough edges of my personality would I want to have smoothed? How would I want my priorities to change? What attitudes would I want to abandon or reinforce?

I've been doing this ever since 1995, when I first read that provocative question in *Becoming Soul Mates*, written by Christian relationship experts Les and Leslie Parrott. "That simple question," they said, "can do more to help you ensure the success of your marriage than just about anything else. Think about it. How would you rate you as a marriage partner? Are you easy to live with? How do you enrich the relationship? What are the positive qualities you bring to your marriage?"[13]

This question is especially relevant in an unequally yoked relationship. You're empowered by the Holy Spirit, guided by God's truth, motivated to follow his commandments, committed to living for him, and yet you're wed to someone who is indifferent or possibly even antagonistic toward those heartfelt values. He could have a myriad of responses to your efforts to live the Christian life and bring your children to faith. We can't anticipate all of them in this book. But this question from the Parrotts is the answer for how to react in any given situation.

The reason it's so convicting is that it's rooted in how Jesus taught us to behave: "So in everything"—which, of course, includes unequally yoked marriages—"do to others what you would have them do to you, for this sums up the Law and the Prophets."[14]

How would you like to be married to you? Let that be the grid through which you evaluate how you'll react to the ever-changing and often-disorienting dynamics of a relationship with an unbelieving spouse. Ask yourself that question so often, and wrestle with its implications so honestly, that it begins to reshape your attitude, decisions, and reactions.

The result will be that you will make the most of your spiritual mismatch.

PART THREE

Your Marriage
as a Mission Field

7 | Before You Tell Your Spouse about God

It took a long time for Leslie to work up the courage to have a serious discussion with me about her faith. Her mouth got dry and her pulse raced every time she thought about doing it. But she felt she had no alternative. She kept looking for the right opportunity, that perfect moment when she imagined I would respond with boundless enthusiasm. Unfortunately, that time never seemed to come.

Then one morning at breakfast, she couldn't contain herself any longer. As I sat across from her with my eyes riveted on the newspaper, she suddenly found herself blurting out of nowhere: "Lee, do you know that you matter to God?"

"I held my breath as soon as the words came out," Leslie recalled as we reminisced about that day. "But nothing even registered with you. It was like you didn't hear a word I said. You never took your eyes off the newspaper. You just muttered, 'Uh-huh,' and then you got up to look for your briefcase, totally oblivious to what had just happened. I was completely deflated!"

Maybe you too have been haunted by the times you have tried to talk to your spouse about God, only to end up tongue-tied, embarrassed, or even making matters worse. "I wrote the hand book on how not to win your spouse to Christ," wrote Christian author Nancy Kennedy. "I trumpeted my every minute change: 'See how loving and humble I am?' I prayed loudly in Barry's presence and made sure he knew he was a sinner destined for hell. I gave him every gospel tract I could find . . . When he wouldn't go [to church], I'd sulk and make him sorry. He was sorry, all right—sorry he married me."[1]

Leslie and I know it's a daunting task to reach your partner with the gospel, and yet there is too much at stake to merely sit idly by. You look across the breakfast table each morning at a spouse you deeply love, and you desperately want to see him receive Christ's gift of eternal life. You want him to become more than just a good person; you want to see his attitudes, priorities, and character shaped and molded by Jesus. You want him to experience the love, joy, and peace you have found through a personal relationship with your Savior. You want your spiritually divided home to be united behind your mutual devotion to Christ. You want to see your values mesh so that you both approach your marriage, finances, relationships, and parenting in a way that honors God.

Sometimes you want all of this so much that your heart aches. And when the response from your spouse is disinterest, displeasure, or disapproval, you feel deflated, defeated, and disheartened. Will the day ever come, you wonder, when you will be able to kneel next to your spouse as you worship the Lord, when you will hold hands as you sit in church together and drink in teaching from the Word of God, or when you will finally rest easy in the confidence that both of your eternal destinies are safe and secure?

"I can't count the number of times I cried about your hard heart toward God," Leslie told me as we discussed this chapter. "And I can't count the times I wanted to give up on you. I'm just glad God didn't give up! And that's what I tell people who are married to non-Christians: it's God who's the Great Evangelist. He's in the human reclamation business. All we have to do is learn to cooperate with him."

Admittedly, that isn't easy to do. But through Leslie's reluctant enrollment in the school of hard knocks, she discovered some principles that just might help you as you reach out with the gospel to your nonbelieving spouse.

YOUR UNIQUE OPPORTUNITY

Two thousand years ago, Jesus gave marching orders to every Christian who would live through history: spread his message as far and wide as you can. Bring neighbors, friends, colleagues, and family members into an eternity-changing relationship with him, and then watch as God transforms their lives with new purpose, new priorities, and new power. Through his death and resurrection, Jesus had opened the door to heaven; now he was mobilizing his followers to help fill it to overflowing with freshly redeemed souls. The apostle Paul picked up that challenge. "Telling the Good News is my duty—something I *must* do," he said.[2]

And guess what? Today, in the twenty-first century, you are on the front lines of that battle. That's right—you! While you may not envision yourself to be a noble missionary on a majestic mission from God, you actually represent one of evangelism's single most strategic groups of people in America. Really! If you are a wife married to a non-Christian, then God has entrusted you to a role that is absolutely brimming with potential.

That is not just an opinion; it's based on new research by Thom S. Rainer, dean of the Billy Graham School of Missions, Evangelism, and Church Growth. One of the startling conclusions of his ground-breaking study into evangelism is this: "The wife is *the* most important relationship in reaching the unchurched."[3] In fact, based on the data that he and his team gathered, Rainer added, "We cannot overstate the importance of wives in bringing formerly unchurched persons to Christ and to the church."[4]

Flesh-and-blood stories put faces on Rainer's mountain of statistics. "The reason I'm in church today is because of my wife," said a resident of Florida. "When I saw the change in her life, I decided to try it out. Now I'm a Christian and hardly ever miss church."[5]

Another husband interviewed for the study not only became a Christian through his wife's influence, but he went on to help organize a ministry in his church to equip Christian wives to reach their non-Christian husbands.

"The results have been outstanding," Rainer reported. "In the first three months of the class, four husbands became Christians."[6]

All of which prompted Rainer to wonder why Christian wives are not being trained to reach out to their nonbelieving husbands. Well, that's exactly what Leslie and I want to do in the next two chapters. We feel passionate about this issue, because it was Leslie's godly influence in my life that prompted me to begin investigating Christianity and which quietly nurtured me during the nearly two years before I became a Christian.[7]

From her trial-and-error efforts, we have distilled eight insights in these next two chapters to help you effectively influence your spouse for Christ. See if they can prepare you for the opportunity to help steer your spouse toward God.

PRINCIPLE #1:

Don't Expect More from Yourself Than God Does

Repeat after us—that's right, actually say these words out loud: *"I am not responsible for my spouse's spiritual decisions."* Let that sink in. Repeat as necessary!

We have said it before, but it's important to emphasize it again: God would not lay upon your shoulders the eternal destiny of another human being. The weight would be crushing. The Bible stresses that no individual can convert anyone. That's God's job. "No one can come to me unless the Father who sent me draws him," said Jesus in John 6:44.

As much as you would like to make your spouse's spiritual decisions for him, you cannot do it. He—*and not you*—will be held accountable by God someday for the choices he made about God during his life. Your role is simple: love God and love your spouse. Live out your faith as authentically as you can in front of him. Ask God to use your life to point your partner's eyes toward him. In short, cooperate with the Great Evangelist.

"There is an inevitable tension in evangelism," said Rebecca Manley Pippert in her classic evangelism book *Out of the Salt Shaker and Into the World*. "On the one hand, we should feel an urgency about sharing the gospel . . . At the same time we need to learn to relax. Since it is the Holy Spirit's job to convert, that should ease some of our anxiety."[8]

So don't let misplaced guilt weigh you down. Don't fall into the trap of thinking that if you were just a better Christian, if you were just more aggressive about trying to get him to understand the gospel, or if you were just more articulate, then he would fall to his knees in repentance and receive Christ. Don't let your actions be driven by an inappropriate sense of responsibility for your spouse's spiritual state, because inevitably that will cause you to cross the bounds of pushing too hard for his conversion.

No, your responsibility is for you to live out your life, as best you can, in a Christ-honoring way. And as my friend Don Cousins likes to say, "If you honor God with your everyday life, he'll honor you for a lifetime."

The truth is that seldom are spouses the ones who pray with their partners to receive Christ. More likely, you're going to be one of several influences God will use in touching your spouse's life. Other Christians in the workplace, neighborhood, or elsewhere in his relational world are going to be in silent partnership with you. Evangelist Cliffe Knechtle put it this way:

> A person's coming to Christ is like a chain with many links. There is the first link, middle links, and a last link. There are many influences and conversations that precede a person's decision to convert to Christ. I know the joy of being the first link at times, a middle link usually, and occasionally the last link. God has not called me to only be the last link. He has called me to be faithful and to love all people.[9]

So remember: you have not failed as a Christian or as a spouse if you never have the opportunity to pray with your partner to receive Christ. You may be one of many links that leads him into a relationship with God. If so, you can celebrate with all of the other people who God also used in the process. Or your partner may choose, of his own volition, to ignore Christ's outstretched hand toward him, despite your every encouragement for him to follow God. That is beyond your control. As for you, you must do what God has told you to do: be faithful to him and live out your Christian beliefs as authentically as you can through the enabling power of the Holy Spirit.

PRINCIPLE #2:

Showing Your Faith Is a Powerful Way of Sharing Your Faith

If Leslie had tried to debate me on the historical reliability of the New Testament right after she became a Christian, we probably would have ended up in an argument. If she had read me the Four Spiritual Laws, I would have scoffed at her naïveté. But what ultimately made me receptive to the gospel was the undeniably positive and winsome changes that I observed in her life. I saw her day in and day out, in those quiet, unguarded moments, and she couldn't have consistently been faking it. Something—or was it Someone?—was beginning to subtly transform her. That's what intrigued me! That's what God used to begin opening my heart.

It is much more powerful to show your spouse your faith than merely to share it verbally. Said Bill Hybels and Mark Mittelberg in their book *Becoming a Contagious Christian*: "Before we can become highly contagious Christians, we must first live in a way that convinces people around us that we actually have the disease ourselves!"[10] To quote an old adage, "your spouse probably doesn't need a *definition* of Christianity as much as he needs a *demonstration* of it."

As we have discussed in previous chapters, the Bible specifically says that nonbelieving husbands "may be won over without words by the behavior of their wives, when they see the purity and reverence of your lives."[11]

We don't believe this means wives should *never* speak a single word to their spouse about God. It would seem pretty awkward for you to remain inexplicably silent if your husband asks you what happened in church that day. Besides, other verses encourage Christians to be prepared to define and defend what they believe if the right opportunity arises.[12] Here's what the apostle Paul is underscoring: *it's how we live out our faith that will ultimately have the biggest impact on our partner.*

After all, talk is cheap. Jesus did more than merely say that he loved the world; he demonstrated it through his life as he served the poor, healed the sick, and eventually gave his very life as a ransom. And as Christian wives and husbands live quiet but determined lives of faith in front of their spouse, as they humbly reach out to serve their partner out of hearts genuinely renewed by Christ, and as they lovingly sacrifice to meet the needs of their mate, then their behavior becomes like salt that's savory and like light that gently illuminates the love of Christ for them.

There are three aspects of the Christian life that I found especially winsome in Leslie: the attractiveness of authenticity, the influence of genuine conviction, and the lure of the abundant life.

The Attractiveness of Authenticity

The very minute you told your spouse that you're now a Christian, his hypocrisy radar started to scan your life. Since then he has been searching day and night for signs of duplicity or false piety in you, because that will give him one more reason to reject your faith. And frankly he may have some justification for being skeptical. This may not be the first time you have gotten excited about something that you believed would change your life.

Hybels and Mittelberg point out that family members are "the ones who have seen you go through all kinds of phases before: earth shoes, eccentric diets, *tae kwon do* classes, pyramid marketing schemes, subliminal tapes you played under your pillow each night to improve your attitude, and the like. Now you're coming along and saying, 'I've found what's been missing in my life all these years. It's Jesus Christ!' And they're thinking, 'Yeah, isn't that what you were saying about those herbal food supplements a couple of years ago? How long is this *fling* going to last?'"[13]

I know that when Leslie told me she had become a follower of Jesus, I wondered how long this would endure. Was this going to be a brief foray into faith that was going to quickly fade away or slowly morph into a more bizarre expression of spirituality? But the more she integrated her beliefs into her everyday lifestyle, the more convinced I became that this was real.

As I scanned Leslie's life with my hypocrisy radar, I never expected her to be perfect. That's not realistic. I was looking for whether she would have integrity. What does that mean? Warren Wiersbe points out that the word *integrity* and the word integer, which means a whole number as opposed to a fraction, come from the same root. This can help us pin down what integrity really means—it suggests wholeness, completeness, or entirety. Another related word is *integrated*, which is when all aspects of your life are working together in harmony.[14]

So for a Christian, integrity means a wholeness or integration between your beliefs and your behavior. A person with integrity has consistency. What she believes is how she acts. What she says is what she does. Her faith isn't segregated into one area but marbled throughout all aspects of her life.

Of course, every Christian falls short of perfectly expressing his or her faith. That's where the disciplines of humility and confession come in. For example, let's say you're talking to your husband and you lapse into some rather cruel gossip about someone you both know. Your husband's hypocrisy radar is going to go, *Beep! Beep! Beep!*

But what if you said later, "You know, I really shouldn't have said what I did. It was wrong and I apologize. I really want to grow in my character so that I'm not hurting other people with my words. I hope you'll forgive me." *That's* living with integrity. When we fall short, we're humble enough to confess it to God and others. Sometimes that's the very best way to demonstrate the change God is doing in our lives.

Please don't inadvertently fuel any expectations in your spouse that you're suddenly going to be changed overnight into the perfect Christian. Let your husband know that living the Christian life is a process of constant growth and development as you increasingly apply Christ's principles to everyday situations and yield yourself more and more to the power of the Holy Spirit.

The Influence of Genuine Conviction

One of the most winsome aspects of Leslie's changed life was that despite our difference of opinion about Christianity, she was determined to live out her faith with earnest conviction. She didn't water down her beliefs in the hope that they would somehow become more palatable to me. She was willing to take a firm stand for what she believed. I couldn't help but admire that.

We had lived for so long in a muddy mess of make-it-up-as-you-go morality that there was something refreshing about her newfound faith, which gave her sharp distinctions between right and wrong. For instance, my philosophy was that the ends justified the means. If I had to step over the line into illegality in order to beat the competition to a news story, I was willing to do it if I felt I could get away with it. But as Leslie began to demonstrate scrupulous honesty in the small circumstances of everyday living, I couldn't help but respect her.

She wasn't pointing an accusing finger at me or berating me because of my character flaws, my indifference to the suffering of others, or my self-absorbed and self-destructive lifestyle. Through her life, though, she was providing a powerful counterpoint to my immoral behavior. She was modeling Christlike character and God-honoring values. When she didn't back off, even when it meant we would disagree over something, it intrigued and impressed me.

As we mentioned in a previous chapter, Leslie didn't major on the minors. She didn't develop a holier-than-thou persona and get into squabbles over every little issue in our marriage. She didn't put herself on a pedestal as the final arbiter of good and evil. Using a combination of grace and savvy, however, she made it clear that her absolute allegiance was to God and his ways.

The Lure of the Abundant Life

Jesus said in John 10:10: "I have come that they may have life, and have it to the full." When Christians are really living that kind of abundant life—where there's joy, meaning, excitement, purpose, direction, forgiveness, and grace—then their spouses may very well sit up and take notice. In fact, here is an astute observation that Hybels made: as your partner is watching your life, he is doing a quiet evaluation, asking himself whether he would be a winner or a loser if he too began to follow Jesus. He is wondering: *Would Christianity be an upgrade over my current situation?*

"People considering Christianity want to know if they're going to be trading up or down when it comes to the quality of their life," said Hybels.

> If you're driving a BMW, would you trade it for a Hyundai? No. And unchurched people are asking, "If I buy into what Bill's living, is it a trade up or a trade down?" Dallas Willard said, "It is the responsibility of every Christian to carve out a satisfying life under the loving rule of God." Why? Because when people around you see John 10:10—a life in all its fullness—then people living lesser lives want to know more about a life like that.[15]

So here's the question: *are you living the kind of Christian life that your spouse would see as a trade up?* He's probably not thinking about eternity at this point. (Heaven, of course, is the ultimate upgrade!) Instead, he is focused on tomorrow, next week, and next month. If your Christian life is strangled by legalism, parched by gloom, pinched by a desire to control, smothered by somberness, or numbed by boredom, then nobody in his right mind would want that kind of life for himself.

As agnostic-turned-Christian Sheldon Vanauken said: "The best argument *for* Christianity is Christians: their joy, their certainty, their completeness. But the strongest argument *against* Christianity is also Christians—when they are somber and joyless, when they are narrow and repressive, then Christianity dies a thousand deaths."

We are not saying you should pretend that the Christian life is one big party. There will be sorrow, sacrifice, and strife as part of it—Jesus warned us about that.[16] How you handle those moments of pain and difficulty, however, may speak the loudest to your nonbelieving spouse. The reason is that the person without God lacks hope at those times, but as a follower of Jesus you have his strength, power, direction, comfort, and promise of eternity to sustain you.

What Christian wouldn't agree that following Jesus is the very best way to live? Christians need to embrace that sentiment fully and cooperate with the Holy Spirit as he manifests those nine gifts that are available to all Christians: love, joy, peace, patience, kindness, goodness, faithfulness, gentleness, and self-control.[17] That's a prescription for the kind of purpose-driven, God-enabled life that's hard for any spouse to ignore.

So think through how you might be able to exhibit these qualities in daily life. How can you be loving when your next-door neighbor is being annoying? How can you exhibit patience when you are backed up in traffic? How can you show kindness to the single mom who is living down the block? How can you reach out with goodness to the boss who is expecting too much from you? How can you demonstrate self-control when your "wants" outstrip your family's income?

"As Christians," said Michele Halseide, ". . . our highest calling is to be a walking advertisement for [God's] incredible power and attributes."

PRINCIPLE #3:

You Must Diagnose Your Spouse's Spiritual Condition to Effectively Reach Out to Him

Non-Christians are not all the same. Your spouse may be a highly opinionated atheist who is openly hostile to Christianity, or he might be someone who has a general belief in God but is dubious about the claims of Jesus. He may be a devout follower of another religion. His mind may be shut tight or wide open toward Jesus. It's important for you to discern your partner's receptivity to the gospel so that you can be prepared to nudge him closer to Christ if the appropriate opportunity arises.

In an evangelism training course I coauthored, we talk about four species of nonbelievers—cynics, skeptics, spectators, and seekers.[18] These categories refer to the person's receptivity toward Christ (so they would still be applicable if your spouse believes in another religion). Ask yourself whether your partner fits into one of these categories, and then see if these next steps might be appropriate in his case.

The Cynical Spouse

This described me at the time Leslie became a Christian. These spouses aren't open to being influenced spiritually. In fact, they are running in the opposite direction from Christ. They may express animosity when you make an attempt to bring up Jesus, responding with sarcasm or even anger. They can be highly opinionated and often have some negative religious experience in their background. If you want a mental picture of a cynic, imagine someone with their eyes closed tight, their fingers plugged into their ears, and their head turned away. For obvious reasons, these are the most difficult spouses to approach.

What can you do if your husband is a cynic? If he will engage with you at all on spiritual issues, one suggestion is ask questions that seek to get at the reason behind his hostility—*but be prepared to duck!* You might say, "You're awfully negative toward spiritual matters; what happened to make you so angry about the topic of God?" Listen with empathy. He may not be interested in answers to spiritual questions as much as he needs someone who cares about the wounds that are keeping him from God.

Getting him to discuss these issues will at least start him thinking about spiritual matters. By listening without being judgmental, you are signaling that you are sincerely interested in this dimension of his life and that you are a safe person to talk to.

Another possibility is to appeal to his curiosity by saying, "You sound like an atheist I read about. He was a law-trained journalist who spent two years investigating Christianity and became convinced it's true. Would you be interested in reading his book?" If he's willing, then give him a copy of *The Case for Christ*, which retraces my own journey from atheism to faith and includes interviews with thirteen scholars who provide compelling evidence for Christianity.

Also, flip to the end of this book and read the open letter I wrote to nonbelieving spouses. Consider whether it might be appropriate to photocopy it and show it to your partner, especially since he could probably relate to the part where I talk about my reaction to Leslie's conversion.

Still, these spouses are the toughest cases. The chances are you're going to have to wait until something happens to him—perhaps a crisis that rocks his life—before he becomes more receptive to spiritual matters. For example, all Americans were stunned by the September 11, 2001, terrorist attack on the World Trade Center, the Pentagon, and the jetliner above Pennsylvania. For many non-Christians, it highlighted the fragility of life and made them feel vulnerable and uncertain about the future.

Many nonbelievers crowded into churches the following weekend. At the church where Leslie and I serve, I met an agnostic who hadn't been in church for twenty-seven years. When I asked why he came, he said, "It was like a magnet. I don't know why, but I just had to come!" Sometimes it takes a life-shattering event to get a cynical spouse to begin asking questions about God. In the meantime, these partners make great prayer projects!

The Skeptical Spouse

These spouses may be slightly open to spiritual issues, but they are plagued by doubts. They are not actively pursuing God on their own. They may filter all beliefs about him through a mindset that says: "I don't believe miracles are possible or that the supernatural exists; now, go ahead and tell me about God if you want to." For a mental image of a skeptic, picture someone with their arms defiantly crossed in front of him, as if to say, "I dare you to try to convince me of the impossible!"

If this describes your partner, a good approach is to encourage him to distill his doubts into specific questions. You might say, "I'm really interested in hearing about your objections to Christianity. Could you list them for me?" Most likely, he has never done this before; his doubts are probably more like clouds of vague questions, concerns, misgivings, and confusion that are swirling in his head. If he will actually take the time to write out his objections, this is a tremendous breakthrough. One lawyer responded to a challenge like this by writing an eight-page handwritten summary on yellow legal pads!

With your spouse's list as a starting point, you can now pinpoint the roadblocks between him and God. You can encourage him to investigate whether there are reasonable responses to his obstacles. If you used to struggle with some of the same issues, this can provide common ground from which you could begin a discussion. In any case, you could point your spouse toward some of the resources that we list at the end of this book as a way to get answers to his questions or clear up his misconceptions about God. My book *The Case for Faith*, in which experts provide answers to the eight most common objections to Christianity, might be helpful.

"My husband really liked the challenge of making that list, and when he did, it was a real turning point," said a woman from Chicago, whose husband became a Christian in 1997. "It got him off dead center and started him thinking about God for the first time since college. When I saw his questions, my heart jumped. I knew there were good answers! And once he spelled out his issues, he actually got excited about investigating them."

That's what happened to Dr. Vic Olsen, a brilliant surgeon. He and his wife, Joan, didn't believe in God because they thought modern science had established that the Bible is mythology. But they spelled out their objections and put Christianity to the test, investigating it from a scientific, legal, archaeological, medical, and even a detective's perspective.

Not only did they end up committing their lives to Christ, but they then redirected their careers, using their medical skills to serve the needy for many years in poverty-stricken Bangladesh. Olsen wrote a book whose title says it all: *The Agnostic Who Dared to Search*.[19]

The Spectator Spouse

This category describes Leslie during the first part of our marriage. As a spectator, she wasn't hostile toward spirituality, nor was her path toward God impeded by a host of skeptical questions. In a sense, she was in spiritual neutral. She was indifferent to God and not motivated to check him out.

If you want to visualize a spectator, imagine someone sitting in the bleachers at a football game. Spectators may watch others pursue faith in God, but they're not interested in getting off the bench, suiting up, and getting into the fray themselves. Sometimes they grew up in a home where Christianity was a dry and inconsequential ritual rather than a dynamic, fulfilling, exciting relationship with Christ. The result: they emerged spiritually numbed.

Because spectators don't recognize the relevance of God to their lives, it's helpful to get them thinking about matters of ultimate importance: *Where did they come from? Why are they here? What is their purpose in life? What is their destiny?* These people may be so caught up in the fast-pace grind of living that they have never paused to explore these deeper issues that can lead them to God.

You might say to your spouse, "It's easy to get so busy that we never stop to ask what the world is all about. Do you ever wonder about the meaning of life?" Encourage him not to wait until tough times come or tragedy strikes before he begins pondering these matters.

You can use examples from your own life about the way God has made a difference in everyday situations. Help him understand that Christianity makes sense *now*, not just for eternity. Hopefully, he has already observed Jesus at work in you; in fact, your living illustration of God's daily relevance may very well be what moved your spouse through cynicism or skepticism into being more spiritually open.

Once he begins thinking about ultimate issues, the spectator spouse might be more receptive to the idea of visiting a church. It is extremely important to bring him to a place of worship where both the reality and relevance of Christ are emphasized. (We will talk about selecting churches in the next chapter.) He also might be willing to read a book that talks about how God relates to our daily living. I wrote *God's Outrageous Claims*—which deals with such practical issues as business ethics, loneliness, sexuality, forgiveness, and doubt—just for this purpose.

Also, it's helpful to expose spectator spouses to other Christians who are living out their faith in an authentic and vibrant way. Who knows? If he gets around some other contagious Christians, he might just catch the disease!

The Seeking Spouse

These spouses are beginning to express an interest in Christianity. They're open to exploring whether there might be any credibility to the faith. They're willing to seek out information, evidence, and answers. If you would like a mental image of someone who's seeking, imagine a person with arms outstretched in an expression of receptivity toward God.

I became a seeking spouse after Leslie's lifestyle convinced me I should go to church. That's where I heard the gospel explained in a relevant way, and I became determined to figure out whether Christianity was based on wishful thinking or solid evidence. Suddenly, I found myself launched on the most exciting and rewarding investigation I had ever undertaken as a journalist! After nearly two years of intensive study, I came face-to-face with the realization that Christianity is true.

It is always great news when your spouse hits the seeking stage, because the Bible says nobody seeks God of his or her own volition.[20] If your spouse has become a seeker, it's because God has already started doing something inside of his heart to begin drawing him toward Christ. And the Bible says if he sincerely seeks God, he is going to find him.

"You will seek me and find me when you seek me with all your heart," says Jeremiah 29:13. Hebrews 11:6 says God "rewards those who earnestly seek him." Jesus said in Matthew 7:7–8: "Ask and it will be given to you; seek and you will find; knock and the door will be opened to you. For everyone who asks receives; he who seeks finds; and to him who knocks, the door will be opened."

Your role as the spouse of a seeker is to gently encourage him to continue down the road toward God. He may be willing to engage in spiritual discussions with you or take your advice on resources that might further his understanding of God. Ask questions that can help you discern the sticking points in his spiritual journey so that you can recommend a course of action for him. You might say, "What are the barriers that are standing between you and God?" Once you identify those, you can prescribe some steps he can take toward eliminating them.

We would also suggest that you encourage your spouse to pray the "seeker's prayer." Don't expect that he will say it in your presence; that is probably much too intimidating for him. Instead, merely suggest that there's nothing to lose by praying, "God, I'm not even sure you exist, but if you do, I really want to know you. Please reveal yourself to me. I sincerely want to know the truth about you. Put people in my life, put books and tapes in my path, use whatever means you want to help me discover who you are." With the idea of this prayer planted in him, your spouse might very well be willing to pray it when he feels ready to do so.

In addition, he may be receptive to reading the Bible as part of the process of seeking the truth about God. Too many critics of Scripture have never taken the time to actually study the Bible with an open mind. Their negative opinions about the Bible were probably formed by what others have told them about it and not what it really says. Of course, we know that the Bible has the power to convict, to encourage, and to enlighten your spouse like nothing else. "For the word of God is living and active," says Hebrews 4:12. "Sharper than any double-edged sword, it penetrates even to dividing soul and spirit, joints and marrow; it judges the thoughts and attitudes of the heart."

We would suggest that you encourage your spouse to read *The Journey*, a Bible "guaranteed not to spontaneously burst into flames if it's read by those who don't yet believe it's God's book."[21] This version of the Bible, based on the readable New International Version translation, has notes specifically geared toward the questions that seekers frequently ask about God.

"You may have never labeled yourself a seeker, but it's not a bad title," says *The Journey*'s introduction. "It shows you're willing to put out some effort to find truth. It means you're a risk-taker, because seeking can lead to finding, and finding can lead to changing. While change doesn't come easy for most of us, a seeker will be willing to change if it means finally coming to terms with truth and where it can be found."[22]

Don't just give your spouse the Bible, however, and wish him the best. The chances are he will open it to Genesis and start reading from the beginning—and quickly get bogged down in Leviticus! Let him know that the Bible is a collection of sixty-six books, and that it's okay to start by reading in the New Testament so he can learn about the life of Jesus.

If he's a nuts-and-bolts kind of individual, suggest he start with the gospel of Luke. Being a first-century "investigative reporter," Luke writes with the kind of straightforward clarity that appeals to lawyers, doctors, scientists, and engineers. If your spouse is more artistic or philosophical, recommend the gospel of John, with its poetic flair and rich texture. If he has a Jewish background, prescribe the gospel of Matthew, since he emphasized the fulfillment of Old Testament prophecies in Jesus.

One caution if your spouse is a seeker: don't expect his progress to be continual. He may sound like a seeker one day but a skeptic the next. That's because he may encounter something in the Bible, a Christian book, or a sermon that is especially convicting or challenging. He may need time to ponder this before he becomes willing to continue in his journey. Just understanding this tendency may help you from panicking when he doesn't seem as interested in pursuing God today as he was yesterday.

Being Open to God

These categories of spouses—cynics, skeptics, spectators, and seekers—can be useful in assessing how you can best help your partner in the spiritual realm. Keep in mind, however, that spouses don't necessarily progress through each of these areas. We have seen cynics jump to becoming seekers overnight after they have been diagnosed with a serious illness, faced another setback in life, or encountered a person or book that rocked their world and prompted them to begin investigating Christianity. And we have seen people in each of these categories who have directly received Christ.

Regardless of your partner's stage of openness to God, there are prayers you can pray, steps you can take, and a Christian lifestyle you can lead in encouraging him in his attitudes toward God. Above all, you must be prepared for the time when an opportunity might arise for you to spell out the gospel in a simple, accurate, relevant, and compelling way. If you are not sure how to do that, turn the page as Leslie and I continue with five more principles in making your marriage a mission field.

8

What to Say When Words Are Hard to Find

You are lounging with your husband in front of the television on a lazy Friday night. He's using the remote control to casually flip through the channels, lingering for only a moment at each stop. When he comes to a Christian station, he lets the program play for a few minutes. Inside, you are cringing at the jewel-bedecked evangelist with the flashy suit, disingenuous smile, and lacquered hair. He is spouting teachings that bear scant resemblance to what you have read in the Bible.

Your husband sighs. "Sometimes I come across these guys on TV, and I have no idea what they're talking about," he says as he lifts the remote to change the channel. "Can't somebody just set out what the Bible says in a way that I can understand it?"

As if to answer his own question, he turns to you. "*You're* a Christian," he says, almost as an accusation. "What do *you* believe?"

Freeze that moment.

There may very well come a time in your marriage when your spouse will ask you a question like that. The chances are it will spring from nowhere. You won't be given a few days to prepare or even a couple of hours to study up. His eyes are going to bore in on you and he is going to be expecting a short, pithy, logical explanation of the gospel. If you can't provide it, you could lose credibility with him, because he will think you don't even understand what you have put your faith in. So what will you say?

If a situation like that makes you recoil in fear, then let us prepare you in case that moment comes. Because 1 Peter 3:15 tells all Christians

139

to be ready to define and defend what they believe, the fourth precept in making your marriage a mission field is this:

PRINCIPLE #4:

Always Be Prepared to Explain What You Believe and Why

Most of my friends in law school took a practice bar exam before they sat down to see if they could pass the real thing. Both of our children took preliminary SAT tests so that they would be better prepared for the one that would count in getting them into college. In a similar way, it makes sense for Christians to take a few dry runs at explaining the gospel so that if their partner ever asks what they believe, they will be ready with an answer.

That's why evangelism training is so important. If the *Becoming a Contagious Christian* training course is taught at your church, it would be worth attending in order to get comprehensive training in discussing the gospel with non-Christians. If it isn't taught yet, you might suggest the course be added. This seminar provides helpful insights on how to relate to non-Christians, how to understand your own particular style of sharing your faith, how to describe what God has done in your life, how to explain the gospel in a compelling way, and how to answer difficult questions that might arise.[1]

Books also can be helpful in providing basic training. Three of the best are *Becoming a Contagious Christian* by Bill Hybels and Mark Mittelberg; *Out of the Salt Shaker and Into the World* by Rebecca Manley Pippert; and *How to Give Away Your Faith* by Paul Little. While these books weren't designed specifically for reaching non-Christian spouses, they do contain some principles that can be applied in mismatched marriages.

In the meantime, we want to get you ready to explain the fundamentals of the gospel without overwhelming your spouse. We want to keep it basic. When evangelical leaders got together a few years ago to succinctly summarize the gospel, their work consumed ten pages.[2] You probably won't have your spouse's attention that long! On the other hand, my friend

Judson Poling telescoped the entire sixty-six books of the Bible down to a three-second sound bite: "God made us, we blew it, Christ paid for it, we must receive Him."[3] That might be a little too sketchy for your partner! What we need is something in between.

We suggest that if your partner asks you to explain the basics of the faith, open your Bible and show him three verses from Romans. It's a good idea to mark these verses ahead of time so that you will be ready. These verses form what is known as the Roman Road, because they take you on a journey that results in an understanding of the gospel. Ask your partner to set aside the issue of whether the Bible is the inspired Word of God; that can be fodder for a later discussion. For now, tell him you merely want to explain what Christians believe. Here's what you might say:

- Romans 3:23: *For all have sinned and fall short of the glory of God.* "The Bible tells us that all have fallen short of how God wants us to live. That's pretty obvious, isn't it? We don't live up to our own standards of behavior; that's why our conscience bothers us sometimes. So it makes sense we fall short of God's standards, which are above ours. I certainly know that I've fallen short."
- Romans 6:23: *For the wages of sin is death, but the gift of God is eternal life in Christ Jesus our Lord.* "We've already talked about the fact that we've all fallen short of God's standards, and this verse tells us we're in a real predicament. It says the wages of sin is death, which means eternal separation from God. In other words, this is the consequence of falling short. You see, God is perfect and we're not, and so our wrongdoing separates us from him. Unless we're somehow reconciled, that separation continues forever in eternity. On our own, we're totally without hope.
- "The good news comes in the second half of the verse. We don't have to suffer this spiritual death on account of our sins, because *the gift of God is eternal life in Christ Jesus our Lord.* He lived a perfect life and died on the cross as our substitute to pay the penalty for all of our wrongdoing. He graciously offers us

forgiveness and heaven as a gift—one we could never earn or obtain on our own. But it's not enough just to know this; we have to act on it."

- Romans 10:13: *Everyone who calls on the name of the Lord will be saved.* "This verse shows that if we are willing to humbly receive Jesus as our forgiver and leader, then we will be saved from the consequences of our wrongdoing. Just like a Christmas gift doesn't become ours until we receive it, Christ's gift of forgiveness and eternal life doesn't become ours until we receive both the gift and the Gift-giver. When we do that, the separation between us and God is bridged, because all of our sins—past, present, and future—are fully paid. So we can now begin a relationship with God that will last the rest of our lives and then continue forever in a perfect way in heaven."[4]

One of the most common misunderstandings about Christianity concerns the concept of grace. Many people—especially men, who are taught to be self-sufficient and self-reliant—believe that the door to heaven is only opened for those who somehow earn God's good favor. In fact, every other religion I have encountered is based on the idea of people working their way toward salvation. If this is your spouse's viewpoint, you could pique his curiosity by saying, "There's a big difference between religion and Christianity." When he asks what it is, you might say:

"Religion is spelled D-O—people *do* good deeds, like praying, being nice to others, or giving money to the poor, in order to try to earn their way to heaven. The problem is, they never know how many good deeds they need to do. Even worse, the Bible says they can never do enough to merit eternal life.

"But Christianity is spelled D-O-N-E. Jesus has *done* for us what we could never do for ourselves. He lived the perfect life and died as our substitute to pay for all of our wrongdoing. But merely knowing that isn't enough. We have to humbly receive what he has done for us. We do that by asking for his forgiveness and leadership in our lives."[5]

Then it's a good idea to describe for your spouse how the gospel has affected you personally. What benefits have you derived from your relationship with Christ? How has he nurtured and encouraged you, given you strength to face difficult challenges, and comforted you in times of grief? Don't assume your partner has been observant enough to notice all of this on his own. Talk with candor and clarity about how your life has changed for the better now that you are a follower of Jesus. This will help him recognize that the gospel is more than a formula, but it is a life-changing reality that transforms a person's entire world.

After explaining the gospel, ask your spouse in a nonthreatening way, "What do you think?" Give him an opportunity to react. He may acknowledge that he understood what you said, enter into a discussion with you, or merely shrug it off. If he raises questions, do your best to respond. We suggest reading some of the books we've listed in Appendix 3 as a way of preparing yourself to deal with objections that your spouse might raise. In particular, Cliffe Knechtle's *Give Me an Answer* and Paul Little's *Know What You Believe* and *Know Why You Believe* can equip you to provide a basic defense of the faith.

If your spouse brings up an issue that baffles you, don't panic! The best response is to simply say, "That's a great question, and frankly, I don't have a great response for you right now. But if you're willing to keep an open mind, I'd be glad to help you get an explanation." With that, you might refer him to some of the resources at the end of this book. A good idea is to offer to read the book with him. That way, the two of you can wrestle with his questions together.

It is essential to note that your spouse's immediate reaction to the gospel is not as important as his eventual response. He may nonchalantly thank you for clarifying what Christians believe and then quickly go on to other subjects. That's okay. Now that he understands the message of Christ, he may need some time to mull it over. What's important is how he ultimately decides to react to it—and that may be a long time in coming.

Since he has brought up the issue, though, this gives you the opportunity to say at a later date, "Remember when you asked about what

Christians believe and I showed you the Roman Road? Have any questions come into your mind since then?" Or you could get him a book about Christianity, saying, "Since you brought up the question of what Christians believe, I thought you might find this book interesting."

In the end, you may be surprised at how little your partner knows about Christianity. So many churches are soft on the gospel or have drifted away from the historic faith that a lot of people have grown up to be biblically illiterate. Jay Leno illustrates that when he goes "Jaywalking" and asks people on the street to answer basic questions about the Bible. When challenged to name one of the Ten Commandments, one person furrowed his brow and then declared: "Freedom of speech!" In one study, when non-Christians were asked if they knew why Christians celebrate Easter, half of them couldn't give an accurate answer.[6]

So it is possible that your spouse's resistance to Christianity is based on misinformation or confusion rather than a well-thought-out analysis of the faith. That is why it's worth it for you to be prepared to clarify the gospel in everyday language and to respond to some of the most commonly asked questions about Christianity. You might want to team up with another Christian of the same gender from an unequally yoked relationship and practice with each other. If the opportunity arises for you to spell out spiritual answers for your partner, you will be thankful that you were ready.

PRINCIPLE #5:

If Your Spouse Agrees to Visit a Church, Make Sure It's Geared for Seekers

Our friend Natalie was thrilled. After years of being totally indifferent toward God, her husband, Jack, agreed to go with her to church on Easter. She was praying this would provide a breakthrough for him. But when we saw her a few weeks after the holiday, she was more glum than ever.

"It was a disaster," she said. "Jack didn't want to go to my church, because it's too far from our house, so we went to the one down the block.

The service was so boring! There wasn't anything in the sermon for Jack. At the end, the pastor really pressed for people to walk the aisle, and everybody's eyes were on Jack and me. We were the only strangers in the room! It was extremely uncomfortable."

"How did Jack take it?" I asked.

She shook her head. "I'd say he's done with church for a while."

Many churches seem oblivious to the Jacks of the world. Their services are geared for the "already convinced" and not for those who are spiritually seeking. Their sermons are littered with "Christianese" that's indecipherable to visitors; they assume that nobody has questions about the validity of the faith; and they make newcomers feel uncomfortable by inappropriately highlighting them. One study showed that ninety-one percent of non-Christians believe that church isn't very sensitive to their needs.[7] Often, bringing your nonbelieving spouse to one of these churches can actually set back the evangelism process.

Other churches, however, have been shaped to meet the needs of people who are checking out the Christian faith. Everything that these seeker-sensitive churches do—from their style of ministry, to their children's program, to the language they use, to the topics they address—is thought through from the perspective of nonbelievers. Typically, they are contemporary, creative, relevant, authentic, well-organized, and highly focused on their mission of reaching spiritually confused people.

That is a good description of Willow Creek Community Church in South Barrington, Illinois, where Leslie's friend first took her and where Leslie later brought me. Currently, more than seven thousand churches from eighty denominations are part of the Willow Creek Association (WCA), a network of like-minded ministries around the world. Another excellent example is Saddleback Valley Community Church in Lake Forest, California, where I am now a teaching pastor. *The Purpose-Driven Church*, written by Saddleback's visionary founding pastor, Rick Warren, has helped pastors around the world to create churches where seekers would be willing to come to hear the message of Christ.

In my book *Inside the Mind of Unchurched Harry and Mary*, I spell out in great detail why a seeker church like Willow Creek attracted an atheist like me and kept me coming back week after week during the seeking process. Essentially, it is because the church was friendly without smothering me; it gave me freedom to investigate Christianity without unduly pressuring me; and it dealt with issues and questions of concern to me without trying to pawn off simplistic answers. I was impressed by its excellence, intrigued by its authenticity, challenged by its teachings, and emotionally moved by the very real presence of God.

One misconception about seeker churches is that they water down the gospel to avoid offending seekers. "There's a rumor that if you want to attract unchurched people, you've got to tell them what they want to hear," said Mittelberg, who is in charge of evangelism for the WCA and wrote *Building a Contagious Church.* "We've found just the opposite. People are looking for leaders who have the guts to tell them the truth. Being seeker sensitive means learning to speak the language of the people you want to reach so you can give them the message full strength."[8]

The right church can be an invaluable tool in helping you reach your spouse for Christ. Here are some tips:

- *Don't necessarily think that your current church is the best one to bring your partner to.* Remember Linda, the friend who led Leslie to Christ? She knew if she were to bring Leslie to her church, Leslie wouldn't be able to relate to the music, the believer-focused sermon, or the rituals of a traditional service. Instead, she brought Leslie to Willow Creek, because she knew its seeker emphasis would appeal to her. After getting Leslie comfortably enfolded there, Linda then returned to her own church.
- *Always investigate a church personally before inviting your spouse.* Just because a church has a reputation for being seeker friendly doesn't mean it will sync up with your partner. Sit through a service yourself and imagine seeing everything through your spouse's eyes. Evaluate the message, music, authenticity of the leaders, and attitude of the congregation. Then decide if it's a good fit for him.

- *Make sure you know the topic being addressed in the sermon before you bring your spouse.* One study showed that fifty-four percent of unchurched people want to know the sermon title in advance—mainly because they don't want to waste their valuable time with a subject that has no relevance to them.[9] You can find out the theme of each week's service by calling the church or checking its web site.
- *Check out more than the church's weekend services.* Most seeker churches offer a wide range of seminars, events, and programs to help people find God. For instance, some have "seeker small groups," where nonbelievers meet with a Christian leader on a regular basis to discuss spiritual matters. While most seekers prefer to investigate Christianity anonymously, these groups are excellent for those who would like to do their spiritual journey in community with others. One church reports that eighty percent of seekers who join and stay in these groups end up becoming Christians.

Since finding the right church, with the right emphasis, and the right "feel" is so important, it is a good idea to begin conducting research far in advance of when your spouse might even be interested in attending a weekend service. The Internet can be helpful. The WCA's site has a "church finder" feature that can direct you to a member church in your area.[10] You can glean a lot of useful information by visiting the web sites of local churches you are considering. And by logging on to the homepage of your local newspaper, you can search its archives for any articles about seeker-sensitive churches in your community.

Still, the best research is personal. Ask formerly mismatched Christians for their advice on which churches might be appropriate for your nonbelieving partner. And don't forget to investigate the church yourself. You know your spouse better than anyone. You know his personality, temperament, attitudes, and preferences. Match those with a church where he will be comfortable enough to return time after time during his seeking process;

where he will be challenged by the Bible-focused, relevant teaching; where he will encounter authentic and enthusiastic Christians; and where he will be convicted by his need for Christ's forgiveness and grace.

PRINCIPLE #6:

Diagnose the Emotional Barriers Keeping Your Partner from God

What is keeping your spouse from God—*really?* He may casually dismiss Christianity as being silly, he may insist that all religions are wishful thinking, or he may claim to have well-reasoned objections to the faith. But if you peer down beneath the surface, you may be surprised at what is actually keeping your partner from considering Jesus. He may not even realize it himself, but he may have deep-seated emotional or psychological barriers between himself and God. If you can discern what those roadblocks are, then you can become better equipped to help him get beyond them.

For example, he may have a psychological aversion to intimacy that keeps him from relating to God—or anyone else—on a deep and meaningful level. "Some of the people most threatened by intimacy are warm and gregarious at a superficial level," writes John Guest. "They can chat and laugh and be very embracing in their personality style, but you never get close to them and they don't want you to. So we're not talking about a frigid personality style. We are talking about a wide range of personality styles that are mere facades behind which folks choose to live, sometimes in utter aloneness."[11]

Here's the point: since the core of Christianity is a deep, transparent, trusting, and dependent relationship with Jesus Christ, this kind of intimacy-adverse person is motivated to come up with all sorts of excuses why Christianity is not for him.

Instead, said Guest, he may find refuge in the New Age Movement, where people retreat inward in search of the god they think is inside instead of seeking after the true God who wants to interact with them in warm and profound friendship. They may find it more comfortable to chant a meaningless mantra over and over or to merely meditate, rather than pray a personal, vulnerable, and honest prayer to a God who wants a relationship with them.

"The focus of such a religion is withdrawal, not engagement; self-searching, not God-searching; getting into oneself, not adoration of God," Guest said.[12]

Another sign to watch for is if your partner is consumed by pursuing some of the substitutes that our society offers for true intimacy, such as pornography, or if he is dependent on alcohol to lubricate his social interaction with others.

Your spouse may be oblivious to these dynamics in his life. But if you have noticed that he has a tendency to keep people at arm's length, then ask yourself this question: *Could that be part of the reason why he's keeping God at a distance too?*

Frankly, I think some of my initial resistance to Jesus stemmed from this kind of intimacy issue. I found, though, that as my marriage to Leslie grew stronger and richer over time, I became more willing to open up myself to deeper relationships with others. I think that helped pave the way for my eventual openness to Christ.

I believe there's a lesson in that for other Christians who suspect that intimacy avoidance is at least part of the reason for their partner's tendency to keep God at bay. Focus on deepening the intimacy of your marriage. There are plenty of resources to help you do that. For instance, a couple of helpful books are *The Two Sides of Love* by Gary Smalley and John Trent, and *Risking Intimacy* by Nancy Groom.[13] As the trust and authenticity of your marriage increase and as your partner reaps the benefits of experiencing a profound marital connection, then his receptivity to relating personally to God may also grow.

The Father Barrier

Other nonbelieving spouses have father issues. They have felt abused or abandoned by their earthly father and therefore have an unstated but very real resistance to the idea of a relationship with a heavenly Father. So without even realizing why they are doing it, they may steer clear of God.

In fact, psychologist Paul C. Vitz, who received his doctorate from Stanford University and is a professor at New York University, studied the lives of influential atheists through history and discovered an extraordinary pattern: many of them had been abandoned by their father at a young age, their father died when they were small, or they had a terrible relationship with their dad.

Just go down the list: Friedrich Nietzsche, the world's most famous atheist and coiner of the phrase "God is dead," had an extremely close relationship with his father—until his dad died just short of Nietzsche's fifth birthday. Scottish skeptic David Hume's father died when Hume was two. The father of the most prominent British atheist, Bertrand Russell, died when Russell was four. The father of Jean-Paul Sartre, the French existentialist, died when Sartre was fifteen months old. The father of Albert Camus, the French atheist, died when Camus was only one. Atheistic British journalist Richard Carlisle's father died when Carlisle was four, and English freethinker Robert Taylor's father died when Taylor was about seven. Samuel Butler was beaten and terrorized by his dad and felt fear and hatred of him. Albert Ellis, the psychologist who called all religion irrational, was abandoned by his father. Madalyn Murray O'Hair, the founder of American Atheists Inc., hated her father so much that she once attacked him with a ten-inch butcher knife as she screamed, "I'll see you dead! I'll get you yet! I'll walk on your grave!"[14]

Let's face it: it can be difficult for someone who has felt abuse from his father or suffered abandonment due to his father's divorce or death to want to reach out to the God who is repeatedly portrayed in Scripture as our heavenly Father.

Most don't go to the extreme of atheism. But if their earthly father spewed anger at them, they might assume their heavenly Father would be similarly vengeful and shy away from wanting to relate to him. If their dad abandoned them when they were a child, either emotionally or physically, they may resist a relationship with a heavenly Father out of the fear that he might someday abandon them and break their heart again. They may have a shattered self-esteem, thinking that their father must have had good grounds for abusing or abandoning them because they lack any intrinsic value as a person. Consequently, they have difficulty conceptualizing the idea of a heavenly Father who offers to love them unconditionally, just the way they are.

Ask yourself this question: *how was your spouse's relationship with his father?* Was it negative, abusive—or virtually nonexistent? Did his father bow out of his life due to disinterest, divorce, or death? This can be an important clue concerning why he won't even consider the possibility of relating to his Father in heaven. How can you help him?

- First, simply being aware of this dynamic will be beneficial to you if you get an opportunity to talk to your spouse about God. Don't *compare* God to an earthly father, but *contrast* the two by talking about how God is always perfect, always loving, always present, and always attentive, while earthly fathers, unfortunately, are fallible.
- Second, see if your partner would be willing, perhaps a little bit at a time, to express his feelings about his dad. Sometimes talking about this relationship can defuse the anger that has built up—and it might open the door to some gentle observations about how God is different from his natural father. If he is open to it, visiting a good counselor can help him make progress.
- Third, congratulate him on his own parenting. When he is a good father to your children, let him know it. Then when the opportunity comes up, let him know that his loving behavior as a dad is a little bit like how his supernatural Father feels about him.

"Dave's dad was an absentee father," Sharon told us about her husband. "It really angered him. Then one day we were at Disneyland with our daughter and she got lost. We were panicked! We looked everywhere and even had the security guards searching. You can imagine how relieved we were when we found her! On the way home, I told Dave I thought that's a little like how God feels about us when we've wandered away from him and finally return home. That blew him away! Before Dave was a dad, he couldn't relate to that, because he never thought his own father cared very much about him. But now that he's a father, he could understand the emotions that the father felt toward the Prodigal Son [in Luke 15]. This began to open his mind to the possibility of a heavenly Father who longs to be united with his lost son."

It can be tricky to deal with these subtle psychological barriers of intimacy and father issues. On top of that, it is a little dangerous to play amateur psychoanalyst! Still, diagnosing the obstacles between your partner and God can be a big step toward helping him overcome them.

PRINCIPLE #7:

Master the Art of Asking Great Questions

Jesus used questions to make important points or crack open spiritual conversations. He asked his disciples, "Who do you say I am?" as a way of crystallizing his true identity. He inquired, "What good will it be for a man if he gains the whole world, yet forfeits his soul?" to force his followers to confront what's really important. He asked Peter, "Do you truly love me?" to probe his depth of commitment.

In a similar way, you can use creative questions to stimulate dialogue with your spouse about spiritual matters. This is much less threatening and confrontational than trying to preach at him. Questions lead to conversations; conversations lead to insights; and insights lead to understanding. Rather than trying to impart information, questions stimulate the other person to come up with answers. Questions confer respect; we honor our partner when we sincerely ask him what he thinks.

"We can learn to ask good questions," Pippert said. "Too often we allow ourselves to be put on the defensive. The dynamics are greatly changed when we turn the tables and begin to direct the conversation by asking questions."[15]

By nature, most people don't like to be told what to believe. Think about how teenagers respond when they sense a lecture coming from their parents: "Don't preach at me!" they exclaim. Instead, people like to be asked for their opinions, observations, and beliefs—and that can be a good starting point for a conversation about God.

Marriage relationships are deepened when we have meaningful conversations about matters of real substance. Intimacy grows the more we delve into each other's world. We candidly discuss our dreams, our fears, our politics, our plans, our careers, our children—so why should our spirituality be off-limits? Since our view of religion shapes so much of who we are—from our self-image to our hopes for the future—at some point we should be able to ask each other about our beliefs.

Of course, you will have to gauge how receptive your partner will be to questions about his spiritual outlook. A cynical spouse might refuse to engage with you; a seeker might be more than willing. If you sense he would be open to a discussion, don't start by trying to teach him something. Begin with a question that he can't dismiss with a mere "yes" or "no," but which will encourage his thinking about spiritual matters.

"You already know that I'm a Christian," you might say, "but I'm unclear on what you think about God. What do you believe?"

Let him elaborate as much as he wants. Ask him for details and more details. Ask him why he believes what he does. Where did he learn it? Who taught him? Why does he think that source of information is credible? Does he ever have doubts? What kind? How do his beliefs help him to live day by day? Is he open to new ideas? Why or why not? Listen with sincere interest. Resist the urge to jump in with your own opinions. Let your questions help him unfold his spiritual perspective.

The truth is that most people have never really formulated strong beliefs about spiritual matters. They have picked up a few thoughts from college professors; they retain some remnants of what a Sunday school teacher once said; they have read a little Deepak Chopra or *Chicken Soup for the Soul*; and they have been influenced by their peers. Their religious convictions remain murky and ill-defined. One study showed that half of Americans have no philosophy of life.[16]

Sometimes as a spouse goes into great detail about his beliefs, he realizes for the first time that he is not really sure what he believes and why. His words sound flimsy and cliché-ridden even to his own ears. This can be the beginning of the realization that he needs more than just hollow speculations to base his life and eternity on.

Don't use your questions as a pretense for preaching to him. Don't make it a bait and switch, where you say you want to hear his viewpoints when your real motivation is to spout your own. Let his own words create doubts in his own mind. The chances are that in quiet moments for the next weeks and months, he will return to the spiritual uncertainty that your questions have uncovered.

And at some point, it will be natural for him to turn the tables on you. What do *you* believe? Why do *you* believe it? Now that you've been willing to delve into his beliefs in depth, he may be more open than ever to hearing you articulate the gospel and how Jesus has changed your life.

What about Other Religions?

In other cases, however, he will know exactly what he believes. The reason is that he's not an irreligious individual. Instead, he follows another belief system—Judaism, Islam, or Hinduism, for example—or he is an adherent of a faith that masquerades as Christianity but denies essential Christian doctrines, such as Mormonism, Jehovah's Witnesses, or Unitarian Universalism. He is open to his own beliefs but harbors skepticism toward yours.

Again, asking the right questions can be helpful. First, this can assist you in diagnosing whether he truly believes the tenets of this other religion or whether his devotion to it is based on cultural traditions and family loyalty. He may be more receptive to your faith if he has "inherited" a religion that he doesn't really embrace fully.

Second, questions can help you find some common ground. While there are irreconcilable differences between all other religions and Christianity—since Christianity is built around the uniqueness of Jesus as the Son of God and the "Done" rather than the "Do" plan of salvation—there may nevertheless be some similarities in certain basic values, such as honesty, integrity, concern for the poor, and so forth. Helping identify these commonalities can validate your faith in his eyes and possibly make him open to Christian training for your children, where such values can be inculcated.

Third, expressing genuine interest in his beliefs confers respect and may very well cause him to become more respectful of your faith. *Remember: it is important to be tolerant of his beliefs without compromising your own.* You need to become educated about what his faith believes and where it differs from Christianity so that you don't inadvertently water down your own faith in favor of his. Some helpful books along these lines include, *So What's the Difference?* by Fritz Ridenour; *Handbook of Today's Religions* by Josh McDowell and Don Stewart; *The Kingdom of the Cults* by Walter Martin; *The Challenge of the Cults and New Religions* by Ron Rhodes; and *Another Gospel* by Ruth A. Tucker.[17]

Fourth, asking honest questions about his beliefs may cause him to begin asking sincere questions about yours. You may even want to suggest a book exchange. Propose that he read a book about Christianity—for example, my book *The Case for Christ*, which sets forth the historical evidence for Jesus being the unique Son of God—while you read a book about his faith. This can expose him to the evidence for Christianity and generate discussion. You must approach this idea prayerfully, however, and with a mature and knowledgeable Christian walking alongside you.

"In any discussion," said Mittelberg, "remember that there are real and legitimate needs of his that are probably being met by this other religion. Pray and help show him how those needs can be met on a deeper level through Christ. As you have opportunities to answer his questions, do so with an emphasis on the virtues of Christ and the benefits of being in the body of Christ, knowing that the gospel message itself is 'the power of God unto salvation,' as Romans 1:16 [KJV] says."

Also, don't let yourself fall into the trap of rationalizing that all religions are essentially the same and that all spiritual paths lead to heaven. "Only someone who doesn't understand the world religions would claim they basically teach the same thing," said Ravi Zacharias, an India-born Christian and expert on various religious expressions.[18] While it would be comforting to believe that all religions will lead people to heaven, it was Jesus himself who said, "I am the way and the truth and the life. No one comes to the Father except through me."[19]

PRINCIPLE #8:

Remember That This Is a Process You're In for the Long Haul

We live in a lightning-quick world of fast food, instant emails, ATM machines, pocket phones, jet travel, and cable channels that beam breaking news to us twenty-four hours a day, live and in color. When we want something, we want it *now*. For the most part, we are used to getting it.

The spiritual realm seldom works that way. Sure, there are exceptions. God knocked Saul of Tarsus off his horse and instantly transformed him into the apostle Paul. I have brought the gospel to remote villages in Southeast India, where young people heard the name of Jesus for the first time and immediately repented of their sins and received his forgiveness and grace.

But my story isn't like that. Neither is Leslie's. And chances are, yours isn't either. Our journeys to Christ took place over a period of time. We needed to think about the gospel, ask questions, consider whether the Bible is reliable, wrestle with our pride and ego, and finally come face-to-face with our sin before we bent our knees to Christ. For Leslie, that took a matter of months. For me, it took almost two years. Others have spent decades on the road toward Christ. I met a woman whose husband's journey to Christ consumed more than fifty years!

In the midst of the frustration you feel over your spiritual mismatch, it's important to keep reminding yourself that evangelism is most often a process, not an event. Keeping this long-range perspective is absolutely vital. Why?

First, this viewpoint will encourage you to reach out to your partner in small ways that he will be better able to handle. For example, maybe he's not ready to go to church. For many non-Christians, it is incredibly intimidating to walk into a church's alien atmosphere. That may be hard for you to understand, but think of it this way: how would you feel if your Muslim friend invited you to attend a service at her mosque? It would be natural to feel apprehension and anxiety, because you wouldn't know what to expect and you would be afraid of embarrassing yourself by inadvertently doing something wrong. So it is little wonder that many non-Christian spouses feel the same uneasiness about their partner's invitation to church.

But maybe there are smaller steps your spouse would be willing to take. Seeker-oriented churches often sponsor sports leagues, such as basketball, softball, or football teams. Would he be willing to participate in one of those programs? He would probably enjoy the exercise and spirited competition, while you would love him to be rubbing shoulders with Christians. From time to time, seeker churches also put on debates, such as the one between an atheist and a Christian that Mittelberg and I staged at Willow Creek a few years ago.[20] Others host seminars on intellectual issues, such as the evidence for the Resurrection, or more practical topics, such as parenting. Special breakfasts, luncheons, or dinners with big-name Christian athletes, authors, or business-people are common as well.

If your spouse has an altruistic desire to help people in need, you might suggest he participate in a Habitat for Humanity building project, an inner-city tutoring program, or a disaster relief effort organized by a local church. Serving other people alongside Christians can lead to friendships and important spiritual discussions. Or maybe he would be willing to attend a dinner party at the home of some leaders from your church. Who knows where socializing with thoughtful Christians might lead? These are some small steps that can lead to great spiritual progress over time.

Zigzagging toward God

A second reason for keeping a long-range perspective is that it helps you celebrate each step of progress your partner makes along the path toward God. It may not seem much of a victory to have a spouse read a Christian book, for example. But if he had always been hostile toward the faith and had adamantly refused to even consider the claims of Jesus for many years, then this small step takes on new importance. Encouraging him in these little matters might lead to even more significant strides in the future.

Third, when you remember that evangelism is often a long process, you won't get upset when your partner's path toward God isn't a straight line of steady and consistent growth. More likely it will be a circuitous, zig-zag journey where progress is mixed with periods of stagnation or retreat.

Leslie and I were talking about this phenomenon recently. "You used to drive me crazy," she said. "One day you'd be enthusiastic about checking out Christianity and I'd feel very encouraged, but then you'd lose interest for a while or even become hostile again. Or I'd be thrilled because you were starting to go to church, but then you'd stop going for no apparent reason. Or you'd read a Christian book but have absolutely no reaction to it. Or you'd talk about God with me one day but then refuse to discuss the topic for the next month. It was maddening!"

I wasn't trying to play with her emotions! The truth is that sometimes I would learn something convicting in my spiritual investigation and it would set me back. I needed to process it for a period of time before proceeding. Other times I would get nervous because I felt like I was moving too quickly, and so I would disengage for a while. And there were instances when Leslie got too excited about a little step I had taken, and I felt like she and her Christian friends were going to gang up on me. There were a lot of reasons for the start-and-stop nature of my spiritual journey.

Once Leslie came to accept that my spiritual journey might take a very long time, she got off this emotional roller coaster. "I would still get excited when I'd see you going to church or asking questions," she said, "but I would try to be more realistic. I'd remind myself that you may back off for a while. I tried to celebrate each little victory without assuming you were going to keep making progress. You read a Christian book—*hooray!*

You came to Christmas services—*hooray!* I tried to be satisfied with that and not get disappointed when you didn't follow through."

That's easy to say but often difficult to do. You may find yourself tied in emotional knots because of your partner's on-again, off-again spiritual journey. Half the time you are cheering him on, the other half you are shaking your head in confusion. The best thing you can do is trust God. Remember: *he* is the Great Evangelist. He wants your spouse in the kingdom even more than you do. Lean on him, rely on him, and draw strength from him.

That is where prayer comes in. Incidentally, have you noticed that we have listed eight principles for reaching your spouse and that prayer isn't among them? No, this isn't an oversight! We believe wholeheartedly in the power of prayer. That's why we are devoting the entire next chapter to communicating with the Father over your mismatched situation. And to help you get started, we are including a thirty-day prayer guide at the conclusion of this book.

We really believe that the precepts we have described in these last two chapters can be helpful in spurring on your spouse toward God. Yet nothing you do has any power unless it's fueled by the Holy Spirit. We need to be in frequent and fervent prayer over what to do, how to do it, when to do it, and what not to do. Fortunately, you are not in this alone! God is there. He's listening, he cares, and he's waiting for you to embark on the great adventure of praying for your spiritually mismatched marriage.

9

The Power of a Praying Spouse

BAPTISM SERVICES WERE ALWAYS MY FAVORITE WEEKENDS AT Willow Creek Community Church, where I served as a teaching pastor for several years. I reveled in seeing so many people publicly proclaim their faith in Jesus Christ and testify to his transforming influence in their lives. The biggest highlights for me were baptizing my own son and daughter—once the children of a caustic atheist. But I will never forget another incident that taught me again about the awesome power of prayer.

We were baptizing about seven hundred freshly redeemed people that weekend. We spent the first part of the service explaining the gospel, and then the baptism candidates began filing onto the massive stage to be baptized by one of several pastors. They were told they could invite someone to come up with them, since many were frightened at standing in front of four thousand spectators.

A woman in her sixties, accompanied by her tough-looking, construction worker–type husband, walked over to me to be baptized. I greeted her warmly and then asked a question: "Have you received Jesus Christ as the forgiver of your sins?"

"Yes, I have," she replied, her face radiant and smiling. "Absolutely!"

I was just about to baptize her, but I was stopped cold by what I sensed was a leading by the Spirit. I turned to the man standing nervously by her side.

"You're her husband," I said. I meant the words as a question, but they came out more like a statement.

He nodded. "Yes, I am."

I looked him straight in the eyes and said firmly, "Have you given *your* life to Jesus Christ?"

For a moment he didn't say anything. His face began to screw into a knot. I thought he was going to explode in anger or start yelling at me! Then suddenly he burst into tears. "No, I haven't," he sobbed. *"But I'd like to right now!"*

I was stunned! His wife's jaw dropped open. I wasn't sure what to do—should I signal a "time-out"? Then I realized there was no reason to wait. In the next few moments, standing in front of an auditorium packed with people, I led him in the sinner's prayer as he repented and received Christ's gift of eternal life. And then, with all three of us weeping tears of joy, I baptized him and his wife—together.

After the service, as I was stepping down from the platform, another woman ran up to me, threw her arms around my neck, and kept sobbing, "Nine years! Nine years! Nine years!"

I managed to untangle ourselves and ask, "Who are you? And what do you mean, 'Nine years'?"

She gestured toward the stage. "That was my brother who you led to the Lord and baptized with my sister-in-law a few minutes ago," she said. "I have been praying for him for nine long years, and I haven't seen one shred of spiritual interest that whole time. But look what God did today!"

Though nine years is a long time, I don't have any doubt that she was glad she never gave up in their prayers for her brother.

NEVER GIVE UP!

I'm sure you celebrate her husband's conversion every bit as much as I do, and yet maybe you're thinking, "Nine years? That's nothing! She was just getting started! I've been praying for my spouse for twelve or fifteen or twenty-five years—and I still haven't seen any spiritual progress!"

Chances are you have wanted to give up. You have done the prayer drill; now you would like some sort of evangelistic shortcut to reaching your partner. But as that woman would tell you: *never give up praying!*

After all, Jesus didn't. He never stopped praying for people who were far from God—including those who were bitterly opposed to him. In fact, these prayers continued right up until his death. Based on the imperfect tense of the Greek in the biblical accounts of the Crucifixion, British pastor John Stott said, "Jesus seemed to have prayed for his tormenters actually while the iron spikes were being driven through his hands and feet." Over and over and over, Jesus kept repeating his prayer, "Father, forgive them; for they know not what they do."[1]

So here is the question for us: If Jesus refused to give up praying for the very soldiers who were in the process of cruelly murdering him, then how in the world could we ever stop praying not only for our own enemies but also—*especially*—for those who we love the most, including our own spouse?

Once I was speaking at a conference when I noticed a man who was standing by himself in the hallway. His face reflected the most visible peace of God I had seen in a long time. He absolutely exuded contentment! When I asked him about the secret of his happiness, he attributed it to his godly wife who had prayed for him—an agnostic—for twenty-seven years until he finally received Christ in repentance and faith. His conversion changed his eternity, transformed their marriage, and has brought him peace that passes human understanding.

Twenty-seven years! And if you think *that* is a long time, I got a letter from a Christian who prayed for his atheistic brother for forty-eight years and 348 days—until his brother finally received Christ shortly before dying of cancer. "I just *had* to keep praying for him," he told me in a later phone conversation. "I had no choice!"

I hope you too feel a compulsion to pray for the salvation of your spouse. Perhaps these stories have encouraged you to persevere, even though you might be seeing very few signs of spiritual progress. But maybe you are feeling a bit of dissatisfaction with your prayer life. How do you know how to pray for your mate? What should you pray? What should you avoid?

GOD, THE CONVERSATIONALIST

When CNN talk show host Larry King asked Christian commentator Cal Thomas about how to pray, Thomas summed it up in eight words: "You, Larry, are a conversationalist. So is God."[2]

Prayer is a conversation with the Almighty. It can be formal or informal. It can be intense, passionate, and raw, or it can be calm, orderly, and profound. It can be long or short; silent or aloud; at night or during the day; accompanied by tears or laughter; and done while you are sitting, standing, in the midst of a crowd, or alone in your room.

Whenever you feel at the end of your rope, frustrated because you can't seem to be able to do anything to calm the turbulent waters of your stormy mismatched relationship, remember the words of British pastor Ronald Dunn: "Prayer means that I never have to say, 'There's nothing I can do.' I can *always* do something, something great . . . I don't have to just stand there—I can pray something."[3]

Not only does Satan lack a defense against your prayers, but even your spouse can't dodge their effect. Sure, said Dunn, "he can refuse to attend church, and if he does occasionally show up, he can shift into neutral and count the cracks in the ceiling." He can switch off the evangelist on television, rebuff your suggestions that he read a Christian book, discard the tract handed to him on the sidewalk, and hang up on the pastor who calls to follow up on his visit to church.

"But," said Dunn, "he cannot prevent the Lord Jesus from knocking at the door of his heart in response to our intercession. People we cannot reach any other way can be reached by way of the throne of grace."[4]

But what exactly should we be asking God for—that he would override our spouse's free will and force him to love Christ? Well, no, because "forced love" is an oxymoron; for a person to truly love anyone, including God, he or she must have the ability not to love. Rather, we can focus our prayers on three categories as we lift our unbelieving spouse to the throne of God: our spouse, ourselves, and our marriage.

First, pray for your *partner*, that God would:

- Pull your spouse toward himself.
- Open his eyes to the emptiness of life without him.
- Help him see his need for God's forgiveness.
- Remove the confusion he has about God and the life he offers.
- Help him grasp the meaning and importance of the cross of Christ.
- Open his heart to God's love and truth.

Second, pray for *yourself*, that God would:

- Help you live a consistent and attractive Christian life.
- Make you authentic and honest as you deal with life's ups and downs.
- Give you wisdom in knowing how to approach the relationship.
- Expand your knowledge so you will be ready to define and defend the gospel message as opportunities arise.
- Grant you appropriate courage.
- Use you to help lead your spouse into a relationship with Christ.

Third, pray for your *marriage*, that God would:

- Cause depth and trust to grow in your relationship.
- Strengthen the bonds of your marriage.
- Protect your children from conflict arising from the mismatch.
- Open doors for spiritual conversations.
- Guide those conversations in pace, frequency, and content.[5]

There is an adage that if you do something consistently for thirty days, it will become a habit. So to get you started in praying for your spouse, yourself, and your marriage, Leslie and I have included a "30-Day Prayer Adventure" at the end of this book. Please feel free to use it to launch yourself on a consistent mission of prayer for the salvation of your partner. But that's just part of the challenge of prayer.

CONNECTING WITH OUR CREATOR

If prayer is simply a conversation, why does it always seem so hard to engage with God? Our friend Sharon Sherbondy captured that frustration in a funny skit about a stay-at-home mom who has been trying desperately to find the right time and place to talk to God. Finally, her baby falls asleep. She fights the urge to turn on Oprah and instead gets on her knees in the family room, amidst all the scattered toys and baby paraphernalia, and tries to pray.

But she is quickly distracted. "This house is a mess!" she says, opening one eye and looking around. "When's the last time I cleaned up around here?" She gets up to straighten the room but then catches herself and goes back to trying to pray.

When she prays for her husband, though, all sorts of other thoughts flood into her mind. "The man infuriates me," she says. "Why he won't take a few minutes before he goes to work to rinse his breakfast dishes is beyond me!" Soon she is grousing about his insensitivity—until she stops herself, apologizes to God, and returns to praying.

Again and again she gets sidetracked by random thoughts or aching knees . . . until she actually doses off in midsentence—only to be awakened a short time later by the buzz of the dryer. She tries valiantly to resume her prayer but she knows her good dress will be a mess of wrinkles if she doesn't get it. Finally, tied in knots of total frustration, she blurts out: "Father, thank you for loving me and being my God and . . . I just have to go get that dress! I can't stand it! Amen!"[6]

Audiences roar at Sherbondy's portrayal because everyone can see themselves in it. Despite our best intentions to pray with passion, focus, and specificity, often our prayer lives degenerate into disconnected musings and meandering thoughts. We are easy prey for distractions that get us off our knees and back into the maelstrom of our daily lives.

How can we combat this? Sometimes it helps to have some structure to your prayer life. Not only does this give you an informal "agenda" to keep you on track in talking with God, but it also prevents you from becoming lopsided in what you pray about. Prayer involves more than just asking God to turn your spouse from an atheist into a saint—as important as that is! It is vital that we have a fully orbed approach to prayer.

Years ago I developed a prayer process that I call "The Eight A's of Prayer." I've found in my own life that these eight action-oriented words—*avoid, approach, adore, acknowledge, admit, ask, align,* and *act*—help me keep balanced as I converse with God. You might want to consider whether this format might be helpful with your prayer life as you commit to praying consistently, specifically, and fervently.

#1: *AVOID* WHATEVER WILL HINDER YOUR PRAYERS

For our prayer life to be meaningful, we must avoid what Bill Hybels calls "prayer busters." These are the obstacles we create between us and God that can impede our prayer life.

In his classic book *Too Busy Not to Pray*, Hybels lists unconfessed sin as one of the big culprits in disrupting our communication with God. "Your iniquities have separated you from your God," says Isaiah 59:2. "Your sins have hidden his face from you, so that he will not hear." Said Hybels: "If you're tolerating sin in your life, don't waste your breath praying unless it's a prayer of confession."[7]

The Bible also says that unresolved relational conflict—including rifts between marriage partners—can thwart our prayer life. The apostle Peter specifically warned husbands that their prayers will be hindered if they fail to be considerate to their wives and treat them with respect.[8]

God is so serious about having us deal with fractured relationships that the Bible says we should stop in our tracks on the way to church, turn around, and seek reconciliation with those we are in conflict with. Only after doing what we can to repair the relational rift should we then come to church.[9]

Because living in a mismatched marriage can generate conflict between you and your spouse, it is important to take whatever steps you can to resolve strife before you pray. This might mean apologizing for unfair words that you hurled at him in anger or initiating a frank discussion about the tension in your marriage. Romans 12:18 says, "If it is possible, as far as it depends on you, live at peace with everyone."

Of course, we can't control our partner's response to our peacemaking initiatives. Hybels offers this good advice:

> Sometimes . . . the other person would rather continue the warfare than accept your apology. If this happens, look deep into your heart. Have you sincerely tried to restore the relationship, or are you holding something back? Do you really want restoration, or would you rather blame the other person and let the rupture continue? If your attempts have been wholehearted and honest, God will not let the broken relationship stand in the way of your prayers. But if your reconciliation attempts have been halfhearted and self-serving, try again—this time for real.[10]

Other things that can put static in our connection with God include selfishness (James 4:3: "When you ask, you do not receive, because you ask with wrong motives, that you may spend what you get on your pleasures") and uncaring attitudes toward the needy (Proverbs 21:13: "If a man shuts his ears to the cry of the poor, he too will cry out and not be answered").[11] When I detect these shortcomings in my life, I take steps to rectify them as soon as I can.

"Motives are crucial to prayer because prayer is totally based on the relationship between God and us," said Leith Anderson in his book *Praying to the God You Can Trust.*

> Relationships mean everything to God . . . He delights when we are on good terms with Him and is deeply disappointed when we are on bad terms. What all of this means is that God answers our prayers

more on the basis of our relationship with Him than on the depth of our desire to have our prayers answered.[12]

Even our motives concerning our unbelieving spouse can be selfish under the surface. We pray for his or her salvation, but is our primary desire merely to have someone to go to church functions with? We pray for God to save a non-Christian boyfriend, but is our underlying motive that we just want to get God's clearance to marry him? These questions can be convicting to ask—but important to deal with.

#2: *APPROACH* GOD WITH THE RIGHT ATTITUDE

Then I want to make sure I approach God both in faith and in humility. Hebrews 11:6 tells us, "And without faith it is impossible to please God, because anyone who comes to him must believe that he exists and that he rewards those who earnestly seek him."

Faith is more than just believing something and hoping against hope that it's true. In the TV show *Friends*, Phoebe once told her pals that a stray cat was actually her reincarnated mother who had committed suicide. Not wanting to offend her, the others went along. But as much as Phoebe may have had faith that the cat was her mom, that didn't make it true.

Christianity isn't true *because* we believe it; it's true and we believe it. Our faith is anchored to the absolute truth of Scripture and the resurrection of Jesus. So when we approach God, we do so with a confident assurance that what the Bible teaches is true. R. A. Torrey said that it is by studying the Bible, especially God's promises to us, that we learn the will of God.

"We cannot believe by just trying to make ourselves believe. Such belief as that is not faith but credulity; it is 'make believe,'" he said. "The great warrant for intelligent faith is God's Word. As Paul puts it in Romans 10:17, 'Faith comes from hearing the message, and the message is heard through the word of Christ.'"[13]

And we should always approach God with a sense of humility. When Larry King went on a personal quest to understand prayer, Rabbi Marvin

Hier advised him that the best prayers never contain ego. Interestingly, he said a famous rabbi had studied the difference between two names for God, *Adonoi* and *Elohim*, and found that Jews only used the name Adonoi in prayer. He explained:

> This is because Elohim defines God as the creator of the cosmos, of the vast universe . . . and when we think of such a God, he's far from us. He is distant. That is the God that man thinks of when man is in the mode of being a conqueror . . . successful in his career. When man looks at God from that vantage point, he'll always find him at the end of the galaxy.
>
> To find the God named Adonoi you must be willing to be defeated, willing to surrender, to know you cannot be a conqueror all your life . . . A man must know how to say "I surrender" before an all-powerful creator. In that moment of defeat . . . he meets God not in the distant ends of the galaxy, but he meets God as a friend, as a confidant, as someone whose shoulder he can lean upon.[14]

So when we pray, it should not be from the perspective of someone arrogantly demanding what we think should be ours. Instead, we should come as individuals who recognize our brokenness before the Lord and who respectfully and unpretentiously present our requests to him, as a child sits at the feet of a generous and loving father.

As Christians, we know that God is always near us. In fact, he is closer than any individual, because the Holy Spirit actually dwells inside of us. And we can approach our Savior as a friend who cares about us, who wants the best for us, and who delights in talking with us. "You are my friends," Jesus said in John 15:14, "if you do what I command."

#3: *ADORE* GOD FOR WHO HE IS

After ridding myself of "prayer busters" and making sure I have the right attitude, I begin my prayer with a time of expressing my adoration of

God. I worship him for who he is, for what he has done, and for what he will do in the future. Hebrews 12:28 tells us to praise God "with reverence and awe." Adds Psalm 100:2: "Worship the LORD with gladness."

Praising God is not only appropriate because he deserves it, but also because it helps recalibrate us. It positions us appropriately as creatures who are fully dependent on our Creator. And it sets the tone for the rest of the prayer.

This is where real creativity can flow. We might write a poem to God, sing him a song, meditate on one of his attributes (his holiness, power, goodness, or mercy, for instance), read a psalm, paint a picture, admire his creation of nature—anything to highlight his glory and give him honor.

What we are doing is blessing God. That concept sounded odd to me when I was a new Christian. I knew how God had blessed *me*, but how in the world could I bless *him*? Yet King David knew it was possible for us to bless the Lord. "I will bless the LORD at all times; his praise shall continually be in my mouth,"[15] he said. "Bless the *Lord*, O my soul; and all that is within me, bless his holy name."[16]

When I did some research I found that one meaning of the word bless is "to bend the knee"—and that is what David was doing. He was coming before the Lord with humility to praise him.

For us to bless God means that we call God's greatness into our minds and then, in response to that, we choose to worship and glorify and adore and exalt and revere him. In sum, we honor God as God. "Sing to the Lord, bless his name," said David. "Tell of his salvation from day to day."[17]

#4: *ACKNOWLEDGE* GOD'S GOODNESS TO YOU

It's also important to acknowledge God's goodness—in other words, to thank him for all he has done for us. I don't want to be like the nine lepers who were healed by Jesus but who failed to take the time to come back to thank him. I want to be like the one who went out of his way to express his heartfelt appreciation for Jesus' kindness and mercy.[18] Says

1 Thessalonians 5:16–17: "Be joyful always; pray continually; give thanks in all circumstances, for this is God's will for you in Christ Jesus."

Christian ethicist William Law once speculated about who are the greatest Christians. This was his conclusion: "It is not he who prays most or fasts most, it is not he who lives most, but it is he who is always thankful to God, who receives everything as an instance of God's goodness and has a heart always ready to praise God for it."[19]

When we stop to offer our thanks to God, it reminds us that all we have comes from his provision. This has the effect of keeping us humble and safeguarding us from worshiping our material possessions as idols. Deuteronomy 8:17–18 says, "You may say to yourself, 'My power and the strength of my hands have produced this wealth for me.' But remember the LORD your God, for it is he who gives you the ability to produce wealth."

I often think of how Jesus never gave up on a hard-hearted and hardheaded atheist, but kept reaching out with his gift of forgiveness and eternal life. That keeps me grateful to him. "And give thanks, with joy, to the Father, who has made you fit to have your share of what God has reserved for his people in the kingdom of light," says Colossians 1:12.[20]

Leslie said there were times when the issue of my salvation loomed in her mind and she felt discouraged because she saw little progress in my spiritual journey. "That topic dominated my prayers so much that it crowded out my thankfulness for the many ways God had blessed me," she recalled. "At one point I stopped, took a deep breath, stepped back, and considered the incredible ways God had been good to me. I actually made a list of the things I was thankful for. It was a great reminder of God's faithfulness—and it did wonders for readjusting my perspective."

#5: *ADMIT* YOUR WRONGDOING TO GOD

You give your twelve-year-old son permission to go bowling with some friends. While he's gone, however, a neighbor stops by and mentions she saw him going into that PG-13 movie that you had forbidden him to see.

Later you are preparing dinner when your son comes bounding

through the back door and opens the refrigerator in a search for a pre-dinner snack. You decide not to tip your hand.

"So, how was bowling?" you ask casually.

"Um . . . well, good. It was fine. We had to wait a while to get a lane. But we had a good time."

"Did you beat Jimmy this time?"

"Uh . . . I beat him one game out of three. He's pretty good, you know."

Now, what's the Number One thing you want from your son at this point? You just want him to admit that he went to the movie! You want him to confess that he has deceived you. You just want him to come clean. The longer he denies the truth, the deeper the hole he is digging for himself.

And that is how God feels toward us. He already knows what we have done wrong! It is no secret to him. When we obfuscate and spin, when we duck and dodge, when we rationalize and split hairs, when we pretend everything's fine when it isn't, he's just waiting and waiting and waiting for us to 'fess up. Until then, we are simply lying to him once more by feigning that all's well.

Just as there's going to be a problem between you and your son until he confesses his wrongdoing, there are going to be difficulties in your relationship with God as long as you cover up the truth by claiming everything's fine when he already knows it isn't.

"While unconfessed sin will not break our *union* with God, it will break our *communion* with God," said Hank Hanegraaff, author of *The Prayer of Jesus*.[21] In other words, failing to admit our wrongdoing won't sever our connection to God but it definitely will introduce static into our line. Said Hanegraaff:

The concept of confession carries the acknowledgement that we stand guilty before God's bar of justice. There's no place for self-righteousness before God. We can only develop intimacy with the Lord through prayer when we confess our need for forgiveness and contritely seek His pardon. The apostle John sums it up beautifully when he writes,

"If we confess our sins, he is faithful and just and will forgive us our sins and purify us from all unrighteousness" (1 John 1:9).[22]

Confessing our sins doesn't mean vague generalities like, "Well, God, you know I haven't been exactly perfect." Instead, it's the time for painful specificity. It's when we spell out in agonizing detail how we've fallen short of God's standards. I've been short-tempered and unfair with my spouse. *I've been criticizing him for not acting like a Christian even though he isn't one. I've let my prayer requests to my friends become gripe sessions about him. I've been trying to manipulate him to come to church with me. I've been jealous of other women whose husbands are Christians.*

"I can remember many times when I would begin confessing how I had made mistakes in our relationship," Leslie said to me recently. "As I began doing that, the Holy Spirit would bring into my mind other sins that I had swept under the carpet and wasn't even aware I had committed. It felt so liberating to get those out into the open, to admit them, and to realize that God has wiped my slate clean. I hadn't even been aware of how those sins had been weighing me down."

#6: *ASK* FOR WHAT YOU NEED FROM GOD

Once we have recalibrated our spirit by worshiping God, paid him tribute for his goodness toward us, and cleared the air by confessing our sins, then it's finally the appropriate time to bring our requests to God.

"This is the confidence we have in approaching God: that if we ask anything according to his will, he hears us," says 1 John 5:14–15. "And if we know that he hears us—whatever we ask—we know that we have what we asked of him."

We should not shrink back in bringing our requests to our heavenly Father. Jesus told us to ask for our "daily bread,"[23] which theologian Martin Chemnitz said "encompasses all things belonging to and necessary for the sustenance of this body and life."[24] And for an unequally yoked spouse, the center of the prayer bull's-eye is asking for God to draw her partner to himself. This is where we can pray consistently, fervently, and specifically for ourselves, our spouse, and our marriage, as we detailed earlier in this chapter.

Leslie will tell you how emotionally difficult it can be to ask God to move in someone's heart and yet not see immediate or dramatic results. But God's timing is not our own, and salvation issues are complicated because of the individual's free will. Yet no time spent in prayer is wasted. Inevitably, there is a difference inside the one who prays.

"Something happened when I would pray for you," Leslie told me. "First of all, it was hard for me to stay mad at you when I was lifting you to the Lord. I might be stewing over something you did, but after praying for you my heart would be softened and I'd want to continue to do what I could to make up. Also, it kept your salvation at the forefront of my mind. That made me more alert to opportunities for getting into a spiritual conversation. Finally, praying for you brought me comfort. It reminded me I wasn't alone. My heavenly Father was listening, he cared, and he would soothe my anxieties and fears."

It's true that prayer changes us. It's the mechanism by which we deepen our relationship with God. We may ask God to give us something because we think we need it, when in God's wisdom he knows that the very act of praying gives us what we really need. We emerge more dependent on him, more in love with him, more in tune with his Spirit, more committed to his ways, and more tender to his leadings.

#7: *ALIGN* YOURSELF WITH GOD'S WILL

After we finish expressing what we wanted to say to God, we typically end by saying "Amen." But what does that word really signify? In effect, it means, "May it be so in accordance with the will of God."[25] That is, we want to tell God that ultimately we want what *he* wants. He knows best, he wants the best for us, and so we tell him that regardless of what we have asked of him, everything is contingent on it being consistent with his will. In fact, remember what the apostle John said: "If we ask *anything according to his will*, he hears us."[26]

Think about Jesus' prayer in the Garden of Gethsemane, shortly before he faced the torture of the cross. "My Father, if it is possible, may this cup be taken from me," he said. That was a genuine expression of his heart. But then he also stressed: "Yet not as I will, but as you will."[27]

"We would be in deep trouble if God gave us everything for which we asked," Hanegraaff said. "The truth is we don't know what's best for us."[28] But we can rest assured that our all-knowing heavenly Father does.

We also can be confident that we are squarely within the will of God when we pray for our unsaved spouse. The Bible says that God "wants all men to be saved and to come to a knowledge of the truth"[29] and he is "not wanting anyone to perish, but everyone to come to repentance."[30] At the same time, however, he abides by the spiritual decisions of each person.

Actually, the whole tenor of our prayer from the outset should be that we want to align ourselves with God's will. But as we end our side of the conversation with God by declaring "Amen," that's a good time to affirm that it's God's will, not our own, that we want to prevail.

That doesn't end our conversation with God, however. He very well might have something he wants to communicate to us in return. That's why this final "A" is so vital.

#8: ACT ON GOD'S LEADINGS IN YOUR LIFE

Communication with God was never intended to be a one-way conversation. After we talk to God about what's on our heart and mind, we need to allow him an opportunity to speak to us. He can do that through a variety of ways—through the Bible, through Christian friends, and by giving us an inner impression that is hard to define. "He speaks certain general truths that are true for all time, and he speaks certain specifics that are true for me in my life at this moment," Cal Thomas told Larry King in his interview.[31]

Consequently, I like to pause at the end of my prayer time and invite God to speak to me. When James Dobson of Focus on the Family does this, he says to God, "Lord, I need to know what you want me to do, and I'm listening. Please speak to me through my friends, books, magazines, and circumstances." There are people who like to follow up their daily talk with God by scheduling some time when their mind is a little less active than usual. They may wash the car, mow the lawn, or wash the dishes to let their mental rpms slow down so God's voice might be more evident.

Most of the time, I don't hear anything as I quiet myself and listen for God. That's okay. The important thing is that I made myself receptive to him. When I do sense God communicating to me, however, it is important to distinguish between his voice and my own motivations and desires. We are warned by 1 Thessalonians 5:21: "Examine everything carefully; hold fast to that which is good."[32]

It is like when you are first getting to know a new friend and he calls you on the phone. You might not recognize his voice at first. After a while, though, you become familiar with how he sounds, and as soon as he starts talking you know who he is. Similarly, you learn over time to distinguish God's voice from the background noise of your mind. "My sheep listen to my voice; I know them, and they follow me," Jesus said in John 10:27.

God won't ever ask us to do something contrary to Scripture. And he's consistent; he won't give conflicting orders to two Christians, so it's a good idea to bounce everything off of a mature brother or sister in Christ. One test is to ask whether following this particular leading will accrue to your glory or to God's. If it's primarily yours, it's probably a product of your imagination!

Many times God will use the Bible to communicate what he wants us to do. The Holy Spirit may illuminate a verse in such a way that it seems to leap off the page to you. Or we may feel especially convicted or encouraged by a passage. Leslie and I can identify key turning points in our lives when God used a specific verse of the Bible to redirect us in a certain way.

"I can remember many times when God gave me distinct impressions when I was praying for your salvation," Leslie said to me. "Sometimes

I sensed God wanted me to apologize to you for pushing too hard. Other times I felt that he wanted me to take a stand about something or encourage you in your journey. Most of all, though, the Holy Spirit would reassure me that I'm his child and that he was there for me. That was very meaningful to me."

When you commit to listening for God's voice and following him at all costs, watch out! Amazing things can happen. As God told the prophet Jeremiah: "Call to me and I will answer you and tell you great and unsearchable things you do not know."[33] Was that promise also meant for us? All I know is that when Leslie and I have endeavored to follow God wherever he leads, inexplicable things happen.

I'll give you just one example. Once after praying I had the distinct impression that Leslie and I should send five hundred dollars to a new Christian who was barely surviving financially. Since that's a lot of money, I knew this wasn't merely my imagination speaking! I asked Leslie to pray about it and she too felt God nudging us to take this step.

In fact, we both felt led to mail the money on a particular Saturday morning and to do it from a post office in the same town where the woman lived. That way, it would be received on Monday afternoon. We didn't include our names.

I received a phone call from the woman early on Monday morning. She was frantic. "Please pray for me," she pleaded. "My car broke down Saturday afternoon, and they said it will cost almost five hundred dollars to fix. I just don't have the money! I don't know what to do!"

I smiled. "Okay," I said. "Leslie and I will pray for you."

That afternoon the phone rang again. "You'll never believe what happened!" she exclaimed. "I got my mail and there was an unsigned card and when I opened it five hundred dollars fell out!"

Isn't God amazing? When we sent the money, we didn't know her car would break down that very afternoon—but God knew. We didn't know why we felt compelled to mail the card exactly when and where we did so that it would arrive Monday—but God knew. He answered her prayer even before she prayed it!

Sure, he could have intervened supernaturally to prevent her car from breaking down in the first place. No question about it. But this way her faith was strengthened, and we got to experience the joy of watching God at work behind the scenes.

So as you pray for your spouse, listen for God. As important as it is to have a mentor who can walk you through your spiritually mismatched situation, it's even more important to follow the One who's all-knowing, all-powerful, and who loves your spouse even more than you do!

STORMING THE THRONE OF GRACE

You have prayed for your partner. You have pleaded with God. You have listened for his leadings. And so far you have seen very little impact. Your spouse is still sour toward church, skeptical of the Bible, and cynical about "organized religion." You want to throw up your hands in frustration and quit.

I could tell you story after story of people who reached that point and then—without warning—their spouse suddenly took a huge step forward in his spiritual journey or even received Christ.

Once Leslie was feeling as if her prayers had been bouncing off the gates of heaven. Then she and I got into a big argument and I said some nasty things to her. "Please," she prayed, "soften Lee's heart, God." Even as she said those words, she wondered if her prayers were really making a difference.

Then, out of the blue, I strolled into the kitchen, put my arms around her, and said, "Leslie, I'm sorry. I was wrong. It suddenly occurred to me that I've been harsh toward you lately. Will you forgive me?" That virtually instantaneous answer to prayer seemed like God's way of reaffirming to Leslie that he's listening. It was enough to keep her going for a long time.

Even so, we have to be honest by saying there are also lots of stories where that never happened. There are spouses who will choose to reject God to the end.

"I did everything I was supposed to do," said Karen, whose husband,

Rich, passed away from a heart attack in 1999. "I loved God, I loved Rich, and I prayed that he would open his life to the Lord. As far as I know, he never did. I like to think that he may have reached out to God in those last seconds before he died. But even if he didn't, those years of praying were worth it. They cemented me to God, they developed my perseverance and character, and they brought me peace and strength."

Pray because God wants you to. Pray because God will use that experience to transform your heart. Pray because God is faithful in ways we can't begin to understand. Pray because you can't *not* pray.

"Storm the throne of grace," said John Wesley, "and persevere therein . . . and mercy will come down."[34]

PART FOUR

Managing Other Mismatches

10

Avoiding the Dating Traps

A SCENE FROM *SEINFELD*:

> ELAINE: I borrowed [my boyfriend] Puddy's car and all the pre-sets
>   on his radio were Christian rock stations . . . So, do you think
>   Puddy actually believes in something?
> JERRY: It's a used car—he probably never changed the presets.
> ELAINE: Yes! He *is* lazy!
> JERRY: Plus, he probably doesn't know how to program the buttons.
> ELAINE: Yes! He *is* dumb!
> JERRY: So you prefer dumb and lazy to religious?
> ELAINE: Dumb and lazy I understand.

Donna was intelligent—as an honors biology student at the University of South Carolina, she was elected Phi Beta Kappa her junior year and later chosen outstanding senior for academic performance. She was athletic, serving as head cheerleader at college. She was talented, having acted in television commercials. She was beautiful, winning the Miss South Carolina World beauty pageant.

And she was a Christian. Her mother faithfully brought her to Sunday school and church as a child, and she was baptized when she was five. But her real relationship with God started after a friend took her to a Cliff Barrows crusade in the ninth grade. "God really got a hold on my life," she said.

From then on, Donna's world revolved around church youth groups, missionary trips, and singing in the church choir. As for dating, she abided by a firm rule: she would only go out with Christians. From all appearances, it seemed Donna was on the right track to the right places.

Fast-forward a few years.

Colorado senator Gary Hart was more than twenty points ahead in the race for the 1988 Democratic nomination for president. Many pundits predicted he would sweep the election. His popularity was soaring—that is, until the media took him up on his challenge to follow him around to see whether there was any truth to the rumors that he was a womanizer. That's when they caught Hart—a married man—with another woman. In fact, it was Donna.

One of the most famous photographs of the decade was a picture of Donna coyly sitting on Hart's lap aboard a yacht ironically named *Monkey Business*. Hart's campaign promptly disintegrated, and he was ushered out of the public spotlight in disgrace. To this day, he has never regained his national prominence. Meanwhile, Donna Rice, vilified in the press as "the other woman," fled into hiding, her reputation and career in tatters.

What was it that derailed Donna's life and led her into public humiliation? As we will see, the answer provides a lesson for every person who is dating. Granted, Donna's downfall was unusual because it was played out under the blistering lights of media scrutiny. However, her pain and heartbreak are common stories for Christians who fail to heed God's teachings about unequally yoked relationships.

DONNA'S DOWNWARD SPIRAL

I sat down with Donna and asked her to tell me her story. Was there one major factor that took her life off course? No, she said, that wasn't how it happened. "For me it was a series of subtle left turns," she said. "When I woke up in the middle of this huge scandal and said, 'How did I get here?' I realized I didn't do it in a giant leap. It was just little compromises along the way."

The spiritual shortcuts began toward the end of her college career when the Christian students she had been dating graduated and moved away. Members of the Christian youth group that once made up the nucleus of her life had already dispersed as everyone scattered into different schools and careers. That's when she decided to violate her prohibition against dating non-Christians. She rationalized by telling herself she wouldn't really get serious with any of them. Nobody, she insisted, was going to get hurt.

She graduated from college, drifted away from church, and was no longer reading the Bible. She started dating an older man. One night, after a few glasses of wine, one thing led to another—and he forced her to have sex against her will.

"I didn't realize at the time how violated and ashamed I was," she told me. "I blamed myself for what happened. He called to apologize because he realized that I had been a virgin and didn't want this. I said, 'What didn't you understand? I kept saying no.' He said, 'But I thought you meant yes, and you were just playing a game and this was really what you wanted.'"

This is the "rape myth" perpetrated by pornography—that when women say "no" they really mean the opposite and that they like sex mixed with violence. In Donna's case, the date rape contributed to her ongoing spiritual decline. She didn't realize at the time that she could still guard her virtue even though she had lost her virginity. "It propelled me even further into a lifestyle that was far from my values as a Christian," she said.

She got involved with a man in Florida who, she found out later, was not only cheating on her but was peddling drugs as well. "I left him many times, but kept coming back," she said. "A caretaker at heart, I wanted to 'fix' him and his problems . . . Although I'd felt God calling me back to my Christian roots throughout my twenties, I had a hard time letting go of that illicit relationship. I knew my lifestyle would have to change and I wasn't sure I was ready for that."[1]

He was sent to prison (although, fortunately, he became a Christian many years later). Then Donna met Senator Hart at a New Year's Eve party in Aspen. They ran into each other again by accident five months later, and he asked for her phone number.

At first she didn't know he was married. Even after she found out, however, she went with him and another couple to the Bahamas aboard *Monkey Business*, returning the following morning. He kept calling her day after day. "There was a tremendous amount of conflict because I had already fallen for him," she told me.

This was around Easter 1987, and the film *Jesus of Nazareth* was aired on television. As Donna watched, she felt convicted about how far she had drifted away from God. "I couldn't continue with my lifestyle," she said. "So I made a deal with God. I had been invited to go to Washington, D.C., to see [Hart], and I said, 'You know what, God? I've got to see this person face-to-face and have this confrontation before I can walk away. But I promise as soon as the weekend's over, I'm coming back to you.'"

She wasn't aware someone had tipped off the media that Hart was going to be seeing a woman. Reporters staked out Hart's apartment. The trap had been set.

"I didn't know that within twenty-four hours my whole life was going to be turned upside down, probably history would be changed, and a lot of people would be hurt," she said. "I had this very strong impression not to go. I thought it was my guilt, so I ignored it. I'd been ignoring guilt for a long time. I really think it was God in his mercy wanting to spare me from what was going to happen—but I went anyway."

The media explosion erupted on May 3, 1987. Donna was painted in ugly ways by some of the press, accused of many things she never did. She retreated into hiding. "Everything I had worked on during my twenties— which was success, career, achievement, reputation—was gone," she said.

Even so, God was still there for her.

OPENING THE DOOR OF HOPE

In many ways Donna's story has a happy ending. After years of choosing her own path instead of God's, the scandal with Gary Hart was a very public wake-up call for her. "I said, 'God, it took me falling on my rear end before the entire world for You to get my attention. But You've got it.'"

Like a prodigal daughter, she returned to her Father, abandoning her wayward life and devoting herself to following the way he wanted her to live. She rebuilt her relationship with God through prayer, got back into reading the Bible, arranged for accountability with mature Christians, and experienced the unique comfort of the church.

"There was a time one night when I was in so much pain," she said. "I said, 'I can't go another day; I can't go another hour. God, I just want to feel Your arms around me and hear You talk to me.' I was longing for that. And it was like God impressed on me, 'I'm doing that. Remember when Tammy wiped your tear or Alex gave you a hug? That was Me, because I live in each one of those people.' So the church took on a whole new meaning for me."

Not surprisingly, one of Donna's favorite verses is Romans 8:28: "And we know that in all things God works for the good of those who love him, who have been called according to his purpose." Over and over, God has proven faithful to that promise.

Today, Donna is married to Jack Hughes, who she describes as kind, loving, stable—and a Christian. "Since we've been married, I've learned what true godly love and commitment is—what Jack and I now share," she said.[2]

And God has given her a ministry. Her personal experiences have given her a passion to fight sexual abuse and pornography. Currently, she plays a key role with "Enough Is Enough!" an organization that seeks to protect children from pornography and make illegal pornography unavailable in the legitimate marketplace. Ironically, her former involvement in a sex scandal has now boosted her media visibility in crusading against cyberporn.

"God is the great Restorer," she once told a magazine writer. "In my case, I learned that although God loves me, he doesn't grant us immunity from the consequences of our choices. However, when we mess up, if we ask his forgiveness, he'll redeem those choices, using our mistakes as a 'door of hope' for other people."[3]

That last phrase was a reference to Hosea 2:15, where God promised Israel that he would turn her Valley of Trouble into a door of hope.

WHAT'S WRONG WITH CASUAL DATING?

What can we learn from Donna's story? That all Christians are great guys and all unbelievers are cheaters, drug pushers, and date rapists? No, not at all. The truth is that some Christians act like jerks and some unbelievers are nice folks. The real caution for us is that Donna's slide away from God and into personal anguish began when she rationalized away her principles and started dating non-Christians. Whenever we choose to walk our own path instead of God's, whenever we replace his perfect wisdom with our flawed reasoning, whenever we begin to take those "subtle left turns" away from biblical values, we are venturing into very dangerous territory.

Now, it's true that Leslie and I can't point to a specific verse in the Bible that specifically says, "Thou shall not date a non-Christian." The reason is obvious: dating as we know it in the twenty-first century would have been totally alien in first-century Jewish culture. They didn't have crack cocaine in Jesus' day either. While there is no explicit verse in the Bible that says, "Thou shall not take drugs," we know from a range of verses that abusing our bodies and minds is wrong.

We established in earlier chapters that marriage between a Christian and a non-Christian is contrary to the Bible's teaching—and most people see a dating relationship as a step toward marriage. It is the way that two people allow their lives to intertwine. It is an incubator where love can grow and be nourished. Let's be honest: aren't romance and marriage lurking in most people's minds when they're dating someone? "Why would you date someone you wouldn't consider marrying?" one unmarried Christian woman said to us. "It's like trying to play with fire and not get burned."

It's not just a marriage certificate that makes two people yoked together. We believe that two people who are dating each other can grow so emotionally interconnected, so bonded to each other, that they could be considered yoked. They are in a partnership of sorts, even though it is not as formal or legally recognized as a marriage. And whenever a Christian is yoked with an unbeliever, he or she is defying the commands of God.

As one scholar put it, the command against yoking with non-Christians "is a prohibition against forming close attachments" with those who aren't followers of Jesus if these "temporary or permanent" relationships "would lead to a compromise of Christian standards or jeopardize consistency of Christian witness."[4] Another scholar said that while dealing with nonbelievers is inevitable, "any tendency toward yoking up together must be stopped."[5]

Donna's downfall began when she started rationalizing that she wouldn't really get serious with any of the non-Christians she would date. These would be casual relationships, little more than friendships. What could be wrong with that? That's not becoming yoked to anyone. If the dating isn't intended to be serious or lead anywhere, wouldn't it be okay to date someone who isn't a Christian?

Leslie and I love the way Tim Stafford, a highly respected Christian author and columnist for *Campus Life*, responded to that issue. His answer is exactly on target:

> I used to think . . . some dating is just casual fun—a bunch of friends pairing off to go to a dance, for example, with no serious intentions of romance. That seems harmless, and it usually is. So I used to advise people that dating non-Christians was OK if you kept it light.
>
> I began to change my mind because of the letters I received. I learned that it's very hard to keep the lines clear. What is "just casual fun" for one person might be, under the surface, very serious to his or her partner. Also, feelings change. Dating might begin as a casual relationship but very suddenly develop into something serious.
>
> Then you have a big problem. You've launched into a powerfully emotional relationship, yet you lack any foundation in common beliefs.

You're stuck, having to choose between your faith and your feelings for the other person. Such relationships usually end in heartbreak for both people. I emphasize "both"—it's really no favor to a non-Christian to date him or her when the relationship can't go anywhere. And it's never easy to choose between your faith and someone you care about. When the Bible tells us "Do not be yoked together with unbelievers" (2 Corinthians 6:14), the intent is to protect Christians from relationships where their faith can be compromised.

I've concluded the territory is too dangerous. Too often people end up hurt. Too often what begins as fun ends up with passionate feelings—and bitter tears. Have fun with all kinds of friends, and hang out with groups that are a great mixture of people. But reserve dating for those who share your fundamental beliefs about God.[6]

That is why as Leslie and I raised our two children, our counsel from the outset was crystal clear: only date those who share your faith in Christ. We helped them understand that this wasn't God's way of artificially limiting the field of potential boyfriends and girlfriends. It wasn't a narrow-minded and bigoted restriction that was based on the idea that unbelievers are somehow worth less in the eyes of God. It wasn't an anachronistic throwback to the quaint customs of two thousand years ago.

Rather, it was an expression of God's love for them. He cares about them so much that he wants to spare them the emotional anguish that results when two people become attached to each other and then reach the shattering conclusion that they don't ultimately possess the same worldview and that they cannot share the deepest substance of their souls with each other.

DRAW THE LINE *TODAY*

We encourage single Christians to make a commitment now, rather than later, to only date people who are followers of Jesus. It's much easier to make that decision when hormones aren't raging and when an attractive member of the opposite sex isn't sending off alluring vibes that he or she is interested in getting together.

Tell God *today* that you are going to follow his ways. Draw a line that you vow never to cross. Highlight 2 Corinthians 6:14 in your Bible—then underline it. Then circle it. Write the date of your pledge in the inside cover of your Bible. Ask God to help you stay true to your commitment. Seek out a Christian friend who would be willing to hold you accountable. We really believe that is vitally important advice that can keep you from taking those "subtle left turns" that led to Donna's demise.

But does that always resolve the issue once and for all? Unfortunately, no. We have learned that the best intentions often get thrown out the window in the heat of the dating game. We have seen it in our own family.

Our daughter, Alison, took that stand when she was sixteen. In retrospect, she told us, her own faith was immature at the time. For the sake of deciding whether to date someone, she considered someone a Christian if he went to church, didn't drink, smoke, or engage in other illicit activities, and didn't use profanity.

"But even by those loose standards," she said, "my first boyfriend didn't qualify. He claimed to be reading one of Dad's books and said he wanted to start going to our church—and that was good enough for me at the time. To be honest, all requirements had been abandoned because he had shown interest in me. He was the first guy to do that, and so I decided to cut him some slack. Besides, I figured just because he wasn't a Christian *now* didn't mean he wouldn't be by the time I was finished with him."

What happened in the end? "My first kiss," she said, "and my first broken heart."

So often we see that same pattern repeated. A Christian takes a stand with sincerity and promises never to date unbelievers. But when they are in the midst of the real world, rationalizations start:

- But he's really cute.
- But she's popular—and she likes me!
- But he's nicer than a lot of Christians I know.

- But she's *almost* a Christian.
- But we'll keep the relationship casual.

In helping us research this chapter, Alison interacted with many Christians and non-Christians concerning mismatched dating. The results were fascinating! Time after time Christians knew the right thing to do but found themselves compromising . . . and profoundly regretting it in the end. Sandy was typical:

"I ran into this guy named Brian on the Internet, and we hit it off really well. We met and had a great time together. Everything moved very fast and before I knew it I was in this intense relationship with him. I knew that Brian was not a Christian and that I shouldn't get involved with him . . . but I did.

"Throughout our relationship we fought constantly about the various things we believed which were obviously very important to both of us. One of the big issues was sex. He believed sex before marriage was okay, and that if you didn't include it in the relationship you were placing restrictions on your love. Of course, I strongly disagreed and would take no part in it. We tried desperately to see eye to eye and be together, but he was sexually frustrated with me, and I was frustrated because he was so frustrated.

"Another thing we argued about was abortion. I am strongly against it, and he, of course, is for it. Also, we looked at people differently. Sometimes I would be broken up about a person who is involved in drugs or living on the streets, and Brian would think nothing of it and think I was stupid for being so upset. He very rarely shared my convictions.

"It brings so much turmoil into a relationship when you can't agree on an important issue like sex or even God, for that matter. It is so hard on a Christian to have an encounter with God and not be able to share it with the person we love the most. They don't understand what you're saying, and they look at you like you're insane. They think you're trying to preach at them.

"God is so right when he says you should not be unequally yoked. A lot of Christians who get involved with non-Christians do it because they love them and think they can make them change and become a Christian. But nine times out of ten the Christian is placing herself in harm's way, and she ends up compromising everything that she once stood for. Instead of bringing Brian up, he brought me down. Praise God, though, not down far enough that I couldn't get out.

"Finally, we ended our relationship. Let me tell you it's a lot easier to stay pure and stand firm in my love and devotion to God and my values when I don't have the pressure of his worldly views intertwining with mine!"

Her experiences sound very similar to the stories we have heard from Christians who have married unbelievers, don't they? The good news is that she was able to escape from that relationship before it progressed to marriage and children, when the consequences would have been amplified greatly. The bad news is that she still underwent the emotional anguish of ending a deep and romantic association with someone. And as we were told by many non-Christians, that can be painful for *both* parties.

THE NON-CHRISTIAN'S PERSPECTIVE

One of the most eye-opening results of Alison's interviews about dating were the comments of the unbelievers themselves. Often we think of the damage that a spiritually mismatched relationship can have on the Christian, but the non-Christians end up suffering as well. It was a poignant reminder that we can inflict emotional anguish on people we care about if we venture into dating relationships where we know deep down inside that there's no future.

"The religious differences are tearing us apart," lamented one self-described atheist who is dating someone he called a devout Christian.

Another atheist said he met a Christian girl online. "At the time we were both bored, so we started talking," he said. "It was almost an instant connection. We just clicked. By the time religion came up it was already too late—we were attached to each other. I suppose we could have broken it off then without too much pain, but I don't think either of us realized the extent of the other's beliefs—or the extent we would fall for each other."

Finally they reached the heartrending decision to date other people. "It was one of the most difficult decisions I've made in my life," he said. "I've never met anyone remotely like her. I hate the thought of her being with anyone else!"

Now he is wondering whether his best strategy might be to try to undermine or destroy her faith in Christ. "I have to attack her beliefs," he said. "No matter how delicately I approach the situation it still comes down to me trying to convince her that the Bible is wrong or at least outdated."

The end result is that her faith in Christ might be in jeopardy because of her boyfriend's concerted efforts to sabotage her trust in the Scriptures. Plus, she now has a vested interest in rejecting the Bible. If she abandons it as her guide, she can keep going out with the boyfriend she loves. That's a formula for spiritual disaster!

We have to be honest: *your faith and values as a Christian are at risk when you're dating someone outside the family of God.* Remember Donna's story about how dating unbelievers lured her into doing things that were at total odds with her faith? If you think that you're somehow immune to these risks, read these words from an atheist-turned-Christian who intentionally set out—with devastating results—to corrupt Christian women:

Let me be blunt. When I was a non-Christian, I loved dating Christian girls. I chose to date Christian girls over any others. It was fun (at the time) to be more powerful over them than God. There is a mindset that Christian girls are "clean." I loved the challenge of making them fall. It's sad, but when a Christian girl dates a non-Christian, it's inevitable that it will be easier for the non-Christian to bring down the Christian than it is for the Christian to bring up the non-Christian. One must remember that there is a reason that God tells the believer not to get involved with unbelievers. You may say to yourself that you're stronger than that, but I can tell you that every girl who said that and who I dated, fell.

Let those words from the pen of a former cynic stir you to draw the line right now by vowing to date only Christ-followers! If you think you would somehow avoid the consequences of flirting with danger, remember the words of the apostle Paul: "So be careful. If you are thinking, 'Oh, I would never behave like that'—let this be a warning to you. For you too may fall into sin."[7]

Of course, that raises another issue: if you have promised to date only Christians, how do you know whether someone who claims to be a follower of Jesus is really being honest with you? There's no secret handshake, magic decoder ring, or laminated identification card that can authenticate a person as being a Christian. Fortunately, however, there are steps we can take to avoid being intentionally or unintentionally deceived.

EVALUATING SOMEONE'S HEART

If Harry were filling out a form that asked for his religion, he would check the "Christian" box without hesitating. After all, he was baptized as a baby, and his parents took him to church on a fairly consistent basis when he was a child. He still considers himself a "churchgoer" because he drops by at Christmas and Easter and puts a twenty-dollar bill in the offering plate. He says a prayer from time to time, especially when he is in a jam, and he keeps a leather-clad King James Bible on his bookshelf. Occasionally when channel surfing he lingers on a Christian television program. He generally tries to live by the Golden Rule. If you asked him whether he expected to go to heaven when he died, he would say, "Of course! I believe in God. I'm a nice guy."

Harry met Jennifer at a party at the big brokerage house where they both worked. They were attracted to each other from the beginning. She was a Christian, having received Jesus at a Billy Graham rally as a teenager. Even though she had never been discipled by a mature believer and was between churches at the time, she knew enough to tell Harry that she was looking for someone who shared her faith.

"That's me!" was his reply.

Was Harry being deceptive? Not exactly. In his eyes, he was a heaven-bound Christian. Since Jennifer liked him, she wasn't very motivated to delve too deeply beneath the surface. He was open to visiting churches with her from time to time. And he did seem to speak the right Christian lingo.

Their relationship grew to where they were planning to get married. When he suggested they hold the ceremony at a church not known for its strong doctrinal positions, she acquiesced. Besides, she told herself, its stained glass would look gorgeous in the wedding photos!

Their marriage went smoothly at first. But when Jennifer would ask Harry to go to church with her, suddenly he wasn't interested anymore. She began to see how he would cut ethical corners in subtle ways, like when he pressured her into signing a joint income tax return that fudged on some of its figures. And when Jennifer joined a neighborhood Bible study and started to get very excited about growing in her faith, Harry let her know to count him out.

"Look, there's a difference between being a Christian and a fanatic," he told her. "I believe in God, but I'm not a Holy Roller. That should be good enough. Don't judge me just because I don't practice religion like you do. I think faith is a private thing, so let me believe what I want to believe, and you can believe what you want."

Jennifer's faith really skyrocketed when she started attending a strong, relevant, Bible-believing church. Yet the more she followed Christ, oriented her world around the Scriptures, and built relationships with other Christians, the deeper and wider the rift became between her and Harry. Pretty soon, she was heartbroken. Their spiritual mismatch became the biggest regret of her life.

Her story is more common than you might think. As Leslie and I have interacted with mismatched couples, we have found many instances where the Christian was under the false impression their future spouse also was a believer. And we have seen cases where the non-Christian feigned faith and deceived his future spouse into thinking he was a Christian when he knew he wasn't. Most of them didn't think they were doing anything terrible. To them, religion just wasn't important, and so they couldn't imagine that a spiritual mismatch would make any real difference in their relationship.

So how can a Christian discern whether someone is really a born-again follower of Jesus Christ? It can be very difficult at times. "A true saint and a hypocrite . . . may be similar in outward appearance," said Gerald R. McDermott in his book *Seeing God: Twelve Reliable Signs of True Spirituality.* "Outward devotion to God is no guarantee of inner spirituality."[8]

In other words, just because a person may claim to be a Christian, regularly attend church, speak fluent "Christianese," and perform good deeds doesn't guarantee that he has truly received Christ and that the Holy Spirit therefore dwells in him. Only God really knows the state of someone's soul. "The LORD does not look at the things man looks at. Man looks at the outward appearance, but the LORD looks at the heart," says 1 Samuel 16:7.

But there are some factors we can weigh in trying to figure out whether someone has an authentic faith in Christ. Leslie and I have compiled fifteen questions you should ask yourself about anyone you are considering dating. We don't mean to imply that every one of these qualities should be fully true of any individual, because nobody can live up to the Christian ideal. But as you watch this person's life, pay attention to his reputation among people you trust, talk to others about him, and get to know him in a group setting or as a friend apart from dating, ask whether these characteristics are present to any degree. And if you're already in the midst of dating someone, use these questions as a guideline to help you discern his or her spiritual condition.

FIFTEEN QUESTIONS TO ASK YOURSELF ABOUT SOMEONE YOU MIGHT DATE

1. Can he describe a specific time or era during which he received Christ's gift of eternal life? If he can't pinpoint the time of his conversion, or at least the time frame in which it occurred, then it might not have ever happened. Listen carefully when he talks about his faith. Is he counting on his good deeds, religious rituals, and winning smile to get to heaven, or does he describe coming to the point of recognizing his sinfulness, turning from his own path in life, and receiving Christ as his forgiver and leader? "He saved us, not because of righteous things we had done, but because of his mercy," says Titus 3:5.

2. If he were put on trial on a charge of being a Christian, would there be enough evidence to convict him? Imagine yourself as the prosecutor at his trial: who would you call to the witness stand and what other evidence would you present to persuade a jury that he is a follower of Jesus? Don't dwell too much on externals, since they can be misleading. Even the hypocrites of Jesus' day prayed, fasted, and tithed—and let everybody know it! Who would testify about his character, values, attitude, and his behind-the-scenes deeds that demonstrate the state of his heart? "What good is it, my brothers, if a man claims to have faith but has no deeds?" says James. "Faith by itself, if it is not accompanied by action, is dead."[9] Do his actions reflect a God-changed heart, or is he like those described in Titus 1:6: "They profess that they know God, but in deeds they deny him."

3. Can you tell that the Holy Spirit lives inside of him? Galatians 5:22 says that in true Christians the Holy Spirit increasingly, over time, will manifest nine gifts: love, joy, peace, patience, kindness, goodness, faithfulness, gentleness, and self-control. Of course, nobody perfectly reflects those qualities. But the question is whether the trajectory of his life is toward exhibiting these gifts more and more as time goes by. Is he cooperating with God as the Holy Spirit changes him from the inside out? Or do you see these nine values absent from him or diminishing as time goes by?

4. When he talks about the future, is there room for God? Or does he envision a future only of his own making? Does he talk about seeking God's direction for his life? Does he have plans to serve God and the church in some way? Is he focused on the achievement of temporal success or eternal significance? Does he want to make a difference in the world for Christ? "But one thing I do," said the apostle Paul. "Forgetting what is behind and straining toward what is ahead, I press on toward the goal to win the prize for which God has called me heavenward in Christ Jesus."[10]

5. What does he choose to feed his mind? What kind of books does he read, music does he listen to, video games does he play, Internet sites does he visit, and movies does he watch? Philippians 4:8 says, "Finally, brothers, whatever is true, whatever is noble, whatever is right, whatever is pure, whatever is lovely, whatever is admirable—if anything is excellent or praiseworthy—think about such things." What a person feeds his mind is what he will eventually become. As Paul urged: "Be transformed by the renewing of your mind."[11]

6. Where does the compass of his heart naturally point? When you put a compass on a table, it will automatically seek out north. When this person is at rest, where does his life point? Does he naturally hunger for God and want to know him more? Does his heart tug him toward the Bible, toward ministry to others, toward the church, toward worship, toward prayer, toward fellowship with other believers, toward making a difference for Christ? "But seek first [God's] kingdom and his righteousness," says Matthew 6:33.

7. Does he exhibit the traits of Jesus? Does he forgive those who hurt him or does he enjoy nursing a grudge and plotting revenge? Is he generous toward others? Does he stand up for what's right? Does he care about the poor and the downtrodden? My friend Gary Collins, a Christian psychologist, put it this way: "The Bible knows nothing of true Christians who are miserly, spiteful, habitually unforgiving, self-righteous, or arrogant. Nobody is perfect and we are all tempted to sin, but the true Christ-follower shows signs of becoming more like the Master."[12]

8. Who does he spend his time with? Birds of a feather *do* tend to flock together. You can learn a lot about his discernment and what he values by looking at who he shares his time with. Is he constantly pulled toward the "in-crowd" whose main activities would be anything but pleasing to God, or does he seek relationships with Christians who can encourage him to grow in his faith and lovingly hold him accountable?

"Do not be misled," says 1 Corinthians 15:33, "Bad company corrupts good character."

9. Does he possess humility? Jesus spoke out forcefully against pride, and Micah 6:8 says that true spirituality involves walking humbly with God. Does this individual always have to be right? Does he hog credit or generously praise the contributions of others? Does he constantly put himself first and think he knows better than everyone else? "[Humility] is not a false piety that denies the strengths God has given," Collins said. "It does not involve putting ourselves down and wallowing in insecurity or self-pity. Humility is a quiet recognition that all we have and are comes from God. It is an attitude that is open to new insights and has little concern about inflating our ego or enhancing our image."[13]

10. Is he honest about the little things in life? Integrity means there's a consistency between a person's beliefs and behavior or between his character and creed. Does he have a reputation for being trustworthy, or is he known for trying to cleverly cut ethical corners? One woman said her boyfriend's character was revealed when a waiter accidentally gave them the bill for another table. Instead of pointing out the error, he tried to quickly pay the lesser amount and leave—until she stopped him. "There is no such thing as a minor lapse of integrity," said business guru Tom Peters.[14] Seemingly small acts of dishonesty often reveal the true state of a person's heart. "The godly walk with integrity," says Proverbs 20:7.[15]

11. Through what lenses does he see the world? We all view life through one kind of lens or another. "The term *worldview* may sound abstract or philosophical . . . but actually a person's worldview is intensely practical," said Charles Colson. "It is simply the sum total of our beliefs about the world, the 'big picture' that directs our daily decisions and actions . . . Genuine Christianity is a way of seeing and comprehending *all* reality."[16] Does this individual see an artificial separation between his spiritual life and the rest of his existence, or is his faith integrated into all areas of living? Does he recognize and apply the Bible as the foundation for his whole life?

12. What is his attitude toward other people? Does he use others merely as tools to get what he wants, or does he genuinely care about other people? Is he polite because his parents taught him good manners, or because he sincerely respects others? How does he treat the less fortunate in our society? Does he care about the needy? Does he have a sense of social justice that makes him want to see conditions for the poor improved, or is he uncaring or even cynical about those who have less than he does? "He who mocks the poor," says Proverbs 17:5, "shows contempt for their Maker."

13. Does he take responsibility for his actions? Is he quick to candidly admit when he has made a mistake or does he try to justify his actions even when they were clearly wrong? Does he gloss over his own sinfulness or blame others for things he did? "Healthy believers don't try to pass the buck, pin the blame on somebody else, or refuse to acknowledge our actions," Collins said. Instead, they "admit errors and sinfulness, seek forgiveness from God and from others who might have been harmed, make restitution when possible, and go on—determined not to let a similar situation happen again."[17]

14. Does he care about bringing the gospel to those who haven't heard it? People whose hearts have been transformed by Christ feel motivated to share their faith with others. But someone who's a Christian in name only sees no reason to bring the message of Jesus to those who haven't heard it. As one ancient saint said: "I doubt the salvation of anyone who doesn't care about the salvation of his neighbor." That doesn't mean he has to be Billy Graham, but it does mean he prays for lost friends and takes advantage of opportunities to engage them in spiritual conversations so he might be able to tell them about Christ.

15. Is he willing to postpone immediate gratification so that greater satisfaction can come in the future? Does he live out the biblical teaching that sacrifice and struggle often are necessary to achieve greater long-term goals? Or does he relentlessly pursue short-term pleasure at the expense of long-term consequences? "Healthy religion calls for us to forsake self-indulgent, self-centered living and to commit instead to purity, love, giving, unselfishness, discipline, and sometimes uncomfortable lifestyles," Collins said. "This is not intended to steal away our joy and make life miserable. In contrast, a life of devotion brings inner peace, fulfillment, and the promise of better things to come in the future."[18]

Again, this checklist isn't intended to be rigidly applied. While all Christians are continually growing to become more like Jesus, this is a process that varies in pace from individual to individual and will never be completed this side of heaven. Perhaps these questions have even raised concerns about some areas of your own life that you need to address before God.

In any event, raising these issues can help us diagnose the general condition of the other person's Christian life. Don't flinch from being honest as you seek answers. Keep in mind that self-interest—such as romantic feelings toward the other person—can fog otherwise clear thinking.

THE COMMON THREAD

When Leslie and I talk with Christians about their anguish and despair from being married to a nonbeliever, we think about the common thread in each one of these cases: *it all began with a date.* That is why it's so critically important for single Christians to decide up front to date only authentic followers of Christ, to get into an accountability relationship, and to abide by that commitment. Here's some other advice we'd offer:

- Beware of how quickly romantic bonds can develop. Repeatedly, we have heard from Christians that they fell in love so fast with someone that they didn't know they weren't Christians until it was too late. Consequently, it is important to avoid situations where these romantic feelings can be kindled. For instance, getting together in a group is preferable to being alone with someone until you're sure you want to date him. If your feelings get ahead of you, follow the Bible's advice: flee from anything that might pull you away from God.
- It is important how you decline an unbeliever's request for a date. You could inadvertently chase him further from God if you make him think that you are rejecting him because unbelievers

are inferior to Christians. Don't send the subtle message: "I'm good, you're bad, so stay away from me." It's better to gently explain, "I'm a Christian, and it's important for me to go out with people who share the same values and beliefs so that we're on the same page spiritually. Otherwise, there are important parts of our lives we can't share." That seems to make sense even to most atheists. But what if he says he wants to learn more about Christianity and that you might be the best possible teacher? That brings us to our last point.

- Resist the temptation to do missionary dating. The problem with stories about Christians dating unbelievers and then leading them to Christ is that they are the exception to the rule. The chances are far higher that you will be pulled away from your faith than he or she will embrace what you believe. Remember that it is wrong to knowingly violate God's injunction against unequally yoked relationships. While it is natural and healthy to be concerned about the salvation of a potential dating partner, the best approach is to connect him with a member of the same sex to talk about the gospel, give him a Christian book to read, invite him to your church or Christian youth group, and pray for him. You can take all those positive steps without putting yourself in harm's way.

What Might Have Been

At first, Gail wasn't sure she did the right thing when she followed the kind of advice that Leslie and I have set forth in this chapter. When one of the best-looking and upwardly mobile guys at her college asked her out, she was incredibly tempted to say yes.

She could even talk herself into thinking that Ken was a Christian. They came from the same hometown, and he had attended the same church as she did when they were younger. But as she looked honestly at his life, she had to admit that there would be woefully little evidence to "convict" him if he were accused of being a follower of Jesus. He ran with a fast crowd and belonged to a fraternity notorious for its weekend drinking binges and wild parties.

When she told him she couldn't go out with him, he protested that he was a nice guy with good intentions. But she stuck to her commitment, and he quickly lost interest in her.

And that hurt. She cried. She moped around. She second-guessed herself. She found herself fixated on dreaming about "what might have been." She told herself that maybe she would have been the person to lead him to Christ. It took quite a while for her emotions to calm down. Over time, though, she found herself developing a quiet confidence that she had done the right thing.

Ken went on to date a girl who attended the same campus church as Gail. In fact, Gail had seen Susan a few times at meetings of a campus ministry she was involved with. One day when they ran into each other in line at Starbucks, Gail asked about Ken. Susan said they were having a great time going out together.

"Is he a Christian?" Gail asked.

Susan hesitated. "He's a really nice guy," she said, then changed the subject.

Soon Gail didn't see Susan at any of the meetings of the campus ministry, and after a while she stopped running into her at church. According to friends, she and Ken were regulars on the party scene. Within eighteen months, Susan and Ken were living in an off-campus apartment with their newborn baby.

Gail lost track of them after graduation. A few years later, though, she got word that Ken and Susan had broken up. Now Susan was a single mom, living in a distant town.

Today, thinking about "what might have been" has taken on a totally different meaning for her. What if she had said yes to Ken? What if she had let herself get swept away by him? Gail can't help but imagine herself in Susan's place.

For Susan, it all began with a date. For Gail, everything started with a decision.

11 | When Christians Are Out of Sync

LESLIE AND I WERE CONFUSED BY RACHEL'S REQUEST TO GET together and discuss the turbulence she was encountering in what she called her "unequally yoked situation." Both of us knew her to be a strong follower of Christ, and her husband had told us at a church function that he was a fairly new believer. So the first thing we wanted to know when we met Rachel at a restaurant was how they could be unequally yoked if both of them were Christians. We soon found ourselves dealing with another species of spiritually mismatched relationships that also can introduce stress and frustration into a marriage.

"The problem in our marriage isn't that Stan isn't a Christian," she told us. "He received Christ about eighteen months before we got married. The problem is that we're running at different spiritual speeds. I love to go to church and worship God and study the Bible and pray and participate in my small group, but he sort of just tolerates church. He isn't involved in any ministries. He doesn't talk a lot about spiritual matters. He seems content to be lukewarm in his faith—and it's creating more and more tension in our relationship."

"What kind of tension?" Leslie asked.

Rachel thought for a moment. "Well, I get the sense that if I didn't prod him, he wouldn't bother to go to church on Sundays," she said. "He just lays in bed until I come in and say, 'Are you going with me today?' Then sometimes he gets in a huff and says I'm nagging him and being legalistic and that he can worship God just as much around the house as he can at church."

"What else?" I asked.

"I love to serve as a small group leader in women's ministries," she said, "but Stan isn't serving in any area of the church. He doesn't seem motivated to volunteer. And he's a bit sporadic in his devotional life. I suggested we pray together and study the Bible as a couple, but that has never really worked out. Other things seem to crowd out the spiritual side of our life."

The result, Rachel told us, was an ever-increasing degree of frustration in their relationship. She feels like they're missing a lot of the adventure and excitement of the Christian life, and she's afraid her frequent attempts to encourage him to grow spiritually are being interpreted by Stan as unwarranted criticism and badgering.

The reality is that just because both partners in a marriage are Christians doesn't mean they will automatically be in "spiritual sync." Often, one spouse lags behind—sometimes, *far* behind—the other partner in terms of spiritual development. Sometimes he is indifferent about growing spiritually; other times, he shows some enthusiasm for deepening his faith, but nevertheless his progress is vastly outpaced by his overachieving partner.

Leslie and I have encountered this phenomenon many times as we have discussed spiritual mismatches with Christians around the country. Time and time again, we have seen—like in the case of Rachel and Stan—how running at different spiritual speeds can introduce friction into Christian marriages. Fortunately, however, there are concrete steps that the more spiritually advanced partner can take toward achieving better marital balance.

GETTING IN SPIRITUAL SYNC

We were discussing this once with our friend Tom Holladay, who is one of the most astute Christian teachers we know. Tom is internationally known as a leader at the burgeoning Saddleback Valley Community Church in Orange County, California, where I serve as one of the teaching pastors. One of Tom's areas of expertise is "spiritual formation," or how we can grow more and more to be like Christ. So we were surprised when he told us that he once lagged far behind his wife, Chaundel, in spiritual development.

"When Chaundel and I met, I was a brand-new believer in Christ, and she was a believer who had been in church all of her life," he said. "Her dad was a pastor, and her brother, Rick Warren, was on his way to becoming one of the most respected church leaders in the world. She was *way* ahead of me spiritually."

Chaundel, however, took the right approach in helping Tom to continue developing his spiritual life. Instead of inadvertently discouraging him through subtle criticism, she lovingly encouraged him through genuine and enthusiastic praise for the progress she saw him making.

"She invited me to grow by never expressing disappointment about what I didn't know, and by sharing a genuine excitement with me about any growth that was happening in my life," Tom said. "She never once treated me as if she were the teacher and I were a student who needed to learn. Instead, she always acted as though we were friends who were growing together in Jesus."[1]

The Holladays are a success story—an inspiring example of how the more spiritually advanced partner in a marriage can nurture growth in his or her spouse. While it may be unusual for the lagging partner to morph into a renowned Bible teacher and church leader like Tom, we have seen many cases where the right approach has succeeded in bringing the spouses into better spiritual sync.

These days when we encounter Christians running at different spiritual speeds—like Rachel and Stan—there are eight pieces of advice that we routinely offer. If you find yourself far overshadowing your spouse in spiritual growth, use this as a checklist for how to proceed as Chaundel did—with godly sensitivity, loving concern, and an encouraging heart.

1. ASK THE TOUGH QUESTION: IS YOUR SPOUSE REALLY A CHRISTIAN?

A person who has authentically received Christ as their forgiver and leader will have a natural desire to want to grow in his or her relationship with him. The Holy Spirit, who takes up residence inside people when they cross the line from spiritual darkness into light, will create a hunger for prayer, fellowship, Bible study, and worship. Galatians 5:22 says that over time, as the individual opens his heart up more and more to God, the Holy Spirit will increasingly manifest love, joy, peace, patience, kindness, goodness, faithfulness, gentleness, and self-control. Said the apostle Paul in 2 Corinthians 3:18: "And we, who with unveiled faces all reflect the Lord's glory, are being transformed into his likeness with ever-increasing glory, which comes from the Lord, who is the Spirit."

There are several possible reasons why this transformation process can be retarded or slowed in a Christian. For example, he might be resisting the ministry of the Holy Spirit, failing to yield himself fully to God's work in his life, stubbornly clinging to a pattern of sin, or lacking the discipleship of a mature Christian. If someone who claims to be a Christian, however, exhibits absolutely no outward signs of an inner transformation, we need to ask the difficult question of whether he or she has ever really been "born again," to use the imagery of John 3:3.

The Bible makes it clear that some people who claim to be followers of Jesus really aren't. "Not everyone who says to me, 'Lord, Lord,' will enter the kingdom of heaven, but only he who does the will of my Father who is in heaven," Jesus said in Matthew 7:21–23. "Many will say to me on that day, 'Lord, Lord, did we not prophesy in your name, and in your name drive out demons and perform many miracles?' Then I will tell them plainly, 'I never knew you. Away from me, you evildoers!'"

Those are very sobering words! The truth is that some people sincerely believe they are Christians, but there is no evidence in their lives to back up that assertion. At the root of their problem may be a fundamental misunderstanding about what it means to become a follower of Christ.

Merely being in general agreement with Christian doctrine does not make someone a Christian. Neither does being a member of a church, attending a Christian school, or even believing Jesus is the Son of God who died on the cross for the sins of humankind. "Do you still think it's enough just to believe that there is one God? Well, even the demons believe this, and they tremble in terror!" says James 2:19.[2]

John 1:12 describes what it means to become an authentic Christian: "Yet to all who received him, to those who believed in his name, he gave the right to become children of God." This verse affirms there are two steps to becoming an authentic follower of Jesus: BELIEVE + RECEIVE = BECOME. A person must not only believe Jesus is the unique Son of God who died for our sins, but he or she must receive him as their forgiver and leader. Only then does a person *become* adopted into God's family.

This equation can be an excellent diagnostic tool in trying to discern whether a spouse is a true Christian. Ask him to recount his spiritual journey for you, and listen carefully for a specific moment or era in his life when he received Christ's gift of forgiveness, eternal life, and leadership. If that step is absent or suspiciously vague, it would be wise to review John 1:12 with him—and then to take that step of receiving Christ if he realizes he has never done that before.

Far too often we have seen people who have been sitting in pews of churches for a dozen years or more, nodding in casual agreement with Christian teaching, and yet their lives have never been changed by God and their hearts have never become hungry to grow spiritually. God cannot change a person's life until he or she wholeheartedly gives it to him. An individual cannot strengthen his relationship with Jesus if he has never met him. Without the Holy Spirit's indwelling power, the desire, capacity, and ability to change and develop are sorely limited.

Rather than cling to false security, it is critically important to deal forthrightly with this fundamental issue of whether your spouse has ever really walked across the line of faith.

2. CONSIDER SWITCHING TO A CHURCH WHERE BOTH OF YOU CAN FLOURISH

It happens on Saturday nights when Leslie and I decide to go out for dinner. We have agreed we are hungry, but that's only half the battle.

"How about the steak place?" I ask, my mouth watering for a big T-bone.

She wrinkles her nose. "Well, I don't know," she says. "How about the Italian place down the block?"

"Too Italian," I say. For me, Italian food is Chef Boy-R-Dee. Anything too authentic is . . . well, too authentic.

"Mexican?" I ask, sizzling fajitas dancing in my head.

"Pizza?" she counters.

We're stuck. Neither side wants to give in. Then at the same time, we blurt out the one restaurant we both love. "Seafood!" we exclaim. And it's decided.

In a way, this can happen in the spiritual realm. Christians hunger for a church where they can be fed spiritually, but what kind of experience does each person want? A mainline liturgical church? A high-energy charismatic congregation? A cutting-edge evangelical church? A highly relevant seeker church? A megachurch or house church? There are dozens of different denominations and even more variety within each one.

Leslie and I have seen cases where a church is well-suited to the temperament, personality, style, and taste of one spouse, but the other partner is languishing spiritually because he or she doesn't connect with the church's leadership, approach to worship, or philosophy of ministry. As difficult as it can be to change fellowships, this might be necessary if both partners are going to thrive in their faith.

Try attending a few other local churches together. First run the church through a doctrinal grid to make sure it's teaching the uncompromised Word of God, and then see if the atmosphere of the congregation might be more conducive to both of your spiritual journeys.

Does the worship style free you to unreservedly express your love to God? Is the teaching relevant, challenging, honest, and grounded firmly in Scripture? Are small groups available so you can get to know some other Christians in depth? Is the church successfully reaching out to spiritual seekers in the community? Are members actively engaged in meaningful ministry? Does the church minister to the poor, the hurting, and the disenfranchised? Does the church emphasize missions? Are the leaders mature Christians who have unquestioned integrity and an authentic faith? Avoid "toxic" churches that are legalistic and controlling, as well as "feel-good" churches that are heavy on psychology but light on the gospel.

Some personal compromise might be required. The very, very best church for you might be stifling to your partner, so you might have to settle for a church that is good for you while at the same time being appropriate for him. Be honest with each other as you evaluate possibilities. Take your time. Keep in mind that no church is going to be perfect, since they are all made up of imperfect people like ourselves!

Remember Stan and Rachel? One key to stimulating Stan's appetite for spiritual growth was to change churches. It was difficult for me, as a pastor, to recommend they experiment with other congregations, but both Leslie and I sensed this was a necessary step. Stan needed a smaller, more structured, and more traditional church instead of our contemporary megachurch. Stan and Rachel were able to find a congregation where both of them felt comfortable—and six months later, Rachel called to say that Stan was starting to flourish and she was once again finding ways to enthusiastically serve and grow.

3. HELP YOUR PARTNER DISCOVER HIS SPIRITUAL GIFTS

Todd grew up in a church where the leaders always seemed to be scrambling for volunteers to tend to the babies in the nursery, sweep out the sanctuary before services, or wash the windows. He frequently felt pressured to participate in this way, at one point spending an entire summer teaching Sunday school to a class of rowdy and inattentive third graders. That prompted him to give up on volunteering and to shy away from church.

"Never again," he said when his wife asked why he wasn't interested in getting involved in their local congregation. "I've done my time. Nobody's going to guilt-trip me into volunteering for some mind-numbing job." The result was that he became a "pew potato," a mere spectator whose spiritual growth became stunted.

All of that ended, though, when his wife gave him a book on spiritual gifts. After taking assessment tests, he learned God had given him a spiritual gift of administration. He loved to organize things, to keep track of paperwork, to create "to do" lists and then check off each item as it's accomplished, to computerize records, and to help pull off a ministry event by making sure all of the myriad details were efficiently handled. When he was exercising that gift, he found great satisfaction, fulfillment, and joy.

Today, having wed his spiritual gift with his passion for sports, Todd is deeply involved in administrating an elaborate athletic ministry at his church. This has enabled him to build new relationships with other Christian men, and now he is finally flourishing in his faith.

We have seen that happen time after time. People who have been stagnant, unchallenged, bored, and ineffective in their Christian life have suddenly sprung into spiritual overdrive when they have learned that God has specifically wired them up to participate in ministry in a particular way. At Saddleback Valley Community Church, we use the acronym "SHAPE" to describe how God has formed us to accomplish certain tasks in the kingdom:

- *S* stands for *Spiritual gifts.* The apostle Paul said in 1 Corinthians 12:1, "Now about spiritual gifts, brothers, I do not want you to be ignorant." The Bible says each Christian is given at least one divine enablement to serve in a specific area of ministry, whether it's evangelism, administration, mercy, teaching, leadership, hospitality, shepherding, encouragement, helping, and so on.[3]
- *H* is for *Heart.* "There are certain subjects that you feel passionate about and others you couldn't care less about," Saddleback's senior pastor, Rick Warren, said in his book *The Purpose-Driven Church.* "That is an expression of your heart."[4] Maybe you get particularly excited about working with high

school students, visiting the sick in the hospital, or creating a sense of community in a small group.

- **A represents our *Abilities*.** God also has given us natural skills—music, athletics, gardening, decorating, repairing, drawing, writing—that we can employ in the church. Says 1 Corinthians 12:5: "There are different kinds of service, but the same Lord."

- **P stands for our *Personality*.** "The Bible gives us plenty of proof that God uses all types of personalities. Peter had a sanguine personality. Paul had a choleric personality. And Jeremiah's personality was definitely melancholy," Warren said. "There is no 'right' or 'wrong' temperament for ministry. We need all kinds of personalities to balance the church and give it flavor."[5] For instance, two people may both have the same spiritual gift of teaching, but one might be an extrovert who enjoys teaching in front of a large group while the other might be an introvert who prefers to work alone in creating small-group curricula.

- **E is for *Experiences*.** "At Saddleback, we help people consider five areas of experience that will influence the kind of ministry they are best shaped for," Warren said. "(1) Educational experiences: What were your favorite subjects in school? (2) Vocational experiences: What jobs have you enjoyed and achieved results while doing? (3) Spiritual experiences: What have been the meaningful or decisive times with God in your life? (4) Ministry experiences: How have you served God in the past? And (5) Painful experiences: What are the problems, hurts, and trials that you've learned from?"[6]

When a once-sidelined, ineffective, and stagnant Christian discovers how God has shaped him to make an eternal difference through a local church—*watch out!* Suddenly you can't keep him away from participating in ministry! He finds a unique kind of excitement, enjoyment, and inner reward in experiencing God working through his gifts, passions, skills, personality, and experiences. And being actively involved as a volunteer in ministry inevitably elevates all other aspects of the individual's spiritual life as well.

One caveat, however: make sure you are participating in a church that not only gives verbal assent to the nice-sounding biblical slogan "every member a minister," but which actually puts that belief into practice. If your church does not enthusiastically unleash all Christians to use their "SHAPE" in meaningful ministry opportunities, then this might be one sign that you should consider aligning with another fellowship.

4. OFFER PRAYERS FOR YOUR SPOUSE THAT GO BENEATH THE SURFACE

"Sometimes it's tempting to try to psychoanalyze and pick apart our spouse to figure out why he isn't responding the way we're responding spiritually," said our friend Brad Mitchell, director of men's ministries at Willow Creek Community Church. "So we ask questions, wonder things out loud (where he can hear us), talk to our friends in disappointed tones on the phone (again, where he can hear us)—all in an effort to unlock his heart and learn the missing piece needed to catalyze his faith or to guilt him into action. But the most important thing a spouse can do is to pray—because God is the only One who can engage their spouse. It will have to happen from the inside out."

Brad's right. We need to offer prayers that go beyond the simplistic, "Please, Lord, get him to church next week." Instead, pray for your spouse's heart. "You don't want him coming to church to please you," said Tom Holladay. "You want him to come to church because of his love for the Lord."

Focus on praying for the sanctification process in your partner. Theologian Wayne Grudem defines sanctification as "a progressive work of God and man that makes us more and more free from sin and like Christ in our actual lives."[7] He points out that we have two roles in sanctification. In our "passive" role, we merely offer ourselves to God and his transformational power in our life. "Yield yourselves to God as men who have been brought from death to life," says Romans 6:13.[8] So pray that your partner would offer himself wholly to God in order that the Holy Spirit would be free to work inside of him in changing his heart, attitudes, priorities, values, and perspective, and giving him new desires to grow in his relationship with God.

In addition, we have an "active" role to play in becoming more like Christ. Paul urges Christians to "work out" the benefits of their salvation in their Christian life.[9] Consequently, it is important to pray that your spouse will strive for holiness (Hebrews 12:14); abstain from immorality and obey the will of God (1 Thessalonians 4:3); and make every effort to grow in character traits that are consistent with godliness (2 Peter 1:5). Pray that God would draw your spouse to what Grudem calls those "old-fashioned, time-honored" catalysts of spiritual growth: Bible reading and meditation (Psalm 1:2; Matthew 4:4 and 17:17), prayer (Ephesians 6:18; Philippians 4:6), worship (Ephesians 5:18–20), witnessing (Matthew 28:19–20), Christian fellowship (Hebrews 10:24–25), and self-discipline (Galatians 5:23; Titus 1:8).

"It is important that we continue to grow both in our passive trust in God to sanctify us and in our active striving for holiness and greater obedience in our lives," Grudem said.

> If we neglect active striving to obey God, we become passive, lazy Christians. If we neglect the passive role of trusting God and yielding to Him, we become proud and overly confident in ourselves. In either case, our sanctification will be greatly deficient . . . The old hymn wisely says, "*Trust and obey*, for there's no other way, to be happy in Jesus, but to trust and obey."[10]

Our ministry partner Brad Johnson, also a teaching pastor at Saddleback Valley Community Church, recommends that you don't forget to pray for yourself too. "Most prayer is, 'Change that man,'" Brad said. "That's fine, but I would also suggest another tack: 'God, change me. Give me patience, wisdom, and strength of character. Build in me,

Lord, a loving heart for this man. Help me to see him as you do and to remember daily that you died on the cross for my spouse. Help me to love him like that.' It's like Ruth Graham once said: 'It's God's job to change Billy Graham. It's my job to love him.'"

5. REMEMBER THAT YOUR ATTITUDE IS EVERYTHING

The Bible has colorful imagery to describe the effects of one spouse trying to change the other through badgering and berating him or her. "Better to live alone in a tumbledown shack than share a mansion with a nagging spouse," says Proverbs 25:24. "A nagging spouse," says Proverbs 27:15, "is like the drip, drip, drip of a leaky faucet; you can't turn it off, and you can't get away from it."[11] Not a pretty picture, right?

Nobody purposefully sets out to nag his or her partner. But that is the effect when we repeatedly point out their flaws, highlight their shortcomings, and criticize their lack of spiritual progress. Many times we are not even aware of how critical we are being. We think we are merely being helpful—but marriage expert H. Norman Wright emphasizes that this attitude of fault-finding is actually counterproductive to producing the change you would like to see in your spouse. Why?

- **Faultfinding wounds your partner.** When you pester him about his lack of spiritual progress, you are saying, in effect, "I don't accept you for who you are. You don't measure up, and I can't accept you until you do. You're not good enough for me. You must do better or I may not love you as much as I used to." Those are devastating messages that can create uncertainty and anxiety in your partner. "A wounded spouse becomes afraid or angry and retaliates through overt or covert withdrawal, resentment, or aggression," Wright said.
- **Faultfinding is contagious.** What's your natural reaction when someone points out your faults? You want to point out *his* faults

in return, right? So when you are critical of your partner for not keeping up with you spiritually, you are prompting him or her to be critical and intolerant of you.

- **Faultfinding doesn't change the heart.** Yes, it may alter short-term behavior occasionally, if for no other reason than your spouse wants you off his back! But fundamentally, pestering your partner won't transform his attitudes.

- **Faultfinding inadvertently reinforces the very behavior you want to change.** When you dwell on your partner's shortcomings, you are subtly reinforcing and encouraging those faults rather than discouraging them. Spouses generally fulfill whatever vision of their life that is painted by their partner, whether it's positive or negative.[12]

It is a far better approach to accentuate the positive and to sincerely and enthusiastically applaud whatever spiritual progress you see in your partner. Spouses have a tendency to become what their loved ones praise in them. Speaking gentle words of respect and encouragement, whether in private or in front of others, can be extremely influential in bringing about a desire to change.

"Respect your spouse for what he *does* do spiritually," advised Holladay. "The Bible tells us that there is nothing like the respect of his wife to bring joy to a man's heart. If he feels nothing but a sense of disappointment from you about his spiritual life, that does not give him much to build on! I'm not saying to go overboard and act phony about this, but just to give genuine recognition and to express real appreciation for what God is doing in and through his life."

6. DON'T EXPECT YOUR SPOUSE'S SPIRITUALITY TO EQUAL YOURS

Each of us relates to God differently. Some experience God most naturally through public worship, private praise times, walking among the grandeur of nature, discovering new nuggets of spiritual truth, journaling their thoughts, writing poetry, playing music, discussing theology, quietly meditating on Scripture, praying fervently, sharing their lives deeply with another Christian, and so on. Unfortunately, it's easy to fall into the trap of thinking that if your partner isn't relating to God in the exact same way you are, then he or she is not growing. The reality may be that he or she is making spiritual progress, but it just doesn't look like the kind of progress you are making.

We saw this in the lives of Susan and Dan. She is an extreme extrovert who thoroughly enjoys interacting with other people. It's not surprising that a lot of her spiritual growth takes place in the context of relationships, where she gets elbow-deep into other people's lives through her ministry of hospitality or goes deep in community with members of her small group. On the other hand, Dan is a soft-spoken, shy introvert. He is less likely to speak up during a meeting of their small group, and he shrinks back from getting involved with church activities that involve a lot of people. Because of that, Susan thought that her husband wasn't growing very fast in his faith.

The truth, though, was that Dan was merely growing in a different way than she was. He tends to be an intellectual who experiences God and deepens his faith through reading weighty theological tomes that illuminate God's attributes and character. Then he writes in a journal about how these new insights can help him change his own character and values to be more like Christ. Because these are private spiritual exercises that he is shy about discussing, his wife wasn't aware that he was actually growing as much as he was. She equated spiritual growth with group activities and public ministry, but that is not the only sign of someone's spiritual development.

It helps when spouses can candidly discuss with each other the way they tend to grow spiritually. That way, they can encourage each other and even join in the other person's spiritual exercises when appropriate. For example, if your spouse experiences God most readily through enjoying the beauty and wonder of nature, it might be a good idea to spend time with him on hiking trips deep in the mountains. Peeking into his world can give you a new appreciation for how he is wired up to relate to God.

And here is another suggestion: agree with each other that when one of you reads a book that ministers deeply to you, the other will read the book too, so that you can discuss its implications for your lives and marriage. This will also help each spouse understand what influences each partner in his or her spiritual growth.

Another way we can make mistakes about our spouse's spiritual growth is through "gift projection." This means that we project our spiritual gifts onto our partner and judge him lacking because he fails to measure up. For example, if your spiritual gift is evangelism, you might think your partner is lagging behind spiritually if she is not as active and successful in sharing her faith with others as you are. You might lament that you have to prod her to get into spiritual conversations with strangers or to build relationships with unchurched neighbors.

It's unfair to judge your spouse for not exercising a spiritual gift that God never gave her in the first place! Yes, all Christians should be attuned to sharing their faith as God opens up opportunities, but those with a spiritual gift of evangelism have a divine enablement that helps them lead more people to Christ than those without the gift. Just because your partner doesn't have the same ministry passions as you do doesn't mean she isn't growing in the use of her own spiritual gift.

7. FACILITATE FRIENDSHIPS BETWEEN YOUR SPOUSE AND CHRISTIANS OF THE SAME GENDER

My own spiritual development began to soar when I got into relationships with other Christian men who stimulated my vision for ministry, encouraged me, prayed with me, and befriended me on a number of levels. Often these kind of friendships can be the catalyst to get spouses on track with their spiritual life. "As iron sharpens iron, so one man sharpens another," says Proverbs 27:17.

"I'd encourage a wife whose husband was lagging spiritually to look for Christian men who might have points of connection or affinity with her husband," Johnson said. "For instance, maybe she's in a Bible study where another woman says, 'My husband just got a new mountain bike. He's been wanting to take up riding for some time, but he's looking for someone to ride with.' She might think, *Hmmm. My husband is an avid mountain biker and her husband is a dedicated Christian—maybe they could connect.* So at the right time she mentions to her husband that her friend's spouse is looking for a biking partner for some occasional rides. Would he be willing to include him sometime?"

Granted, this can become manipulative and so caution must be taken and purity of heart must be sought. But there are potentially tremendous benefits to what Dr. Wayne Oates, former professor of psychology at the University of Louisville School of Medicine, calls "the ministry of introductions"—taking advantage of the right opportunities to introduce the right people to each other for the right reasons.

Another avenue is to see if your spouse would be interested in joining a couples small group. This would expose him to other Christian men in a safe setting where authentic community can be created. Often men are indifferent to attending church because they lack personal relationships with others in the congregation. Church becomes merely an impersonal crowd of faces to them. But they become much more enthusiastic when they have a close friendship with some other men who are part of the same fellowship.

One tip: put a time limit on the first small-group experience. Don't make it an open-ended commitment that your spouse envisions as a lifelong obligation. Create an escape hatch by joining, say, an eight-week Bible study on the book of Ephesians or a ten-week group built around improving parenting skills. This will make it more likely that your spouse will agree to join—and any budding friendships that develop can certainly continue into the future.

8. CHECK YOUR OWN HEART AND MOTIVATIONS

This may be hard to hear, but it's necessary. "Be careful that you're not using church attendance or Bible studies to escape struggles in your marriage," Holladay said. "In twenty-five years of ministry I've often seen wives—and husbands—use the activities and ministries of church to escape the pain of a difficult marriage. If you're doing that, your husband instinctively knows what is happening. It may be that he doesn't dislike church at all . . . just the feeling of separation from you that it gives him."

How do you know if this is happening? "If church or your Bible study or ministry has begun to feel like an escape from the weariness you feel in your marriage, or if you find yourself being irritable when your husband *does* come with you to church, those are pretty good indications that this struggle is happening in your heart," he said. "It is *far* more common than you might imagine."

Another way to check your motivation is to ask yourself whether you want your husband to grow spiritually because you honestly want to see him relating tighter with God—or is it because you are embarrassed that he is not more involved in church? Or because you secretly wish he were more like Darla's husband (who is a widely admired small-group leader) or Jenny's husband (who teaches a popular Sunday school class)?

If you are subconsciously comparing your spouse's spirituality with someone else's, or if you feel a bit chagrined in front of your Christian friends because of your partner's spiritual immaturity, these attitudes inevitably will leak out and poison your interactions with him. He'll sense it in your tone of voice, your disapproving looks, and your subtle remarks.

Make sure your concern for him is being propelled by the proper fuel—that is, a sincere yearning for him to know Jesus in a deeper and more meaningful way and to fully experience the joy and adventure of a sold-out Christian life.

Keep Moving Full Steam Ahead!

Leslie and I have found through the years that these eight steps can help bring Christian couples into more spiritual sync. Keep in mind, however, that God may very well give one partner a more visible ministry than the other. In fact, I've met a number of couples over the years where the wife is in the stronger "ministry to others" role and the husband is in the role of supporting his wife in that ministry.

One final caution: while you're encouraging your spouse's spiritual growth, don't slow down with your own. After all, getting in sync shouldn't mean that you intentionally or unconsciously put the brakes on your spiritual development in order to match his slower pace!

"God has an important plan for how he wants to work in and through you," said Mark Mittelberg, coauthor of *Becoming a Contagious Christian.* "Keep pursuing that plan! It would be a mistake to wait around spiritually; you might get stuck in neutral. Don't flaunt what you're learning or the changes you're experiencing, but don't hide them, either. Sometimes there's a side benefit: the progress your spouse sees in you may wind up motivating him to grow!"

Into the Future of Your Mismatch

WHILE LESLIE AND I HAVE BEEN WRITING THIS BOOK, WE CON-tinue to run into Christians who find themselves wed to spiritual cynics, skeptics, spectators, or seekers. As they have told us about their experiences—from the encouraging to the incredibly sad—our hearts have been deeply touched time after time. We have celebrated with some of them, given hugs of sympathy to others, and prayed for them all.

We know that you have a story too. Sometimes it's important to remind yourself: *the end of your story hasn't been written yet!* There are still ways God can use you to affect the outcome. We hope you will continue to persevere, trust in him, and use this book as a resource for ideas and encouragement.

In the meantime, maybe you can see a bit of your own situation reflected in a few of the most recent stories we have encountered. We wish all of these stories were upbeat and positive, but it doesn't help to sugarcoat reality:

- There's Joan, whose mismatched marriage to Jim has lasted fifteen years. When we ran into her the other day at church, she told us she has seen no change in her spouse. He is still totally disinterested in spiritual matters. "The only good news," she said, "is that he has stopped trying to discourage me from going to church. Now he tolerates me and the kids coming on the weekends. We've sort of reached an impasse." Trying to encourage her, we said this sounded like a positive development.

"I suppose so," she said without much enthusiasm. Then she added wistfully: "But I wanted so much more for our marriage."

- Then there's Margaret, one of the sad stories. She's a single mom now, raising her two young daughters by herself. Her church involvement had been a lightning rod for her husband. A heavy-drinking construction worker, Dan became increasingly belligerent toward her, using her newfound faith as an excuse to berate and verbally abuse her. Then one day he slapped her and pushed down their daughter who had risen to her defense. When Margaret asked for counsel, we told her God never intends for anyone to live with a physically abusive spouse who puts herself and her children in danger. Now they're separated; Dan still refuses to seek counseling.

- A more heartening story occurred just yesterday, when I was speaking at a church and met a woman who was spilling over with excitement. She had invited her husband to come hear me speak on Sunday morning about the evidence for Christianity. Instead, he insisted on taking their son deer-hunting over the weekend, which was the opening of the season. "I'll tell you what," he said to her. "If we bag a deer early enough, I'll come on Sunday." She prayed fervently that he and their son would get a deer on Saturday—and, sure enough, they did! He came to church on Sunday, heard my talk, and now he is more open to pursuing God. She's wondering, *Where might this lead?*—and she continues to pray.

- Ted is a "spiritual widower." As a wild-living college student, he met an equally free-spirited bartender named Jennifer, who was rebelling against her rigid, legalistic Christian upbringing. Several years and two children later, Ted agreed to attend a seeker church at the invitation of a colleague. Soon Ted became a Christian. But Jennifer wants nothing to do with it. She even refuses to let Ted bring their son or daughter to church with him. "She can't understand that her childhood experience has nothing to do with authentic faith," Ted said. "Or she won't understand.

Her mind is shut. She won't talk to me about church or God or religion." Ted's saddest experience was when he was baptized. "It should have been an incredible celebration," he said. "But I had to go through it without Jen. It broke my heart."

- Finally, there's Greg and Pam. We saw them at church a few weeks ago, holding hands as they strolled into the auditorium. Nobody would have guessed that their spiritual mismatch had put them through six years of terrible marital anguish. A Christian since childhood, Pam married Greg even though he was an agnostic. She rationalized that he was nicer than most Christians she knew and that his conversion would just be a matter of time. But the more she encouraged him to seek God, the more he resisted. Years of turmoil followed. In the end, it wasn't a cataclysmic event that brought him to Christ. Instead, God used Pam's consistent and compassionate faith to slowly erode his skepticism. "Six years is a long time to be spiritually isolated," she told us. "But still, how could I not be grateful? It could have been sixteen years. Or sixty!"

Maybe it *has* been sixteen years for you. Or perhaps you look into the future of your mismatched relationship and fear that the conflict will last for sixty. Regardless, you need to remember that God has the power to bring good out of your difficult circumstances if you trust him. You might want to commit Romans 8:28 to memory: "And we know that in all things God works for the good of those who love him, who have been called according to his purpose."

If in the depths of your despair you begin to question whether God is actually powerful and loving enough to fulfill that promise in your life, remember this: God was able to take the very worst thing that could ever happen in the history of the universe—the death of the Son of God on the cross—and create from it the very best thing that could ever happen in the history of the universe, which is the opening of heaven to all those who want to follow him.[1]

If he is strong and caring enough to do that, then you can have confidence that he can draw something good from your spiritually mismatched marriage. What kind of good? For me to get an answer to that question, I only have to look as far as Leslie.

THE OPPORTUNITY IS YOURS

When people look at Leslie today, they see a woman of deep and profound faith. They see someone wholly devoted to prayer and radically dependent on God. They see a person with a childlike trust in her heavenly Father, a calm confidence in his sovereign control of the world, and a relentless commitment to pursuing his will for her life. They see someone whose heart is soft toward people who are far from God and whose character is deeply rooted in Christ.

I had to wait until Leslie was out of the room to write that paragraph, because she would hate me saying all of that about her. She would insist that she still has a very long way to go in her journey of transformation. While I know that is true for all of us, I like to look at how far she has already come! The qualities of Leslie today are a far cry from the tentative, immature, and often-wavering faith that she started out with. What happened in the intervening years to make such a difference?

She survived a spiritual mismatch.

In the crucible of that experience, God re-formed and reshaped her heart, her character, and her faith. For example, it was during this era that Leslie learned how to pour herself out in authentic, heartfelt prayer. Formula prayers—with their complete sentences, stilted formality, and tidy theology—just wouldn't cut it. She needed to express her rawest emotions to God. She needed to bring him her anger, frustration, fear, and pain, and that meant her prayers weren't always polite or fancy. Sometimes they were shouted. Often they were messy. And more than a few were stained with tears.

Also, it was during this time that Leslie learned how to be dependent on God. Initially, she wanted everything to happen on her timing, but she came to understand that his ways are above her own. Instead of trying to take things into her own hands, she discovered it was best to merely open her hands in surrender to God. In short, he taught her the joy of obedience. After all, the Bible says even Jesus learned obedience through suffering.[2] Why should we think it would be any different for us?

In addition, Leslie's character was shaped during these challenging years. How could she come to the point where she could forgive me for my cruel words or icy silence? She couldn't—until she learned to allow the Holy Spirit to empower her. How could she become more persevering and patient? How could she love me when I was acting in an unlovable way? How could she stand firm for God when I kept trying to get her to waver? It wasn't going to happen on her own. She needed God to work through our difficult situation in order to bring about this kind of character development.

With all my heart, I am truly sorry for the ways I frustrated Leslie during our mismatched time. I regret my immaturity, defensiveness, and hostility. At the same time, though, I praise God for the way he managed to take those circumstances and use them to create who Leslie is today. I don't think there's any way she would have become who she is without enduring those trials.

And here's my point: regardless of whether your spouse ever bends his knee in repentance, *you* can be transformed to be more and more like Jesus—not *despite* your present circumstances but *because* of them.

A FUTURE WITH HOPE

When researchers studied the lives of 413 high-achieving people, they found a common theme: nearly all of them had been forced to overcome difficult obstacles to become who they were. It was this very process of going through difficult times that stretched them into becoming something they might never have otherwise become.[3]

That's a little bit like what God can do in your life. He can take your heartbreaking experience of living with a recalcitrant unbeliever and fashion you into someone whose faith has a character, depth, and authenticity that it would never have had.

But you are inside the crucible right now. That means it may be difficult—or impossible—for you to see this. You may be so focused on the question of whether your spouse will come to Christ that you are missing something that's not in doubt. While a lot may be uncertain about the future of your mismatched marriage, one outcome is absolutely assured: *God will use this experience to transform you into a man or woman of faith that you never otherwise would have become.* That is, if you cooperate with him.

"We also rejoice in our sufferings," said the apostle Paul, "because we know that suffering produces perseverance; perseverance, character; and character, hope. And hope does not disappoint us, because God has poured out his love into our hearts by the Holy Spirit, whom he has given us."[4]

This era of being spiritually mismatched is a special time of opportunity for you. Leslie and I have tried in this book to give you specific ideas for how you can enrich your relationship, avoid the hidden land mines that could decimate your marriage, and even reach out to your partner with the gospel as opportunities arise. We hope you will pray about putting these suggestions into practice and then, as God leads, follow through with a new attitude or new approach. Please remember that our prayers are with you as you ask God to use you in your spouse's life.

At the same time, this can be the most formative period of your life. This spiritual mismatch may be the difficult obstacle that God will use more than any other to conform you to Christ. It is the time when you will learn to live as a missionary in your own home. You will become a person of passionate prayer. You will develop character and fortitude and strength. You will hone your empathy and compassion for the lost. You will forge a faith that is steady and immovable. More and more, incrementally over time, you will become the person God wants you to become. Not because you are strong, but because God is. Not because you are able, but because you can do all things through Christ who gives you strength.

Oh, yes—and there's one more thing you are bound to learn firsthand. It is something that will revolutionize your spiritual life. It is something that will give you confidence as you face the future. You will find that regardless of whether your mismatch lasts six months or sixty years, whether your spouse never becomes a Christian or becomes the next Billy Graham, one truth will endure above all else:

GOD *IS* FAITHFUL—EVEN IN THE MIDST OF A SPIRITUAL MISMATCH.

Notes

Chapter 1: Entering in the Mismatch

1. When we tell anecdotes about people we've counseled, we change the first names to avoid invading their privacy or causing problems in their marriage. When both a first and last name are used, however, you'll know that it is the actual name of the individual.

2. Linda Davis, *How to Be the Happy Wife of an Unsaved Husband* (New Kensington, Penn.: Whitaker House, 1987), 143.

3. Paul Barnett, *The Second Epistle to the Corinthians* (Grand Rapids: Eerdmans, 1997), 345. Barnett says: "Paul does not ban social interaction with 'unbelievers' (1 Corinthians 5:9–10; 10:27), even envisaging them entering the assembly of believers (1 Corinthians 14:22–24). Nor does Paul discourage believers from remaining in the bonds of marriage with unbelievers (1 Corinthians 7:12–15)."

4. Frank E. Gaebelein, gen. ed., *The Expositor's Bible Commentary: Romans, 1 Corinthians, 2 Corinthians, Galatians* (Grand Rapids: Zondervan, 1976), 359.

5. Jo Berry, *Beloved Unbeliever* (Grand Rapids: Zondervan, 1981), 21.

6. 1 Kings 16:33.

7. Quoted in Terry Mattingly's religion column of July 5, 2000, distributed by Scripps Howard News Service.

8. 1 Corinthians 7:12–13.

9. George Barna, *Absolute Confusion* (Ventura, Calif.: Regal, 1993), 240–41, 247, 258, 270, 272, 274, 283, 285, 291.

10. David W. Smith, *Men Without Friends* (Nashville: Thomas Nelson, 1990), 24–31.

11. See Mark Wingfield, "Researcher Proposes Biological Theory for Why Women More Religious Than Men," *American Baptist Press* (Nov. 30, 2000).

Chapter 2: In Leslie's Words: A Story of Loneliness, Fear, Perseverance, Faith

1. Ronald B. Shwartz, *The 501 Best and Worst Things Ever Said About Marriage* (New York: Citadel, 1995), 114.
2. Linda Davis, *How to Be the Happy Wife of an Unsaved Husband* (New Kensington, Penn.: Whitaker House, 1987), 10 (emphasis in original).
3. John 16:33 NASB (emphasis added).

Chapter 3: In Lee's Words: A Story of Anger, Resentment, Conviction, and Renewal

1. Gerard Egan, *Interpersonal Living* (Monterey, Calif.: Brooks/Cole, 1976), 45.
2. Ken Auletta, "The Lost Tycoon," *The New Yorker* (April 23, 30, 2001), 156, 158. Turner conceded the article's accuracy in Larry King's column in *USA Today* (April 30, 2001), 2.
3. Linda Davis, *How to Be the Happy Wife of an Unsaved Husband* (New Kensington, Penn.: Whitaker House, 1987), 50–51.
4. Michael Fanstone, *Unbelieving Husbands and the Wives Who Love Them* (Ann Arbor, Mich.: Servant, 1994), 71.
5. 2 Peter 3:9.

Chapter 4: The Players: God, Your Spouse, and a Mentor

1. TEV.
2. Phil Callaway, *Who Put the Skunk in the Trunk?* (Sisters, Ore.: Multnomah, 1999), 97.
3. Exodus 20:3: "You shall have no other gods before me."
4. Mark 12:30.
5. Psalm 96:4–5.
6. James 4:8a.
7. Psalm 27:1.
8. Eugene Peterson, quoted in *The Book of Wisdom* (Sisters, Ore.: Multnomah, 1997), 399.
9. Callaway, *Who Put the Skunk in the Trunk?*, 107 (emphasis added).
10. Gary Smalley, *Making Love Last Forever* (Dallas: Word, 1996), 110.
11. 1 Corinthians 13:4–8a.
12. James 1:2–4.
13. Isaiah 54:5.
14. Isaiah 54:10.

15. See Luke 15:1–31.
16. See Bill Hybels and Mark Mittelberg, *Becoming a Contagious Christian* (Grand Rapids: Zondervan, 1994), 16–24.
17. NLT (emphasis added).
18. See Matthew 20:28.
19. 1 Peter 3:2 LB.
20. Bebe Nicholson, *When a Believer Marries a Nonbeliever* (Alpharetta, Ga.: Priority Publishing, 1997), 118.
21. For example, the KJV and RSV.
22. D. Edmond Hiebert, *First Peter: An Expositional Commentary* (Chicago: Moody, 1984), 185.
23. Augustine, *Confessions* 9.19, 22, quoted in Norman Hillyer, *New International Bible Commentary: First and Second Peter, Jude* (Peabody, Mass.: Hendrickson, 1992), 95.
24. Joyce Huggett, "Lop-Sided Love," *Christian Family* (June 1987), 14, quoted in Michael Fanstone, *Unbelieving Husbands and the Wives Who Love Them* (Ann Arbor, Mich.: Servant, 1994), 84.
25. Carole Mayhall, "Cherish Is the Word," in Ramona Cramer Tucker, *Thirty Days to a More Incredible Marriage* (Wheaton, Ill.: Tyndale, 1998), 96.
26. H. Norman Wright, quoted in *The Book of Wisdom*, 196.
27. Beverly Bush Smith and Patricia DeVorss, *Caught in the Middle* (Wheaton, Ill.: Tyndale, 1988), 68.
28. Ibid.
29. Simon Signoret quoted in *The London Daily Mail* (July 4, 1978).
30. Elizabeth Cody Newenhuyse, "Why Can't He Be More Like . . . ?" in Ramona Cramer Tucker, *Thirty Days to a More Incredible Marriage*, 112–13.
31. Ephesians 4:15 stresses the importance of Christians "speaking the truth in love."
32. See Matthew 5:13–16.
33. See 1 Samuel 18:1–3 NAS.
34. David W. Smith, *Men Without Friends* (Nashville: Thomas Nelson, 1990), 214.
35. For information, see www.Stonecroft.org.
36. For information, see www.cbmc.com.
37. Ted Engstrom, *The Fine Art of Friendship* (Nashville: Nelson, 1985), 131.

Chapter 5: Giving Your Spouse What God Gave You

1. Jack Mingo and John Javna, *Primetime Proverbs* (New York: Harmony Books, 1989), 140.
2. Jo Berry, *Beloved Unbeliever* (Grand Rapids: Zondervan, 1981), 58.
3. J. Allan Petersen, *Reader's Digest* (October 1993), quoted in Ronald B. Schwartz, ed., *The 501 Best and Worst Things Ever Said About Marriage (New York: Citadel*, 1995), 184.
4. Lawrence J. Crabb, *The Marriage Builder* (Colorado Springs: NavPress, 1987), 109 (emphasis in original).
5. Gary Oliver, "When a Spouse Converts," *Christianity Today* (July 9, 2001), 27.
6. J. Stephen Lang, *Biblical Quotations for All Occasions* (Rocklin, Calif.: Prima, 1999), 258.
7. Excerpted from a list of "Fifty Ways to Leave Your Worry," in Phil Callaway, *Who Put the Skunk in the Trunk?* (Sisters, Ore: Multnomah, 1999), 130–31.
8. Phil Callaway, *Who Put the Skunk in the Trunk?* (Sisters, Ore.: Multnomah, 1999); Patsy Clairmont, et al., *Humor for a Woman's Heart* (West Monroe, La.: Howard, 2001); Charles R. Swindoll, *Laugh Again* (Dallas: Word, 1992).
9. Philippians 4:4.
10. Charles R. Swindoll, *Laugh Again*, 34 (emphasis added).
11. Phil Callaway, *Who Put the Skunk in the Trunk?* 152.
12. Ibid., 22.
13. NASB.
14. LB.
15. Matthew 6:14–15.
16. Ruth Graham, *Moody Monthly* (June 1975), quoted in Ronald B. Schwartz, ed., *The 501 Best and Worst Things Ever Said About Marriage* (New York: Citadel, 1995), 49.
17. Romans 12:18.
18. Luke 6:28.
19. James 5:16a: "Therefore, confess your sins to each other and pray for each other so that you may be healed."
20. Proverbs 23:7 NASB.
21. H. Norman Wright and Gary J. Oliver, *How to Bring Out the Best in Your Spouse* (Ann Arbor, Mich.: Vine, 1996), 188.
22. Gary Smalley, *Making Love Last Forever* (Dallas: Word, 1996), 222.

Chapter 6: The Chill, the Children, and the Most Challenging Question

1. C. C. Brooks, "Falling in Love with Your Husband . . . Again," in Ramona Cramer Tucker, *Thirty Days to a More Incredible Marriage* (Wheaton, Ill.: Tyndale, 1998), 88.

2. Bobbie and Myron Yagel, *15 Minutes to Build a Stronger Marriage* (Wheaton, Ill.: Tyndale, 1995), 25–26.

3. Robert T. Michael, et. al., *Sex in America* (Boston: Little, Brown, 1994), 129.

4. Ibid., 127–28.

5. See Genesis 2:24.

6. See 1 Corinthians 7:3–6.

7. Hebrews 13:4 RSV: "Let marriage be held in honor among all, and let the marriage bed be undefiled . . ." We agree with the way Jo Berry explains that verse in *Beloved Unbeliever* (p. 68): "The marriage bed is . . . already pure and holy because it is part of a God-ordained, God-blessed institution. I believe this means that anything that is not physically harmful and is mutually acceptable to both parties is permissible."

8. Robert Moeller, *To Have and to Hold* (Sisters, Ore.: Multnomah, 1995), 41, 45.

9. Mike Mason, *The Mystery of Marriage* (Sisters, Ore.: Multnomah, 1985), 146.

10. C. C. Brooks, "Falling in Love with Your Husband . . . Again," in Ramona Cramer Tucker, *Thirty Days to a More Incredible Marriage*, 88–89. Used with permission.

11. George Gallup Jr., *The Unchurched American . . . 10 Years Later* (Princeton, N.J.: Princeton Religion Research Center, 1988), 36.

12. Michael Fanstone, *Unbelieving Husbands and the Wives Who Love Them* (Ann Arbor, Mich.: Servant, 1994), 109, 110.

13. Les and Leslie Parrott, *Becoming Soul Mates* (Grand Rapids: Zondervan, 1995), 226.

14. Matthew 7:12.

Chapter 7: Before You Tell Your Spouse about God

1. Nancy Kennedy, "When Your Loved One Doesn't Love God" in *Marriage Partnership* (Spring 1999), 40.

2. 1 Corinthians 9:16 NCV (emphasis added).

3. Thomas S. Rainer, *Surprising Insights from the Unchurched* (Grand Rapids: Zondervan, 2001), 83 (emphasis added).

4. Ibid., 49. Rainer's study of 350 formerly unchurched Christians disclosed that 57 percent said relationships played a part in choosing to go to church (p.77). The most commonly mentioned relationship was family members, cited by 42 percent (p. 82). When they were asked, "If a family member influenced you to come to church, which person was most influential," 35 percent said wives. Other responses were 18 percent for children, 16 percent "other," 9 percent parents, 5 percent siblings, and 2 percent parents-in-law (p. 83).

5. Ibid., 70.

6. Ibid.

7. Incidentally, Rainer found that Christian husbands were less influential in reaching their unchurched wives (p. 50).

8. Rebecca Manley Pippert, *Out of the Salt Shaker and Into the World*, 2d ed. (Downers Grove, Ill.: InterVarsity, 1999), 123.

9. Cliffe Knechtle, *Give Me an Answer* (Downers Grove, Ill.: InterVarsity, 1986), 164.

10. Bill Hybels and Mark Mittelberg, *Becoming a Contagious Christian* (Grand Rapids: Zondervan, 1994), 54.

11. 1 Peter 3:1–2.

12. See 1 Peter 3:15.

13. Bill Hybels and Mark Mittelberg, *Becoming a Contagious Christian*, 89–90.

14. See Lee Strobel, *What Jesus Would Say* (Grand Rapids: Zondervan, 1994), 91–92.

15. Bill Hybels, Willow Creek Association Regional Contagious Evangelism Conference, Session 4, Atlanta (June 23, 2001), edited for clarity.

16. See John 16:33b: "In this world you will have trouble."

17. See Galatians 5:22.

18. See: Mark Mittelberg, Lee Strobel, and Bill Hybels, *Becoming a Contagious Christian Participant's Guide* (Grand Rapids: Zondervan, 1995), 128.

19. Viggo Olsen, *The Agnostic Who Dared to Search* (Chicago: Moody, 1990).

20. See Romans 3:11.

21. "Read This First," in *The Journey: The Study Bible for Spiritual Seekers* (Grand Rapids: Zondervan, 1996).

22. Ibid.

Chapter 8: What to Say When Words Are Hard to Find

1. The course is available through the Willow Creek Association at 1-800-570-9812. The International Bible Society will send an experienced trainer to teach the seminar at your church. To reach the IBS, call: 1-888-222-5795.

2. See John K. Akers, John H. Armstrong, and John D. Woodbridge, eds., *This We Believe* (Grand Rapids: Zondervan, 2000), 239–48.

3. Lee Strobel, *Inside the Mind of Unchurched Harry and Mary* (Grand Rapids: Zondervan, 1993), 116–17.

4. Adapted from Mark Mittelberg, Lee Strobel, and Bill Hybels, *Becoming a Contagious Christian Participant's Guide* (Grand Rapids: Zondervan, 1995), 116.

5. Ibid., 64.

6. "Did They Know Why They Were Celebrating Easter?" *Emerging Trends* (April 1991), 5.

7. George Barna, *The Barna Report, 1992–1993* (Ventura, Calif.: Regal, 1992), 69.

8. "Evangelism That Flows," *Leadership Journal* (Summer 1998).

9. George Barna, *Never on a Sunday: The Challenge of the Unchurched* (Glendale, Calif.: Barna Research Group, 1990), 28.

10. See www.willowcreek.com.

11. John Guest, *In Search of Certainty* (Ventura, Calif.: Regal, 1983), 49.

12. Ibid., 51.

13. Gary Smalley and John Trent, *The Two Sides of Love* (Colorado Springs: Focus on the Family, 1999); and Nancy Groom, *Risking Intimacy* (Grand Rapids: Baker, 2000).

14. See Paul C. Vitz, *Faith of the Fatherless: The Psychology of Atheism* (Dallas: Spence, 1999).

15. Rebecca Manley Pippert, *Out of the Salt Shaker and Into the World* (Downers Grove, Ill.: InterVarsity, 1999), 127.

16. George Barna, *The Frog in the Kettle* (Ventura, Calif.: Regal, 1990), 41.

17. Fritz Ridenour, So What's the Difference? (Ventura, Calif.: Regal, 2001); Josh McDowell and Don Stewart, *Handbook of Today's Religions* (Nashville: Nelson, 1992); Walter Martin (Hank Hanegraaff, gen. ed.), *The Kingdom of the Cults* (Minneapolis: Bethany House, revised, updated, and expanded, 1997); Ron Rhodes, *The Challenge of the Cults and New Religions* (Grand Rapids: Zondervan, 2001); and Ruth A. Tucker, *Another Gospel* (Grand Rapids: Zondervan, 1989).

18. Lee Strobel, *The Case for Faith* (Grand Rapids: Zondervan, 2000), 154. This book contains an interview with Zacharias in response to the objection, "It's offensive to claim Jesus is the only way to God." For another discussion of this issue, see my chapter "Jesus is the Only Path to God," in *God's Outrageous Claims* (Grand Rapids: Zondervan, 1997), 184–96.

19. John 14:6.

20. This debate between a Christian, William Lane Craig, and an atheist, Frank Zindler, who was selected by the national spokesman for American Atheists Inc., is available on videotape: *Atheism vs. Christianity: Where Does the Evidence Point?* (Grand Rapids: Zondervan, 1993).

Chapter 9: The Power of a Praying Spouse

1. John Stott, *The Message of the Sermon on the Mount* (Downers Grove, Ill.: InterVarsity, 1985), 119.

2. Larry King, *Powerful Prayers* (Los Angeles: Renaissance, 1998), 18.

3. Ronald Dunn, *Don't Just Stand There . . . Pray Something!* (Amersham-On-The-Hill, Bucks, England: Alpha, 1992), 15 (emphasis added).

4. Ibid., 16.

5. This list adapted from Mark Mittelberg, Lee Strobel, and Bill Hybels, *Becoming a Contagious Christian Participant's Guide* (Grand Rapids: Zondervan, 1995), 12.

6. Sharon Sherbondy, *Quiet Time?* Willow Creek Association Drama Sketch DM9009, 8705, 1991. Script available at www.willowcreek.com.

7. Bill Hybels, *Too Busy Not to Pray* (Downers Grove, Ill.: InterVarsity, 1988), 90.

8. 1 Peter 3:7.

9. Matthew 5:23–24. See also Romans 12:18.

10. Bill Hybels, *Too Busy Not to Pray*, 92.

11. Ibid., 84–95.

12. Leith Anderson, *Praying to the God You Can Trust* (Minneapolis: Bethany House, 1996, 1998), 143.

13. R. A. Torrey, *The Power of Prayer* (Grand Rapids: Zondervan, 1981), 124.

14. Larry King, *Powerful Prayers*, 23–24.

15. Psalm 34:1 RSV.

16. Psalm 103:1 RSV.

17. Psalm 96:2 RSV.

18. See: Luke 17:11–19.

19. Quoted in Mark Water, ed., *The New Encyclopedia of Christian Quotations* (Grand Rapids: Baker, 2000), 449.
20. TEV.
21. Hank Hanegraaff, *The Prayer of Jesus* (Nashville: Word, 2001), 24.
22. Ibid.
23. Matthew 6:11.
24. Martin Chemnitz, *The Lord's Prayer* (St. Louis: Concordia, 1999), 57.
25. Hank Hanegraaff, *The Prayer of Jesus*, 46.
26. 1 John 5:14 (emphasis added).
27. Matthew 26:39.
28. Hank Hanegraaff, *The Prayer of Jesus*, 47.
29. 1 Timothy 2:4.
30. 2 Peter 3:9.
31. Larry King, *Powerful Prayers*, 18.
32. NASB.
33. Jeremiah 33:3.
34. Quoted in Mark Water, ed., *The New Encyclopedia of Christian Quotations*, 777.

Chapter 10: Avoiding the Dating Traps

1. This quote is from an interview with Donna Rice Hughes by my friend, Ramona Cramer Tucker, and published in *Today's Christian Woman* (September/October 1996).
2. Ibid.
3. Ibid. Hosea 2:14–15 says: "Therefore, I am now going to allure her; I will lead her into the desert and speak tenderly to her. There I will give her back her vineyards, and will make the Valley of Achor [or, Valley of Trouble] a door of hope. There she will sing as in the days of her youth, as in the day she came up out of Egypt."
4. Frank E. Gaebelein, gen ed., *The Expositor's Bible Commentary: Romans, 1 Corinthians, 2 Corinthians, Galatians* (Grand Rapids: Zondervan, 1976), 359.
5. Fred Fisher, *Commentary on First and Second Corinthians* (Waco: Word, 1975), 359 (emphasis added).
6. Tim Stafford, "Why Can't I Date Non-Christians?" available at http://www.christianityonline.com/campuslife/8c2/8c2078.html [2001. May 25].
7. 1 Corinthians 10:12 LB.

8. Gerald R. McDermott, *Seeing God: Twelve Reliable Signs of True Spirituality* (Downers Grove, Ill.: InterVarsity, 1995), 16, 18.
9. James 2:14a, 17.
10. Philippians 3:13b–14.
11. Romans 12:2: "Do not conform any longer to the pattern of this world, but be transformed by the renewing of your mind. Then you will be able to test and approve what God's will is—his good, pleasing and perfect will."
12. Gary Collins, *The Soul Search* (Nashville: Nelson, 1998), 219.
13. Ibid., 218.
14. Mark Water, ed., *The New Encyclopedia of Christian Quotations* (Grand Rapids: Baker, 2000), 533.
15. NLT.
16. Charles Colson and Nancy Pearcey, *How Now Shall We Live?* (Wheaton: Tyndale, 1999), 14–15.
17. Gary Collins, *The Soul Search*, 133.
18. Ibid., 134–35.

Chapter 11: When Christians Are Out of Sync

1. Quotations from Tom Holladay, Brad Mitchell, Brad Johnson, and Mark Mittelberg are from personal correspondence. They are used with permission.
2. NLT.
3. See 1 Corinthians 12, Romans 8, and Ephesians 4.
4. Rick Warren, *The Purpose Driven Church* (Grand Rapids: Zondervan, 1995), 372.
5. Ibid., 374.
6. Ibid., 374–75.
7. Wayne Grudem, *Systematic Theology* (Grand Rapids: Zondervan, 1994), 746.
8. RSV.
9. See Philippians 2:12–13.
10. Grudem, *Systematic Theology*, 755 (emphasis in original).
11. From Eugene H. Peterson's rendering in *The Message: The Wisdom Books* (Colorado Springs: NavPress, 1996).
12. H. Norman Wright and Gary J. Oliver, *How to Bring Out the Best in Your Spouse* (Ann Arbor, Mich.: Vine Books, 1994, 1996), 21.

e Kreeft in an interview published in my
   book *The Case for Faith* (Grand Rapids: Zondervan, 2000), 39.
2. Hebrews 5:8: "Although he was a son, he learned obedience from what he
   suffered."
3. See Victor Goertzel and Mildred George Goertzel, *Cradles of Eminence*
   (Boston: Little, Brown, 1962).
4. Romans 5:3–5.

41*

Appendix 1

Your 30-Day Prayer Adventure

TO HELP LAUNCH YOU ON A CONSISTENT PATTERN OF PRAYER FOR yourself, your spouse, and your spiritually mismatched marriage, Leslie and I have written this month-long prayer guide.

Our hope is that you will incorporate these ideas into your broader prayer life over the next thirty days. In other words, this isn't intended to represent the totality of your prayers. We trust you will use a format like the eight A's we described in Chapter 9—*avoid, approach, adore, acknowledge, admit, ask, align,* and *act*—to make sure your prayer life is well-rounded.

Use this guide as a way of building your prayers around a theme each day. Take the time to meditate on the daily verse, and then use the text that follows as a starting point for expressing your own desires to God. At the end of the month, you can recycle through the guide or use it as an occasional reference.

Remember that as you pray for yourself, your partner, and your relationship, Leslie and I will be praying for you.

DAY 1:

Pray That God Would Strengthen and Deepen Your Faith

Without faith, it's impossible to please God—Hebrews 11:6

Tell God that you want to have a strong, enduring, unwavering faith in him. Ask him to create circumstances in your life that will stretch your faith and cause you to become more and more dependent on him, more yielded to his will, and more committed to his purposes. Seek from him a strong foundation for your beliefs so that you will stand firm when your spouse or others might try to undermine your faith or draw you away from God. Ask God to draw ever nearer to you so that you can feel confident in his ongoing presence in your life. Don't forget to thank him for the relationship you enjoy with him.

DAY 2:

Pray That God Would Help You Keep Him First in Your Life

Love the Lord your God with all your heart and with all your soul and with all your mind and with all your strength—Mark 12:30

Tell God that you never want to become so focused on your spiritually mismatched circumstances that you take your eyes off God as being first in your life. Express to him that he alone is worthy of your praise and worship. Thank him for the way he meets your needs unlike any person ever could, the way he causes good to emerge even from the difficult times in your life, and the way he loves your spouse even more than you do. Ask him to recalibrate your priorities and to keep the compass of your life pointed toward him as being True North. Pray that nothing in your mismatched marriage would hinder or distract you from your relationship with him.

DAY 3:

Pray That God Would Give You Contentment in the Midst of Your Mismatched Marriage

Satisfy us in the morning with your unfailing love, that we may sing for joy and be glad all our days—Psalm 90:14

Pour out to God all the emotions you feel as a result of your mismatched marriage—any frustration, resentment, fears, and hurts that plague you. Don't hold back; express them honestly and fully. Ask the Holy

Spirit to help you express those ambiguous emotions that you can't even give names to. Then ask God to replace your frustration with contentment; your resentment with forgiveness; your fears with confidence; and your hurts with healing. Ask for his comfort when you are feeling insecure and his encouragement when your situation seems bleak. Then worship him for being a God who invites your honesty and who loves you so much he wants to satisfy you with his steadfast love.

DAY 4:

Pray That God Would Bring a Spiritual Mentor into Your Life to Help Guide, Encourage, and Challenge You

As iron sharpens iron, so one man sharpens another—Proverbs 27:17

Tell God how much you would like him to bring a person into your life who can be an ongoing source of godly counsel. Ask him for someone who loves you enough to tell you the truth—even when it hurts. Tell God you want to grow in knowledge about him, but that your mismatched situation often makes it difficult to be a full participant at church. Express to him your need for a spiritual companion who can at least partially fill the void created by your spouse's disinterest in God. Thank him for caring so much about you that he wants to bring you someone who can be Jesus to you in flesh and blood.

DAY 5:

Pray That God Would Soften Your Heart toward All People Who Are Outside His Family, Including Your Spouse

But God demonstrates his own love for us in this: While we were still sinners, Christ died for us—Romans 5:8

Confess to God any tendency you have had to feel uncaring toward spiritually lost people or to view them as the enemy rather than objects of God's great love. Ask him to fill your heart with the kind of love he feels for his wayward sons and daughters. Ask the Holy Spirit to bring to mind the faces of lost friends, neighbors, colleagues, and family members, and then pray for their salvation. Especially lift your spouse to the Lord, asking that the Lord would open your spouse's eyes to his need for a Savior. Thank God for the truth that he loves your spouse even more than you do and that he wants the very best for him.

DAY 6:

Pray for God's Help in Living an Attractive and Consistent Christian Life in Front of Your Spouse

> *Wives, in the same way be submissive to your husbands so that, if any of them do not believe the word, they may be won over without words by the behavior of their wives, when they see the purity and reverence of your lives—1 Peter 3:1–2*

Tell God of your desire to live out your faith in a sincere, humble, and authentic way before your partner, and ask him to use this "silent witness" as a way of drawing him toward the kingdom. Ask God to help you display the kind of purity and reverence that will be winsome and attractive to your spouse. Admit to God the times that you have put yourself first in your marriage, and ask that he empower you to have a helpful, serving attitude. Seek from God the ability to live with integrity, where there is a consistency between your beliefs and behavior and between your creed and character.

DAY 7:

Pray That God Would Give You Wisdom in Knowing How to Approach Your Spouse Regarding Spiritual Matters

> *If any of you lacks wisdom, he should ask God, who gives generously to all without finding fault, and it will be given to him—James 1:5*

Confess to God that apart from his wisdom, you are not sure how to share your faith with your partner. Ask God to give you the discernment to know when to discuss spiritual issues and when to back off. Tell God that you need his help to determine when to let your Christian lifestyle speak for itself and when to take advantage of an opportunity to get into a spiritual conversation with your partner. Ask God to guide any discussions that might take place. Praise him for not only being a wise God, but a God who graciously makes his wisdom available to all those who ask him for it.

DAY 8:

Pray That God Would Expand Your Knowledge and Make You Ready to Share Your Faith as Opportunities Arise

> *But in your hearts set apart Christ as Lord. Always be prepared to give an answer to everyone who asks you to give the reason for the hope that you have. But do this with gentleness and respect—1 Peter 3:15*

Tell God that it is your sincere desire to be ready to explain his message of hope to anyone, including your spouse, whenever God opens the opportunity to do so. Ask him for a spirit of humility, gentleness, kindness, and respect so that your demeanor illustrates God's grace as your words describe it. Tell him that when he wants you to spell out the gospel, you are going to need his courage to act and his clarity to communicate the message accurately. Ask that the Holy Spirit would anoint your words and help you to speak the truth in love. Then praise God for what the gospel represents: his unfailing love for failed human beings.

DAY 9:

Pray That God Would Help You Treat Your Spouse with the Kind of Grace That He Has Shown You

> *He does not treat us as our sins deserve or repay us according to our iniquities—Psalm 103:10*

Thank God for the undeserved forgiveness he has showered on your life. Praise him for casting your sins into the deepest part of the sea. Tell him that you never want to take his amazing grace for granted, but that you always want to stand in awe and wonder at his unending love. Then ask that he empower you to show that same sort of compassion and forgiveness toward your spouse. Ask him to help you always see your partner as someone infinitely valuable to God because he is etched with God's very likeness. Confess that your natural tendency is to return evil for evil, but that with God's help you want to return love instead.

DAY 10:

Pray That God Would Help You Live Out Christian Principles, Values, and Morality in Your Marriage

> *You became imitators of us and of the Lord; in spite of severe suffering, you welcomed the message with the joy given by the Holy Spirit—1 Thessalonians 1:6*

Express to God your desire to live out a Christian lifestyle as far as you are able in your spiritually mismatched situation. Ask God for the power to fulfill his values and morality in a marital environment where your spouse may be resistant or hostile. Seek God's wisdom for how to stand firm and do the right thing even when you are under pressure to compromise what you believe. Ask for discernment to determine when it's best to give in on inconsequential matters and when it is crucial to stand firm. Most of all, ask for God's blessing on your marriage and offer him thanks for his willingness to guide and protect you.

DAY 11:

Pray That God Would Give You the Humility and Courage to Reconnect with Your Spouse When You Begin to Drift Apart

> *Love is patient, love is kind. It does not envy, it does not boast, it is not proud. It is not rude, it is not self-seeking, it is not easily angered, it keeps*

no record of wrongs. Love does not delight in evil but rejoices with the
truth. It always protects, always trusts, always hopes, always perseveres
—1 Corinthians 13:4–5

Commit to God that when conflict in your relationship begins
to create a chasm between you and your spouse, that you will seek
reconciliation over recrimination. Ask God to give you the humility,
courage, and love to reach out to your partner and to thaw the iciness
that would otherwise threaten your marriage. Ask God to give you a
godly patience, a listening ear, a sincere empathy, and a love that does
not fail. Tell God that you never want to allow bitterness to feed the
tensions between you and your mate. Express to him your desire that
as far as you are able, as much as it depends on you, you want to be at
peace with your partner.

DAY 12:

Pray That God Would Help You Encourage Your Spouse by Painting a Picture for Him of What He Could Become

Do not let any unwholesome talk come out of your mouths, but only what
is helpful for building others up according to their needs, that it may
benefit those who listen—Ephesians 4:29

Confess to God those specific instances where you have leveled
unduly critical or overly harsh words at your spouse. If you have a habit
of discouraging your partner or speaking disrespectfully to him, then
ask God to break it. Tell God you want to encourage your spouse to
become all he can be. Ask for God's help in returning positive words
for negative ones and becoming someone who cheerleads your mate.
Seek God's assistance in casting a vision for your spouse of what he can
become. Offer your worship to God for the way he isn't condemning
toward you, but instead nurtures you and gently helps you grow to become
more like Christ.

DAY 13:

Pray That God Would Help You Inculcate Christian Values in Your Children

> *Train a child in the way he should go, and when he is old he will not turn from it—Proverbs 22:6*

Thank God for how much he loves your children and wants the best for them. Express to him the challenges you are experiencing in raising them with Christian values in a home where one parent doesn't embrace those principles. Ask God to protect your children from the fallout of your mismatched relationship. Then seek his help in raising your children to love God and follow his ways. Seek his creativity in using examples from everyday life to bring biblical teachings alive for your kids. Ask God to bring the right people into your children's lives to influence them for Christ. And ask God to shield them from any marital conflict that might otherwise create anxiety in them.

DAY 14:

Pray for God's Help in Living Out the Golden Rule in Your Marriage

> *So in everything, do to others what you would have them do to you, for this sums up the Law and the Prophets—Matthew 7:12*

Admit to God how difficult it is to remain a loving servant when your spouse is hostile or indifferent toward the spiritual values you love so much. Ask God to keep you focused on asking this question of yourself: *"How would I like to be married to me?"* Ask him to hold up a mirror so you can see yourself as your partner does. Seek God's power to use the Golden Rule as a yardstick by which you can measure your attitudes, behavior, and servanthood on a regular basis. Tell God it's your heart's desire to live a Golden Rule lifestyle in front of your spouse—and that he would use this to soften his heart toward the gospel.

DAY 15:

Pray That God Would Relieve You from Feeling that You're Responsible for Your Spouse's Spiritual Decisions

When [the Holy Spirit] comes, he will convict the world of guilt in regard to sin and righteousness and judgment—John 16:8

Ask God—the Great Evangelist—to release you from the undue pressure of thinking that your spouse's salvation depends on how well you live out your faith, how accurately you convey the gospel, or how often you encourage him to go to church. Pray that you would always feel an urgency about your partner's eternity, but that you would also learn to relax in the knowledge that God is the One who must draw him into the kingdom. Ask God to help you be a good witness for him, while at the same time remembering that it is your partner who must decide for himself whether he will receive forgiveness and eternal life through Christ.

DAY 16:

Pray for God's Help in Creating the Kind of Intimacy in Your Marriage Where Spiritual Conversations Might Flourish

A man will . . . be united to his wife, and they will become one flesh —Genesis 2:24

Express to God your desire that your marriage relationship will go ever deeper and that true intimacy will be reached between you and your spouse. Ask for God to work in your hearts so that the subtle barriers between the two of you will diminish. Pray for the kind of authentic and transparent relationship where the really important matters of life—such as spiritual issues—can be discussed in an environment of openness, sincerity, and trust. Thank God for his creation of marriage—where 1 + 1 = 1—and ask that someday you and your partner will be able to relate not only on a physical, emotional, and intellectual level, but on a spiritual plane as well.

DAY 17:

Pray for God's Power to Forgive Your Spouse When You Would Rather Hold a Grudge

> *For if you forgive men when they sin against you, your heavenly Father will also forgive you. But if you do not forgive men their sins, your Father will not forgive your sins—Matthew 6:14–15*

Ask God to search your heart so that you can confess any ways in which you are consciously or subconsciously withholding forgiveness toward your partner. Tell God that it is your desire to live in harmony with your mate. Mentally drop the rope in any tug-of-war with your partner and stop trying to punish him by nursing a grudge against him. Ask God to cleanse you of any bitterness and to help you adopt his heart of compassion and mercy. Instead of harboring acrimony, ask God to help you become a vessel of his grace. Pray for God to bless your spouse. Ask that God will use your attitude of forgiveness to help him recognize his need for forgiveness from God.

DAY 18:

Pray That God Would Help You Choose Joy

> *Be joyful always; pray continually; give thanks in all circumstances, for this is God's will for you in Christ Jesus—1 Thessalonians 5:16*

Candidly describe for God what has been sapping the joy from your life. Specifically list the situations, the people, and the conflicts that are chasing away your enjoyment. Then ask for him to help you stop seeking happiness, which is based on circumstances beyond your control, and instead to seek joy, which comes from Jesus' presence in your life. Tell him you want to laugh again. Ask that the Holy Spirit would manifest joy in you. Tell God you want to always remember that he is in control, which makes it possible for you to be lighthearted. Also, ask that your joyful and abundant life will be winsome and attractive to your spouse as he considers Christianity.

DAY 19:

Pray That God Would Use Your Experiences as a Mismatched Mate to Mold You into Someone You Never Otherwise Could Have Become

> *And we know that in all things God works for the good of those who love him, who have been called according to his purpose—Romans 8:28*

Worship God for being so powerful and loving that he can take even the most distressful circumstances of your marital mismatch and cause good to emerge. Tell God that you want him to use this situation as a way of honing your character, increasing your dependence on him, and molding you to become more like Jesus. Offer him your full devotion. Express to him your total trust. Pray that at the end of your life you will look back on the tribulations of your mismatch and feel overwhelming gratitude for how God used them to transform you in ways you never otherwise could have changed. Thank God in advance for what he will do in you and through you.

DAY 20:

Pray That God Would Draw Your Spouse to Himself

> *No one can come to me unless the Father who sent me draws him —John 6:44*

Ask God for your heart's desire: that he would draw your partner into the kingdom of God. Admit to him that you are powerless by yourself to bring about anyone's conversion. Ask God to use whatever tools he wants to reach your partner—you and your life; the witness of Christian friends and colleagues; the content of Christian books and tapes; the proclamation of a local church; and the Word of God itself. Pray that God would soften your spouse's heart toward the gospel and that he would have the courage to respond to it. Most of all, thank God for his patience, his love, and his grace—without which nobody would have any hope.

DAY 21:

Pray That God Would Bring Christian Friends into Your Spouse's Life to Influence Him for Christ

> *He told them, "The harvest is plentiful, but the workers are few. Ask the Lord of the harvest, therefore, to send out workers into his harvest field"*
> *—Luke 10:2*

Pray that God would bring a Christian friend, colleague, neighbor, or family member into your partner's life so that he might shine the gospel into his heart. Ask that God would knit them together and create a strong relationship of mutual respect so that the Christian can have a spiritual influence on him. Pray for common ground that they can construct their friendship on. Ask that God would work on your spouse's heart so that he would be receptive to this person's advice and counsel. Pray for protection for this new friend and that his witness would not be tarnished or compromised in any way. Ask for God to empower him to make a spiritual difference in your spouse.

DAY 22:

Pray That God Would Stop Satan from Blinding Him to His Need for a Savior

> *The god of this age has blinded the minds of unbelievers, so that they cannot see the light of the gospel of the glory of Christ, who is the image of God*
> *—2 Corinthians 4:4*

Since the Bible tells us that our battle is not against flesh and blood but against the powers of this dark world and the spiritual forces of evil, pray that God would stop Satan from continuing to blind your partner to the truth of Scripture and his need for forgiveness through Christ. Offer thanks to God that he is more powerful than any evil spirit and that he has given you the full armor of God so that you will be able to stand firm when evil comes. Ask that God would open your spouse's eyes to the truth of the gospel and his free offer of forgiveness and eternal life through Jesus.

DAY 23:

Pray That Your Spouse Would Become a Seeker of God

> *You will seek me and find me when you seek me with all your heart*
> *—Jeremiah 29:13*

If your spouse has been a spiritual cynic, skeptic, or spectator, pray that God would transform him into a seeker of God. Ask that the Holy Spirit would create a thirst in him for spiritual truth. Pray that he would seek God urgently, making his spiritual journey a front-burner issue in his life. Ask that he would cast off his cynicism or skepticism and instead seek God with a sincere and open heart. Pray that when he comes face-to-face with the truth about God, that he would have the courage to respond to God. Then thank God that he loves you and your spouse so much that he sent his one and only Son to seek and to save the lost.

DAY 24:

Pray That Your Spouse Would Turn from Sin and Embrace Christ as His Forgiver

> *Repent, then, and turn to God, so that your sins may be wiped out, that times of refreshing may come from the Lord—Acts 3:19*

Ask God that he would lead your spouse into confronting and admitting the wrongs he has committed and recognizing his desperate need for cleansing through Christ. Pray that your spouse would recognize that the path he is currently treading is a dead end, but that by following Jesus he can walk the road to eternal life. Ask that God would help your partner see that the cross of Christ means release from guilt and shame, forgiveness of all sin, reconciliation with the God of the universe, and an open door to heaven. Thank God for the willingness of his Son to pay the penalty for your spouse's wrongdoing so that he might be set free.

DAY 25:

Pray for God to Help Your Partner Recognize the Emptiness of His Life without Christ

> *I have come that they may have life, and have it to the full—John 10:10*

Pray that God will help your spouse recognize that all of the ways he is trying to find fulfillment in life—from his career to his hobbies to his accumulation of wealth—will never really satisfy the deepest needs of his soul. Pray that he would come to realize that only God can fill the vacuum at the center of his life. Ask that he will come to recognize the difference between success and significance, discovering that true meaning only comes through serving God and fulfilling his purposes in the world. Pray that God would put people in his path who would show him the kind of abundant life that is available to those who follow Christ.

DAY 26:

Pray That Your Spouse Would Understand God's Message of Grace

> *For it is by grace you have been saved, through faith—and this not from yourselves, it is the gift of God—not by works, so that no one can boast —Ephesians 2:8–9*

Pray that God would illuminate his gospel of grace to your spouse so that he would understand that forgiveness and eternal life cannot be earned through trying to live a "good" life or doing acts of kindness. Express to God your willingness to be the bearer of his good news if he opens up the opportunity. Pray that your partner would see the difference between trying to *do* good deeds and the fact that Christ has *done* on the cross all that he needs to be saved. Ask that he be able to distinguish between the false teachings of other religions that there's salvation by works and the Bible's true teachings that eternal life is a gift that cannot be earned.

DAY 27:

Pray That Your Partner Will Come to Accept the Truth of Scripture

> *For the word of God is living and active. Sharper than any double-edged sword, it penetrates even to dividing soul and spirit, joints and marrow; it judges the thoughts and attitudes of the heart—Hebrews 4:12*

Offer God your heartfelt gratitude for the guidance, wisdom, encouragement, and power that he has made available to us through the Bible. Ask that he would open your spouse's eyes to the truth of Scripture and his need to apply its teachings to his life. Pray that God would bring people or resources into his life to help him realize that the Bible truly is the unique Word of God and to answer his questions or concerns about its authenticity. Pray that the Holy Spirit would illuminate the Bible's words and bring understanding so that your partner would come to grips with the gospel. Ask too that God would continue to use the Bible to bring you hope in the midst of your mismatch.

DAY 28:

Pray That God Would Open the Door for Your Spouse to Have Spiritual Conversations

> *How, then, can they call on the one they have not believed in? And how can they believe in the one of whom they have not heard? And how can they hear without someone preaching to them? And how can they preach unless they are sent? As it is written, "How beautiful are the feet of those who bring good news!"—Romans 10:14–15*

Bring this request to God: that he would create opportunities for your partner to enter into meaningful spiritual conversations with Christians who will be willing and able to define and defend the gospel. Ask that God would create a hunger in your partner to learn more about him. Volunteer to be God's messenger to your spouse, but also ask that "serendipitous" conversations take place between him and other people who are Christians, whether it's a pastor, a friend at work, or a neighbor. Ask that the tenor of the discussion be frank and open, with your spouse getting an opportunity to find answers to his toughest objections to Christianity. Pray that God would lead and guide the conversations.

DAY 29:

Pray That God Would Lead You to a Church Where Your Spouse Can Investigate Christianity at His Own Pace

> *They devoted themselves to the apostles' teaching and to the fellowship, to the breaking of bread and to prayer. Everyone was filled with awe,*

and many wonders and miraculous signs were done by the apostles. All the believers were together and had everything in common. Selling their possessions and goods, they gave to anyone as he had need. Every day they continued to meet together in the temple courts. They broke bread in their homes and ate together with glad and sincere hearts, praising God and enjoying the favor of all the people. And the Lord added to their number daily those who were being saved—Acts 2:42–47

Pray that when your spouse is receptive to visiting a church that you will be able to bring him to a place where faith is authentic, the congregation is committed to Scripture, there's a willingness to reach out to spiritual seekers, and where the gospel is explained in relevant, creative, and persuasive terms. Pray that the Holy Spirit would ambush him as he sits among people who are sold out to Christ and whose lives reflect his love, compassion, and grace. Ask too that your partner would be open to classes, seminars, or events where he could meet credible Christians and see how the gospel is lived out in their everyday lives. Thank God for his church—his agent of redemption.

DAY 30:

Pray That Your Spouse Will Surrender All of Himself to Jesus Christ and Commit to Following Him Wholeheartedly

And he died for all, that those who live should no longer live for themselves but for him who died for them and was raised again—2 Corinthians 5:15

Make your most heartfelt desire known to God: that your spouse would yield his life to Jesus Christ, receive his freely offered gift of forgiveness and eternal life, and become wholly devoted to him and his ways. Pray that your partner would discover his spiritual gifts and serve God unreservedly. Even ask that God would then use your mate as his ambassador to reach out to others with the life-changing and eternity-altering gospel of Christ. Pray too that he would become a husband with godly character, a father with godly values, and an employer or employee with godly motivations. Thank God that he has been faithful in loving your spouse even when your spouse has lacked faith in him.

Appendix 2

Application Guide: Questions and Suggestions for Reflection or Discussion

PART 1: THE CHALLENGE OF A MISMATCHED MARRIAGE

Chapter 1: Entering into the Mismatch

1. You've read the story of how Lee and Leslie became spiritually mismatched. What's your story? Trace the account of how you ended up unequally yoked. Describe the spiritual journeys of yourself and your spouse.

2. On a scale of one to ten—with "one" representing strong hostility and "ten" representing extreme openness—how would you rate your spouse's current attitude toward Christianity? How has this changed over the time you have been married? What do you think is fueling his or her attitude?

3. Do you feel optimistic, pessimistic, or uncertain about the future of your mismatched marriage? Why? If you feel pessimistic, what do you need in order to feel more hopeful? In what specific ways do you want God to help you? When you've identified them, pause and express them to the Lord.

4. If you intentionally violated God's command by marrying a nonbeliever, have you confessed it to God and experienced his forgiveness? First John 1:9 says, "If we confess our sins, he is faithful and just and will forgive us our sins and purify us from all unrighteousness." Pray right now so that you can feel God's forgiveness.

5. Identify what you hope that God will accomplish in yourself, your spouse, and your marriage as you are reading this book. Then pray that God would use this book in those ways. Ask that you would emerge encouraged, equipped, and empowered to survive your spiritual mismatch and to influence your spouse for Christ.

Chapter 2: In Leslie's Words

1. Leslie described several emotions that she experienced—for example, frustration, guilt, fear, loneliness, anger, resentment, and confusion. Are there one or two of these emotions that especially plague you? What circumstances prompt them? Give examples of when these feelings have surfaced. What are some constructive ways you can deal with these emotions?

2. Leslie's perceptions of Lee changed after she became a Christian. How has your view of your spouse's habits, character, and priorities changed as you have become more mature in your faith? What steps can you take to avoid becoming judgmental or negative toward him or her?

3. Leslie talked about the way her values began to clash with Lee's, especially in the area of their finances. Have you found yourself disagreeing with your mate over any issues? What are some examples?

4. Have you lived under false guilt because you have felt you are somehow responsible for your partner's spiritual decisions? Did Leslie's discussion of this issue help ease that emotion? Why or why not? In the future, how can you avoid feeling undue pressure for your spouse's conversion?

5. When Jesus spoke in John 16:33 (NASB), he mentioned both peace and courage: "These things I have spoken to you, so that in me you may have peace. In the world you have tribulation, but take courage; I have overcome the world." In what specific ways could you use God's peace at this time? For what do you need courage? Use the answers to these questions as the basis for praying to God.

Chapter 3: In Lee's Words

1. After delving into the mind of a non-Christian spouse, what surprised you the most? Which emotion that Lee described—his jealousy, hurt, frustration, resentment, fear, and anger—was the most unexpected to you? Did you experience an "Aha!" moment where you suddenly gained an insight into your spouse's behavior? If so, what was it?

2. Lee talked about feeling jealous of Jesus. Do you think your own spouse might be feeling a similar kind of emotion? What are two or three steps you can take to alleviate these fears in your partner?

3. Does your mate show flashes of anger over your church involvement or other religious activity? In light of Lee's description of his own eruptions of rage, what might be the underlying causes of your spouse's outbursts?

4. Did any of Lee's insights create a desire in you to initiate a conversation with your spouse about his feelings concerning your faith? Specifically, what would you say to him? Ask God for guidance about whether you should approach this subject with your partner, and if so, how to do it.

PART 2: MAKING THE MOST OF YOUR MISMATCHED MARRIAGE

Chapter 4: The Players: God, Your Spouse, and a Mentor

1. Like Leslie, have you come to the point where you have drawn a line and declared, "As far as I can, with the power of the Holy

Spirit, I'm going to make this marriage work"? If so, how has this influenced your marriage so far? If not, why not take this step right now—and seal your commitment with a prayer?

2. What steps are you taking to keep God first in your life? What are some practical ways you can practice the spiritual disciplines of prayer, Bible study, fellowship, and so forth, in a manner that doesn't inflame problems in your marriage?

3. How can you live out the kind of "respectful, pure behavior" that 1 Peter 3:2 says will speak volumes to your spouse? For Leslie, this meant practicing servanthood; listening sincerely to Lee; allowing Lee to feel needed; building on their common ground; refraining from comparing him to Christian husbands; and loving him as her partner, not her project. Which of these principles do you need to implement the most? Why? How will you go about doing it?

4. Leslie's mentor, Linda, played a crucial role in coaching Leslie. What did Linda do for Leslie that you would love to have someone do for you? If you have someone like Linda in your life, what insights from this chapter could you discuss with her to make her mentoring more effective? If you don't have a mentor, what are some concrete steps you're going to take to find a person to fill that role?

Chapter 5: Giving Your Spouse What God Gave You

1. What are some ways you can make your relationship a "Christian" marriage by living out godly principles in your own life? Can you think of three things you can start doing today? How do you think your spouse would react?

2. On a one-to-ten scale, with "one" being the depths of gloom and "ten" being the height of hilarity, how much joy is there in your marriage? What steps can you take to move your marriage higher on the scale? Have you ever made the conscious decision to be joyful? If not, do so right now—and ask God to help you live out that choice.

3. Identify at least one way in which you've been nursing a grudge against your spouse, and then work through the PEACE process. Afterward, evaluate how this has impacted yourself, your partner, and your relationship.

4. Describe how you believe your husband will behave if he were ever to become a fully devoted follower of Jesus. Now go back through that description and ask how much of it is realistic. If you have a Christian friend who's wed to a believer, ask him or her to give you a candid assessment of what you can expect if your spouse were to become a Christian.

5. Write a Top Ten list of the things you love most about your partner. Print it out on high-quality paper and present it to him or her over a romantic dinner. Identify what you have in common and resolve to build on that foundation.

6. Describe an incident where your mismatched situation caused conflict in your marriage. How might the Stop-Look-Listen approach have helped you in that circumstance? Looking back, can you think of a win-win solution that might have defused the situation? Which part of Stop-Look-Listen do you need to work on personally? Why?

7. When conflicts arise, what are the ways you haven't been fighting "fair"? What are three specific steps you can take to handle the next argument in a constructive way?

Chapter 6: The Chill, the Children, and the Most Challenging Question

1. How would you describe the relational temperature of your marriage at the present time: hot, warm, tepid, cool, chilly, or icy cold? If there's a chill in the air, which suggestions in this chapter could you implement to heat it up?

2. Discuss which aspects of your temperament or personality keep you from reconciling with your spouse when a distance begins to develop between you. Ask God to make your heart more open

to initiating a reconnection when your spouse seems to be pulling away.

3. How have you and your partner handled the spiritual or moral education of your children up to this point? How would you rate your spouse's openness to Christian training for your kids?

4. Discuss three ways you can provide Christian input to your children without causing a disruption of your mismatched marriage.

5. With as much honesty as you can muster, answer this question: "How would I like to be married to me?" What changes would you want in your behavior? What rough edges of your personality would you want to have smoothed? What attitudes would you want to abandon or reinforce? Then pray for God's help in continuing to grow into the kind of person he wants you to be.

PART 3: YOUR MARRIAGE AS A MISSION FIELD

Chapter 7: Before You Tell Your Spouse about God

1. At some point, most Christians seem to make the mistake of pushing too hard for their spouse's conversion. Have you? What are some examples of ways you may have been overzealous or otherwise acted inappropriately? What was your spouse's reaction?

2. What unspoken message do you think your current lifestyle is sending to your partner about Christianity? What may be causing his or her "hypocrisy radar" to go off? What specific steps could you take to live out your faith in a way that's more winsome and attractive to him or her?

3. Have you said or done anything for which you should apologize to your partner? Ask God to bring any unresolved instances to mind—and then ask him for the courage to act with integrity by asking for your spouse's forgiveness.

4. Are you living the kind of life that your spouse would see as a trade up? Why or why not? Identify three of the gifts of the Spirit—love, joy, peace, patience, kindness, goodness, faithfulness, gentleness, and

self-control—in which you need to grow. What are concrete steps you can take to nurture the development of those qualities in your life?

5. Which category best describes your partner's attitude toward Christianity—the cynical spouse, the skeptical spouse, the spectator spouse, or the seeking spouse? Have you seen a change in this status since you've been married? Which suggestions in this chapter might be helpful in moving your spouse toward God? Pray for God to help you discern how you can encourage him or her to grow in spiritual openness.

Chapter 8: What to Say When Words Are Hard to Find

1. Imagine your spouse suddenly turning to you and asking what Christianity is about. How ready would you be to respond? Practice explaining the Roman Road to a Christian friend so you can get comfortable with doing it. Try the same thing with the Do vs. Done illustration.

2. If your partner agreed to attend church with you, how do you think he would react to the style of the church you're currently attending? What aspects do you think he would benefit from? Which do you think would confuse him? If your church isn't a suitable place to bring seekers, is there another one in your community you could try? Which one and why? Visit that church's weekend services to see if it would be appropriate for your partner.

3. Do you think your spouse might have intimacy issues that are keeping him from Christ? Why or why not?

4. Describe the relationship that your spouse had with his father as he was growing up. Do you think this could be creating a barrier between your spouse and his heavenly Father? Why or why not? Do any of the steps described in the chapter sound appropriate for helping your spouse with this issue?

5. Pretend your spouse is suddenly very open to discussing God. Come up with the three best questions you could ask him in order to stimulate his thinking.

6. Does your spouse have a well-developed philosophy of life or set of beliefs about God? If so, what is it? Pretend you had the opportunity to respond to him. What would you say?

Chapter 9: The Power of a Praying Spouse

1. How would you evaluate your current prayer life: fully satisfying, fairly satisfying, generally satisfying, somewhat unsatisfying, or greatly unsatisfying? Have you had an experience like the woman in the drama, where you constantly found yourself being distracted as you have tried to pray? Describe what happened. What two or three things did you learn in this chapter that will help you stay focused in your prayers and have a more fulfilling prayer experience?

2. This chapter described "The Eight A's of Prayer"—*avoid, approach, adore, acknowledge, admit, ask, align,* and *act.* Which one of these elements do you most often find missing from your prayer life? Why do you think it gets overlooked?

3. Which "prayer busters" might be hindering your communication with God? How can you eliminate them?

4. Do you see God as a distant, detached, and disinterested deity, or as a confidant who eagerly wants to listen to your prayers? Why do you hold that view? How does the Bible describe God's willingness to hear your prayers?

5. What are three creative ways you can express your adoration to God through prayer?

6. Think about why you're grateful to God—and then take the time to list as many reasons as you can. Use that as a basis for expressing your thanks to him.

7. What specific wrongdoing in your life is God just waiting for you to admit to him? Pray the prayer of King David from Psalm 139:23: "Search me, O God, and know my heart; test me and know my anxious thoughts. See if there is any offensive way in me, and lead me in the way everlasting."

8. Have you ever felt God leading you to do or say anything? Describe what happened.

9. Try using "The Eight A's of Prayer" for a week and then evaluate whether it's helping you. Also, turn to the "30-Day Prayer Adventure" and begin implementing those themes into your daily talks with God.

PART 4: MANAGING OTHER MISMATCHES

Chapter 10: Avoiding the Dating Traps

1. Have you made a firm commitment to only date people who are followers of Jesus? If so, what has been the most difficult part of living up to that decision? Have you felt tugged to compromise? Describe what happened. If you haven't made that commitment, make it now by telling God that with his help you want to never become unequally yoked.

2. Tim Stafford gave an eloquent argument against "casual" dating of non-Christians. What was the most persuasive part of his explanation?

3. If you've ever dated someone who wasn't a Christian, did you find your faith threatened or strengthened by the experience? Did you find yourself taking "subtle left turns" like Donna described? How so?

4. If you're currently dating someone—or wondering whether you should—ask yourself the fifteen questions listed in the chapter. Remember, nobody can fully embody all of these values, but they are good guidelines for evaluating whether a person is a follower of Jesus. At the end, do you think this is someone you should date? Why or why not?

5. Go through the fifteen questions again—but this time, ask them about *yourself.* Which questions did you find most convicting? Why? Which ones were encouraging? How so? Use the results as a basis for praying that God would continue to nudge you down your journey toward maturity in Christ.

Chapter 11: When Christians Are Out of Sync

1. Describe your level of spiritual maturity versus your spouse's. In what areas is he or she lagging behind? What do you think is responsible for his or her lack of interest in spiritual growth?

2. Ask yourself the tough question: is your spouse *really* a Christian? Use the equation from John 1:12 as a grid for determining whether he has become a child of God: BELIEVE + RECEIVE = BECOME. Is the problem that he doesn't believe in his need for forgiveness and eternal life through Christ? Or that he has never prayed to receive Christ as his forgiver and leader? See if your partner would engage with you in discussing how John 1:12 applies to him.

3. Is your church a place where your spouse can stretch and grow spiritually? What inadvertent obstacles might be in the way of your spouse fully engaging there? Should you consider attending another church where both of you might flourish? Why or why not?

4. Does your spouse know his or her spiritual gifts? Walk him or her through the SHAPE acronym—spiritual gifts, heart, abilities, personality, and experiences—and see if this helps him or her discover how he or she can grow in the excitement and adventure of serving God.

5. Imagine a continuum with *faultfinder* on one end and *encourager* on the other. Where would you fall in terms of the way you relate to your spouse? What are two or three steps you can take to move more toward the *encourager* end?

6. List some ways you and your partner are different. Are you thinkers or feelers? Extroverts or introverts? Just-settle-it types or play-it-by-ear people? In what other ways are your personalities, preferences, and priorities at odds? How much might these factors explain the different ways in which you're growing spiritually?

Conclusion: Into the Future of Your Mismatch

1. Romans 8:28 says, "And we know that in all things God works for the good of those who love him, who have been called according to his purpose." In what ways have you seen God drawing good out of your mismatched circumstances? What are some ways he might accomplish this in the future?

2. Imagine being at the end of your life. Describe what kind of a person you hope you will be at that point. What qualities do you want God to have developed in you? How could God use your mismatched situation to hone your character, develop your values, transform your attitudes, enrich your prayer life, reshape your heart, deepen your faith, and help conform you more to the image of Christ?

3. The book ends with these words: "God is faithful—even in the midst of a spiritual mismatch." Describe how you have seen God's faithfulness in your life despite the turmoil of your mismatched marriage. Then take a moment to thank God for being faithful even when we're not always faithful in return.

4. Reflect on all that you have read in this book. If you could pinpoint a few principles, ideas, or suggestions that stand out to you, what would they be? Why did they have such an impact on you?

5. Read the open letter to non-Christian spouses that is printed at the end of this book. Do you think it would be appropriate to photocopy this for your partner? Why or why not?

6. Discuss at least three specific changes you are going to make as a result of reading this book. How are you going to implement them? Pause to ask for God's blessing on your marriage—and for his help in living faithfully and abundantly in a mismatched marriage.

Appendix 3

Resource
Guide

WHAT DO CHRISTIANS BELIEVE?

Know What You Believe, by Paul Little. InterVarsity Press. A fine
   introduction to the basic components of Christianity.
Christianity 101, by Gilbert Bilezikian. Zondervan. A thorough but
   readable summary of basic doctrines of the Christian faith.
The Journey. Zondervan. Full text of the Bible, in the readable and
   accurate New International Version translation, with helpful notes
   that answer common questions asked by seekers.
This We Believe, by various authors. Zondervan. With clarity and
   passion, Christian writers help readers understand the gospel's
   simple but profound message.

WHY DO CHRISTIANS BELIEVE
WHAT THEY BELIEVE?

The Case for Christ, by Lee Strobel. Zondervan. Former atheist
   retraces his spiritual journey through interviews with experts who
   offer evidence for Jesus being the unique Son of God. Student
   edition also available.
Mere Christianity, by C. S. Lewis. HarperSanFrancisco. This classic
   book by Oxford scholar presents compelling reasons for believing
   Christianity is true.

2274

Know Why You Believe, by Paul Little. InterVarsity Press. A clear affirmation of the reasonableness of the Christian faith.

Jesus Under Fire, edited by Michael Wilkins and J. P. Moreland. Zondervan. Combining accessibility with scholarly depth, this book helps readers judge for themselves whether the Jesus of the Bible is the Jesus of history.

Resurrection, by Hank Hanegraaff. Word Publishing. A stirring and persuasive defense of the central event in Christianity.

More Than a Carpenter, by Josh McDowell. Here's Life Publishers. Easy-to-read introduction to the historical evidence concerning Jesus.

Jesus Among Other Gods, by Ravi Zacharias. Word Publishing. An insightful defense of the uniqueness of the Christian message. Student edition also available.

Is the Bible True? by Jeffery L. Sheler. HarperSanFrancisco and Zondervan. A journalist explores how modern debates and discoveries affirm the essence of the Scriptures.

The New Evidence That Demands a Verdict, by Josh McDowell. Nelson Reference. A wide-ranging resource that compiles vast amounts of evidence for the Christian faith.

The Baker Encyclopedia of Christian Apologetics, by Norman Geisler. Baker Books. A comprehensive reference volume that examines virtually every key issue, person, and concept related to Christian "apologetics," or defense of the faith.

Scaling the Secular City, by J. P. Moreland. Baker Books. A heavy-duty book that explores both the philosophical and factual basis for the Christian faith.

Reasonable Faith, by William Lane Craig. Crossway Books. Scholar explores such issues as faith and reason; the existence of God; reliability of the New Testament; and evidence for Christ and the Resurrection.

A Search for the Spiritual, by James Emery White. Baker Books. A guidebook that helps seekers find satisfying support for the Christian faith.

DO CHRISTIANS HAVE ANSWERS TO OBJECTIONS?

The Case for Faith, by Lee Strobel. Zondervan. Through interviews
   with experts, former skeptic presents answers to the top eight
   objections to Christianity, such as why God allows suffering,
   doesn't evolution explain life, how could a loving God let people
   go to hell, and how can Jesus claim he is the only path to God.
   Student edition also available.

Give Me an Answer That Satisfies My Heart and Mind, by
   Cliffe Knechtle. InterVarsity Press. Well-reasoned responses, in
   question-and-answer format, to the toughest questions concerning
   Christianity.

Reason to Believe, by R. C. Sproul. Zondervan. Excellent responses to
   common objections that skeptics raise to Christianity.

The New International Encyclopedia of Bible Difficulties, by
   Gleason L. Archer. Zondervan. Scholar offers explanations of
   apparent conflicts and contradictions in the Bible.

When Skeptics Ask, by Norman Geisler and Ron Brooks. Victor
   Books. A handbook of evidence for the Christian faith.

When Critics Ask, by Norman Geisler and Thomas Howe. Victor Books.
   Responses to major Bible difficulties from Genesis to Revelation.

HOW CAN CHRISTIANS SHARE
WHAT THEY BELIEVE?

Becoming a Contagious Christian, by Bill Hybels and Mark
   Mittelberg. Zondervan. Outstanding and thorough description of
   how Christians can naturally share their faith in a way that reflects
   their own style. Also available as a training course.

Out of the Salt Shaker and Into the World, by Rebecca Manley
   Pippert. InterVarsity Press. This book explains Christianity as a
   lifestyle, helping people feel relaxed and enthusiastic about sharing
   their faith.

How to Give Away Your Faith, by Paul Little. InterVarsity Press. A classic book on how ordinary people can effectively share the extraordinary gospel.

Building a Contagious Church, by Mark Mittelberg. Zondervan. A powerful biblical blueprint for turning any church—regardless of size, style, or setting—into one that reaches spiritual seekers.

Inside the Mind of Unchurched Harry and Mary, by Lee Strobel. Zondervan. Former skeptic explores the mindset of non-Christians and suggests ways we can reach them personally and through our churches.

OTHER RESOURCES FOR UNEQUALLY YOKED CHRISTIANS

Beloved Unbeliever, by Jo Berry. Zondervan. Based on interviews with women married to unbelievers, this book offers Bible-based counsel and encouragement in dealing with spiritual mismatches.

When a Believer Marries a Nonbeliever, by Bebe Nicholson. Priority Publishing. Formerly mismatched author offers insights on living a godly life, building a strong marriage, prayer, and overcoming barriers to belief.

How to Be the Happy Wife of an Unsaved Husband, by Linda Davis. Whitaker House. This book draws on personal experience and Scripture to provide wisdom and compassion to unequally yoked women.

Caught in the Middle, by Beverly Bush Smith and Patricia DeVorss. Tyndale House. Having experienced spiritual mismatches, two authors discuss how to live a fulfilled life with a non-Christian husband.

Unbelieving Husbands and the Wives Who Love Them, by Michael Fanstone. Servant Publications. British pastor provides counsel to unequally yoked wives based on his personal interaction with spiritually mismatched couples.

Appendix 4

A Letter to Your Spouse

DON'T YOU WISH YOUR SPOUSE COULD SIT DOWN AND TALK WITH someone who had once been spiritually mismatched but who is now a Christian? Someone who can relate to his circumstances, help defuse the marital tensions stemming from the mismatch, and encourage him to check out Jesus for himself?

Well, I decided to do the next best thing: I have written him (or her) a letter. It starts on the following page. My goal is to talk to your spouse in an honest, unvarnished way about my experience of finding out Leslie had become a Christian. My hope is that the letter will help your partner see that your marriage can still thrive despite your different spiritual perspectives, and that it's worthwhile to personally investigate the truth about Jesus.

My suggestion is that you read the letter yourself. See if you feel it would be appropriate for your partner. If you believe he or she might be receptive, ask God to use it to strengthen your marriage and prompt your spouse to consider the claims of Christ.

Then photocopy the letter and give it to your spouse, saying, "I've been reading a book about people from different spiritual perspectives who are married to each other. One of the authors wrote an open letter. I thought you might find it interesting."

Give him time to read the letter on his own. Later ask, "What did you think of it?" Don't press the issue, but the letter could very well open up a conversation about your marriage. At that point, Leslie and I trust that the insights you have gleaned from this book—and, more importantly, the guidance of the Holy Spirit—will lead you into the right kind of discussion.

Dear Friend,

I got some bad news a while back—my wife told me she had become a Christian. As an atheist, I thought there could be nothing worse. I had given up fairy tales a long time ago, but now here was my wife believing in a deity she couldn't see and in an ancient legend about someone who came back from the dead. Right away I figured she was going to turn into a Holy Roller who would nag me about my bad habits, ruin our sex life, and try to drag me off to church every Sunday. No thanks, I told her. Believe what you want, I said, but I'm not interested.

I don't know how you reacted when you found out your spouse is a Christian. Maybe you've known for a while, or maybe this is fresh news to you like it was to me. But my guess is you're not terribly enthused about it. Believe me, I can relate. You're probably feeling like I did—a victim of bait and switch. I married the fun, free-spirited, try-anything-once Leslie, and now I was afraid she was going to turn into a sexually repressed prude who would spend all her time serving the poor at some skid-row soup kitchen.

You may be wondering what the future holds. I sure did. What would become of my marriage? How was Leslie going to change? Was she going to start to pity me as a hell-bound pagan? Would there be an argument at every turn—over how we'd spend our money, what we'd do on weekends, the way we'd raise our children, and on and on? I looked down the road of our relationship and imagined it paved with problems all the way to the horizon.

And sure enough, the conflict came. I found myself resenting her newfound church friends. I felt like she was judging me for my drinking and swearing, though she never directly said anything about them. But do you know what? Most of my worst-case scenario never occurred.

I found that if I cut her some slack and let her live out her faith without hounding her about it, there were some positive results. Her Christian values of forgiveness, empathy, humility, and love brought a constructive new dynamic to our relationship. It was hard to be critical of her sincerity, her character, or her concern for the less fortunate. In fact, after a while I found many of the changes in her were winsome and attractive.

We reached an accommodation on most issues. She went to church, I didn't. I went to bars, she didn't. The kids? It was okay with me if she brought them to church. A little moral education couldn't hurt. I figured she had as much right to develop her beliefs as I did to follow my nonbeliefs. We still had a lot of common ground to build our marriage on. And we hadn't stopped caring for each other.

Do I regret anything? Sure. Being too reactionary. Trying to squelch her faith. Not giving her the space to become what she felt she wanted to become. Picking arguments over little things that didn't matter. Not seeing the good side of her new beliefs. And resenting it when she would try to interest me in Christianity. I came to understand that she wasn't trying to earn brownie points with God by turning me into a Christian. She had found something that brought her incredible joy and fulfillment, and she just wanted me to experience it. I was a big boy. I could still say "no" if I wanted.

Ironically, I ended up saying "yes." I know that's probably not what you want to hear, but that's what happened. The positive changes in Leslie prompted me to begin investigating Christianity. I did that for nearly two years, using my legal training and journalism experience (I was legal editor of the *Chicago Tribune* at the time). In the end, my conclusion was the last thing I ever would have expected: that Jesus is the Son of God who proved it by rising from the dead. Based on the facts, I became a Christian.

Of course, you can believe whatever you want about Jesus. That's your prerogative. And you can handle your marriage any way you decide. I just thought that maybe some of the things I learned might be helpful to you.

Your marriage doesn't have to be paved to the horizon with problems. There are probably some accommodations you can reach. And some common ground you can build on. Does your spouse want you to become a Christian? Bet on it. But you're an adult. You can make your own decisions. My advice is to check it out for yourself. There's really nothing to lose—and there could be a lot to gain.

No pressure. It's your choice.

Sincerely,
Lee Strobel

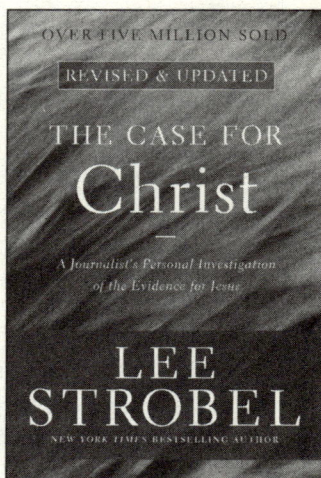

The Case for Christ: A DVD Study

Investigating the Evidence for Jesus

Lee Strobel and Garry Poole

Is there credible evidence that Jesus of Nazareth really is the Son of God?

Skeptics dismiss the Jesus of the Gospels by claiming there is no evidence in the case for Christ. Lee Strobel disagrees. The former legal journalist and one-time atheist knows how to ask tough questions. His own search for truth about Jesus led him to faith in Christ.

Now Strobel invites you and your group to investigate the truth about Jesus Christ leading to the facts that guided Strobel from atheism to faith in Christ. In this revised six-session video with separate study guide, participants will journey along with Strobel on a quest for the truth about Jesus. Rejecting easy answers, you will sift through fascinating historical evidence as you weigh compelling expert testimony. In the end, groups may very well see Jesus in a new way—and even, like Strobel, find their lives transformed.

The six sessions include:
- The Investigation of a Lifetime
- Eyewitness Evidence
- Evidence Outside the Bible
- Analyzing Jesus
- Evidence for the Resurrection
- Reaching Your Verdict

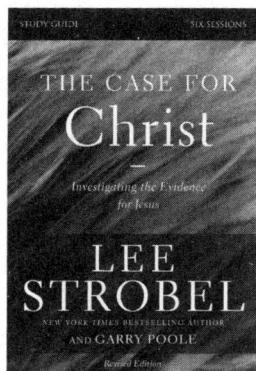

Available in stores and online!

ZONDERVAN®
.com

The Case for Christ — Student Edition

A Journalist's Personal Investigation of the Evidence for Jesus

Lee Strobel with Jane Vogel

There's little question that he actually lived. But miracles? Rising from the dead? Some of the stories you hear about him sound like just that — stories. A reasonable person would never believe them, let alone the claim that he's the only way to God!

But a reasonable person would also make sure that he or she understood the facts before jumping to conclusions. That's why Lee Strobel — an award-winning legal journalist with a knack for asking tough questions — decided to investigate Jesus for himself. An atheist, Strobel felt certain his findings would bring Christianity's claims about Jesus tumbling down like a house of cards.

He was in for the surprise of his life. Join him as he retraces his journey from skepticism to faith. You'll consult expert testimony as you sift through the truths that history, science, psychiatry, literature, and religion reveal. Like Strobel, you'll be amazed at the evidence — how much there is, how strong it is, and what it says.

The facts are in. What will your verdict be in *The Case for Christ*?

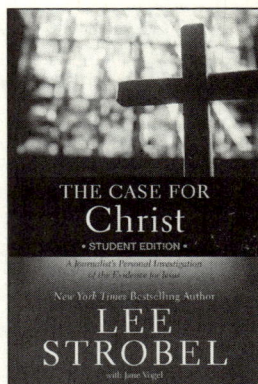

Case for... Series for Kids

Case for Christ for Kids

Lee Strobel with Rob Suggs and Robert Elmer

You meet skeptics every day. They ask questions like:

Was Jesus really born in a stable?
Did his friends tell the truth?
Did he really come back from the dead?
Here's a book written in kid-friendly language that gives you all the answers.

Packed full of well-researched, reliable, and eye-opening investigations of some of the biggest questions you have, *Case for Christ for Kids* brings Christ to life by addressing the existence, miracles, ministry, and resurrection of Jesus of Nazareth.

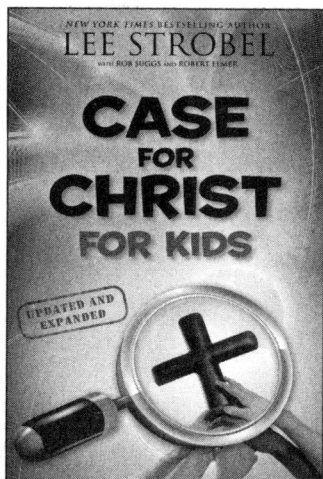

Available in stores and online!

ZONDERVAN®
.com

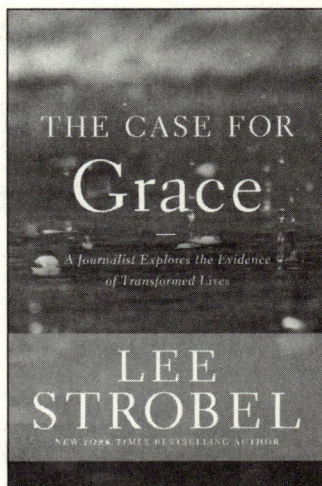

The Case for Faith

A Journalist Investigates the Toughest Objections to Christianity

Lee Strobel, New York Times *Bestselling Author*

Was God telling the truth when he said, "You will seek me and find me when you seek me with all your heart"? In his #1 bestseller *The Case for Christ*, Lee Strobel examined the claims of Christ, reaching the hard-won verdict that Jesus is God's unique son. In *The Case for Faith*, Strobel turns his skills to the most persistent emotional objections to belief—the eight "heart barriers" to faith. This Gold Medallion Award–winning book is for those who may be feeling attracted to Jesus but who are faced with difficult questions standing squarely in their path. For Christians, it will deepen their convictions and give them fresh confidence in discussing Christianity with even their most skeptical friends.

> "*Everyone—seekers, doubters, fervent believers—benefits when Lee Strobel hits the road in search of answers, as he does again in The Case for Faith. In the course of his probing interviews, some of the toughest intellectual obstacles to faith fall away.*"
>
> —Luis Palau, evangelist, radio host, speaker, best-selling author.

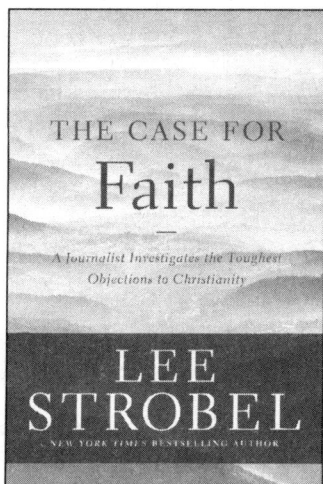

Available in stores and online!

ZONDERVAN®
.com

The Case for a Creator

A Journalist Investigates
Scientific Evidence That
Points Toward God

Lee Strobel, New York Times
Bestselling Author

> "My road to atheism was paved by science... but, ironically, so was my later journey to God"
>
> —Lee Strobel

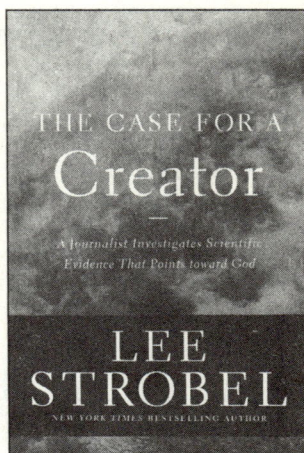

During his academic years, Lee Strobel became convinced that God was outmoded, a belief that colored his ensuing career as an award-winning journalist at the *Chicago Tribune*. Science had made the idea of a Creator irrelevant—or so Strobel thought. But today science is pointing in a different direction. In recent years, a diverse and impressive body of research has increasingly supported the conclusion that the universe was intelligently designed. At the same time, Darwinism has faltered in the face of concrete facts and hard reason. Has science discovered God? At the very least, it's giving faith an immense boost as new findings emerge about the incredible complexity of our universe. Join Strobel as he reexamines the theories that once led him away from God. Through his compelling and highly readable account, you'll encounter the mind-stretching discoveries from cosmology, cellular biology, DNA research, astronomy, physics, and human consciousness that present astonishing evidence in *The Case for a Creator*. Mass market edition available in packs of six.

Available in stores and online!